Brain Rot, Shopping At Costco And Other Joys of Middle Age

The Humorous
KPBX Commentaries
of Doug Hurd

Brain Rot, Shopping At Costco And Other Joys of Middle Age
Copyright © 1996
QBS Publishing
P.O. Box 21056
Spokane, WA 99201
509-448-4305

First Printing 1996
Second Printing 1997
Third Printing 1997

INTRODUCTION

These essays began life as four- to five-minute radio commentaries for KPBX FM, the public radio station that covers a large chunk of eastern Washington, northern Idaho, and parts of Montana and Oregon.

After they aired in Spokane, I would rewrite them and send them to Dan Woodside, who published the revised versions in The Edmonds Paper.

As anyone who has written both for radio and the printed page will tell you, they are not the same animal. I have chosen to go with the original radio scripts, with only minor punctuation and structural concessions made to the printed page.

These particular commentaries were written and aired between 1993 and about the end of 1995. Not every commentary written during that time is included here (mercifully), and I have chosen to arrange them more or less into chapters by subject rather than present them chronologically. Because of this, my daughter may appear as a seventh grader in one commentary and a freshman in the next, but I figure you can deal with that.

After writing these commentaries for almost a decade, I have come to realize that regular listeners have their favorites — usually because something in the commentary touched them personally. If you fit into that category, I hope I've included one of your recent favorites here.

If it's not, well, maybe it will get into the next collection.

Doug Hurd
November 1996

ACKNOWLEGMENTS

There are many people to thank for getting this book from a collection of semi-literate radio scripts to a readable book form.

My thanks to John and Toni Robideaux, Don Hamilton, Lorna St. John and Dennis Magner for reading the entire collection and telling me which commentaries were keepers and which to leave behind.

I am grateful to Anne Phillips and Betsy Newman for their proofing abilities and helpful comments.

I am also grateful to Jack White and Bob Runkle. First, for giving me the time and freedom to write my commentaries in the first place, and second for embracing this book, and helping me to get it out. I also need to thank Ed. Miller and all of the people in the art department at WhiteRunkle for their design help, as well as Lisa Hosmer of Hosmer Design who toiled on the cover design and page layout right up until she got on a plane for Hawaii.

A large debt of gratitude is owed to Dan Mortimore of Mortimore Productions. Dan has let me record my commentaries in his studios for free for several years (his monumental donation to public radio). As a result, I always sound better than I deserve.

And of course, my deepest thanks to Doug Nadvornick, Dick Kunkel and everyone at KPBX for giving me the opportunity to write and air my observations in the first place. Without KPBX, and the support of the KPBX family of listeners, none of these would exist in the first place.

Above all, I owe a special thanks to my wife, Jeannie, and my daughter Allyson for their love, support, friendship and patience.

And for providing me with so many things to write about.

CONTENTS

Brain Rot, Male Menopause and Other Joys of Middle Age

Bloomsday, Coaching Kids and Trucks Called Tacoma

Spring Projects and Other Things You've Bin Gonna Do

The First Seventh Grade Dance and Other Parenting Traumas

DAY-TIMER UPMANSHIP AND OTHER THINGS THEY DON'T TEACH IN BUSINESS SCHOOL

MOONING IN MOSCOW AND OTHER POLITICALLY INCORRECT MEANDERINGS

SHOPPING AT COSTCO AND OTHER THREATS TO MARITAL BLISS

FINDING THE PERFECT ALL-PURPOSE-UNIVERSAL-CHRISTMAS GIFT AND OTHER HOLIDAY TRADITIONS

BRAIN ROT, SHOPPING AT COSTCO AND OTHER JOYS OF MIDDLE AGE

The Humorous KPBX Commentaries of Doug Hurd

DOUG HURD

TIME OUT: PERSONAL WATER CRAFT, CAMPING AND OTHER VACATION THOUGHTS

Coming to Terms with Personal Water Craft

You're at the lake.

You've worked all year for this vacation.

You've saved all year, too. But it's worth it, because you're going to spend a full week with your family at the lake.

Which lake?

Around here, it doesn't really matter as long as it's not Medical Lake which may be the most inappropriately named lake we've got or Long Lake which is to Spokane what the large intestine is to…well, never mind, that's not the point.

It's Hayden Lake.

Or, Coeur d'Alene which is French for "Many Drunk Boat Drivers" or Lake Pend Oreille, which is French for "Always Cold."

Or it's Priest Lake. The true jewel of our natural crown.

Through luck, perseverance and obscene amounts of money, you've secured a cabin at Hills Resort, or Elkins or Linger Longer, or any of the wonderful resort areas along the lake.

Getting out of town late, you arrived in the middle of the night and got the kids settled in.

But now it's dawn and the early light filling your room starts to wake you on your first morning of vacation, and through the fuzzy haze of sleep, you are savoring the smell of the pines and you hear the sound of the lake awakening.

Ngggggg. Ngggggggg. Ngggggggg.

"That's weird," you think. "That sounds like a four hundred pound anopheles mosquito out looking for a human to suck dry. I wonder if they had another radiation leak down at Hanford last week they didn't tell us about."

In your sleepy state, this doesn't alarm you, but it is curious.

NGGGGGG. NGGGGGGG. NGGGGGGG.

You force one eye open. It's six o'clock. You had been thinking that maybe, if you could do it without disturbing anybody, you might put the boat in and wake the kids and go skiing on the glassy lake about 7:00.

So what is this noise?

By this time, you're aware that what ever it is, it's not an "it," it's a "them." There is a pack of them.

NGGGGG. NGGGGGGGG. NGGGGGGGG.

And you now hear voices: "All right! Nice air, Dude!"

You go out on your porch, and there, zooming around on the lake in front of you, there tearing up what had been the glass — the glass that water skiers crave to the point where they will hobble their best friend if it means getting to ski on it first — there you see what has been making the noise, and what, in an instant, you know you will come to loathe with every fiber of your body before your very expensive vacation is out: Jet skis. Sea-Doos. Personal water craft.

Dirt bike motorcycles that float.

NGGGGG. NGGGGGG. NGGGGGG.

"Honey," you say to your wife as you crawl back in bed, any thought of sleeping in, much less skiing on glass, hopelessly ruined for this morning, "Did you pack my 30.06?"

"The one with the big scope? Nope. Want me to go home and get it?" She's been awake, too. Heaven only knows how long.

"But did you remember to get your Jet-ski driver tag?" she asks. "No. So even if you had your 30.06, you couldn't shoot them, could you?"

Apparently she's been awake quite a while.

"I just wouldn't strap him to the bumper when I take him home, that's all," you say.

And so it begins, your vacation.

As the week progresses, you come to discover that personal water craft are everywhere, all the time.

This is not like the occasional drag boat that sits with about six inches of freeboard and has a bored and blown Chevy V8 with chrome exhaust pipes and tucked and rolled upholstery and a little tiny steering wheel that some guy with an expanding belly and a receding hairline roars down the lake in doing 75 in 15 second intervals.

Not at all. In that case the roar is annoying, but we all have compassion for a boat owner who has the bad luck to have that much money and insecurity all at the same time in life.

No, this is something quite different.

This is the democratization of power on the water. Boating made cheap enough for anyone and everyone.

Where two boats will cruise, two jet skis will ... zoom. It is the lake equivalent of taking a 360 Yamaha dirt bike into the tranquil recesses of Yosemite or the back country peaks of Glacier.

Imagine what life in your neighborhood would be like if suddenly, everybody could legally drive high powered go-carts wherever they wanted.

That's about what's happened to the lake.

There is one inescapable fact about jet skis however, one annoying thing that you can't quite put aside, no matter how much you detest them — they sure look like a lot of fun.

So when it happens toward the end of your stay at the lake, that you make the acquaintance of someone who owns one of the very jet skis that you have been contemplating punching an ice-pick through when no one is watching, and that person invites you to take it out for a spin, you have a true crisis of conscience.

Your kids, of course, are begging you to go so you can take them, assuming they haven't already bummed a ride on one.

"Can we, Dad? Can we?"

So against your better judgement and feeling a little like Luke Skywalker going over to the dark side for a while simply because they have neater star cruisers you say, "Well, maybe just for a little while."

And the first thing you think as you hang on for dear life as you accelerate across the waves is, "Whoa! This thing is fun!"

(Of course, that doesn't make it right — illicit sex is fun, too.)

(So I've been told.)

So there you are, out in the middle of the lake, and in no time at all you're jumping waves and taking air and absolutely oblivious to the cold stares of the families boating around you.

NGGGGG. NGGGGGG. NGGGGGGG.

And all you can do is hope that somewhere along the shore, there isn't a vacationer suddenly going over the edge, and saying to his wife, "Honey, bring me my 30.06 will you? The one with the big scope."

A Midsummer's Night of Hide and Seek

There is something happening in the cul-de-sac outside my house on these warm summer nights. It starts about 9:00 and continues until near 11 until an adult goes outside and tells them it's late and to go home and go to bed so we can all get some sleep.

They are playing hide and go seek. At night.

And for the younger boys the ones who are nine or ten — it's nothing less than a rite of passage.

They are being initiated into the Universal and Fraternal Order of Older Kids, as in, "Who were you playing with last night?" "Oh you know, some of the older kids."

Do you remember playing hide and go seek at night?

Scampering, through hedges, and hiding behind fences and under porches until some cranky neighbor made you all go home, grass stained and sweaty? Sure you do. It is the common growing up experience.

It is the perfect kid game. In order to play, you don't have to be big enough to shoot baskets or coordinated enough to hit a baseball. Size doesn't matter. There were no adults to enforce the rules and tell you who you had to play with.

There is really only one requirement: that your parents let you stay up past what used to be your bed time.

Dusk would come, and because you were now fourth grade, and with the older kids who were really old, you know, seventh or eighth grade, your mother didn't make you come in (a totally humiliating experience where she would call so the whole world could hear, "Honey! Time to come in now! Time to get ready for bed!").

But then one summer you got to stay out late.

The first thing a young initiate learns is, every game of hide and go seek had both its protocol and its rules and these were ironclad.

The first protocol rule was, a little kid can't suggest the game.

"Hey, I know," you'd say in your too eager pre-fourth grade voice, "Let's play hide and go seek!" The deadly silence that followed told you in no uncertain terms that you'd committed a horrible social gaffe.

"It's too early," would come the frosty reply. What they meant was, it's not your place to suggest the game. You haven't earned that rite. Only older kids have earned it.

Ten minutes later, of course, an older kid would say the exact same thing, and "Not it" would follow with blinding speed.

It's amazing. Fifteen kids who can't hear their mother calling them in for dinner can hear, "Let's play hide and go seek," and within a nanosecond processes who said it, his social standing, and send the body into full hide and go seek combat alert status. ("Brain to all major muscle groups: This is not a drill, repeat, this is not a drill. We have a game. Confidence is high. Vocal cords: Send the "not it" signal immediately. Ears: Be prepared to identify last person to finish saying "not it." Memory banks: recall and prioritize all hiding places at this location for immediate use. Legs: be ready to move at warp speed seven.")

Since it takes a while to get this internal system up and running, when you're a little kid, you're it a lot.

Each neighborhood has its own ground rules. These include the boundaries. "You can go down to the fire hydrant that way, stay out of the Erickson's front yard because he gets mad, and no farther than this side of 44th. No fair going indoors and you can't hide in cars. Go!"

To the best of my knowledge, the boundaries of hide and go seek are never violated. It is unthinkable. Later on we may cheat on our taxes, our spouses and at solitaire; but as kids the boundaries of hide and go seek are inviolate.

(Well, once in eighth grade when Calvin the Dweeb crashed our game of couples hide and go seek we all took off for the beach and ditched him. We came back about an hour later and Calvin was still looking behind the bushes for us. "Wow, you guys really hide good," he said. Calvin wasn't real swift. But that didn't count.)

About the time you're in seventh grade, you start looking for co-ed games of hide and go seek. Even if you've been playing with girls all along, after your hormones kick in, the presence of girls in the game changes things. You learn that hiding and seeking is also a terrific way to share a small dark place with a girl.

The final phase of the game comes in the eighth or ninth grade, when you start playing in couples. By that time, hide and go seek can quickly degenerate into a thinly disguised hormonally driven opportunity to make out.

Like I said, it's a rite of passage.

Somewhere after ninth grade, your life changes its focus, you get a summer job at McDonald's in the evenings, and the fourth graders you first let play are now seventh graders, and they are showing the game to kids who could barely walk when you learned to play.

And a new rite of passage takes place and the game continues, without end.

But now it's 11:00 and I need some sleep. So maybe I should play the role of the grumpy neighbor who makes them all quit and go home.

But as I lie in bed listening to their voices carry through the night, I realize that my memories of playing hide and go seek on those warm summer nights are among my most enjoyable and unsullied.

They are the essence of being a kid in summer.

And I think how much fun it would be to play again like that.

So, sleepy as I am, I don't want to be the one to end their fun.

"Ally, ally, oxen-free," my brain says as I drift off to sleep.

Summertime Rules

Is your household running on Summertime rules, yet?

Ours is. Finally.

Usually we implement summertime rules the moment school gets out, but we've been a little late this year. Probably has something to do with the weather being so crummy; no one really feels like it's summer, yet.

Usually, the first introduction of summertime rules takes place the first night school is out with the announcement of the first midweek sleepover. Winter rules specify that sleepovers are strictly a weekend activity, so it's something of a summer kick off when the kids get to have one on a week night.

You can tell which parents have been through this before; they're the ones who know the sleepover is coming and rather than fight it, encourage it — but at someone else's house. This usually comes in the form of the parental suggestion pre-emptive strike: "Hey! Since there's no school tomorrow, why don't you have a sleepover tonight…at Lydia's!"

I know that we are now officially on summer rules because I had the Telephone Talk with my daughter. (My daughter is now

12, and faces the real risk of telephone mastoiditis, a condition where a telephone actually takes root and starts to grow into her mastoid bone. When that happens, the receiver must be surgically removed. It's a pretty common problem among pre-teen girls, I'm told.)

Those of you with pre-teen daughters know what the Telephone Talk is. That's where you lay down the rules about how late your child can be on the phone, and at what time outgoing must stop and when incoming calls will start getting impolite greetings. Those of you with younger children still have the Telephone Talk to look forward to.

"Okay, here's the rule: you don't call anyone after 9:00, except the fire department, and only then if the house is fully engulfed in flames. After 9:15, we don't put any more calls through to you and after 9:30 I don't want to get any calls period."

"How am I supposed to keep the phone from ringing?"

I hate it when she asks me a question I don't know the answer to.

"Tell your friends not to call," I reply somewhat lamely.

Actually, I have discovered that you only have to rant and rave at a late caller one time and the word spreads among the sixth grade mafia like a grass fire: Don't call Allyson's house after 9:30, because if her dad answers he gets really MAD! For a while I was telling late callers, "I'm sorry, she broke her leg today, and we had to shoot her." But I stopped when I found out a couple of her friends believed me.

Telephone rules follow the Mother of all summertime rules which is the bedtime rule.

In fact, it is the bedtime rule that is usually a parent's first foray into summertime rules. That's because even a first grader makes the connection between school and bedtime, and the subsequent logic that if there is no school, maybe, just maybe, there is no bedtime. Plus, sooner or later it will occur to them that there is something not quite right about having to go to bed before the sun sets, and all the big kids are still out on the basketball court.

Unfortunately, this rule works at odds with the parental bedtime rule which is non-seasonal and states that the older a parent gets, the earlier bedtime will be. So while the kids want to stay up later, you want to go to bed earlier.

Perhaps because of that, somewhere about 11 years of age the concept of bedtime disappears altogether. And along with it, the concept of getting up in the morning. There is something in me as a parent that says that isn't quite right somehow, but since, like you, I'm just kind of learning the parenting thing as I go along, I let it slide. Besides, I want to go to bed.

Kids aren't the only ones who have summer rules, of course. Adults do, too.

Around our house, the first adult rule to change is the dinner rule. Which changes from, dinner is around six-ish to, maybe we'll have dinner and maybe we won't. (I don't know how it is around your house, but where I live there is some sort of inverse relationship between the outside temperature and the odds we'll have an evening meal. The higher the temperature, the lower the chance of dinner. Above 80, who wants to cook? Above 90, who wants to even be around a hot meal?)

Besides, summertime rules dictate that household chores that used to take place on the weekend have to be moved to midweek, because there are better things to do with weekends than mow lawns. So those get moved to weekday evenings. That's why there's always a lawn mower going, day and night, somewhere in the neighborhood.

Summertime rules also dictate the uniform to be worn (tanktop, shorts, no shoes) as well as the relative priority of play over work. In fact, there is almost no household project thought up during summer rules that can't be shelved until September.

"Honey, the bathtub is leaking and needs to be re-grouted."

"Yeah. I'm going to get to that, um, right after the Interstate Fair."

"That's in September."

"Uhh, yeah."

It would seem that summer rules generally promote family

anarchy, and they would if they lasted forever. But just about the time there seems to be no structure left, fall comes and with it, winter rules?

Not exactly. First come football season rules.

Which means, that maybe re-grouting the bathtub will have to wait until after the Superbowl.

Carefully Planning A Spontaneous Summer

It's June. That means it's summer.

And that means, care free, do-what-you-want days in the sun. Weekends where you wake up, get a whim, and follow it where ever it may lead, at least to the limits of your Visa card, right?

Wrong.

Summer, contrary to what your body is telling you it should be, has become the most structured and rigidly planned season of the year.

"You know, I think I'll call Gary and Dick and get a golf game going tomorrow," you say to your wife on a Friday like today.

"You can't," she replies. "Saturday you're carpooling seven kids from Libby Junior High to Silverwood and back, and Sunday is my office picnic, and next weekend we're taking the kids to Camp Ptomaine and the weekend after that, we're going boating with Tim and Lisa."

"Tim and Lisa? We are?"

"We've been planning it since the Boat Show in January when they were signing away all their future paychecks. It was the only weekend all summer we both still had. Don't you remember?"

Well, if you're a man, the truth is, no. You don't remember.

Welcome to the Summer Planning Paradox Rule and its many corollaries.

The Summer Planning Paradox Rule is simply this: To have a fun-filled, carefree summer, you must plan carefully, and schedule every weekend as far in advance as possible. In the case of family gatherings, vacations and the like, that can mean years in advance.

And corollary number one is, because of the paradox, because of this resistance to what feels like should be the normal order of things, we husbands tend to forget all the advance plans as soon as they're made.

"I never said I'd spend a weekend in a small boat with Tim and Lisa. Are they bringing their yippie little dog?"

"Yes. But it's even — we're bringing our daughter."

"It's not exactly even. Their dog doesn't stay under headphones headbanging to Nirvana all day. Why did you say we'd do this?"

"I didn't. You did."

"Oh. I did?"

Which brings you to corollary number two: Whatever you plan probably won't seem like a good idea when the time comes to do it.

There's a couple of reasons for this. First of all, there's the weather which is always pretty iffy, but most of all, it's just darn hard to know in January what, out of all the choices you have in life, you will want to do most on, say, the third weekend in June.

Now, to a man, the obvious answer is, just don't make plans. Just get to that weekend in June and wing it.

To which the women, who are much more tuned into these things and tend to know how the social calendar really looks, answers, "Sure. Just tell me which of the three available weekends between Memorial Day and Labor Day you want to wing it on. And what do you think the odds are that your friends — any friends — you want to wing it with, don't already have something scheduled, huh?"

Three weekends all summer? That's all that aren't already committed to some activity?

Actually, by this time, if you still have three full weekends left, you probably haven't got kids left at home, or haven't got a life.

Or both.

Three weekends still open after the first week in June is a lot considering office picnics, picking up and dropping kids off at every sports camp ever invented, traditional camping weekends with friends from college, and the three or four weddings you can count on having to attend each summer.

Which brings us to corollary number three: Just as bad drives out good, those things you have to do on summer weekends will expand and crowd out what you want to do.

Now, what you have to do is divided into two categories: what you really have to do, which might include dropping off and picking up your kids at camp (there goes two weekends per summer camp per kid) and what you have to do because you don't know how to get out of it, which is like the extended family vacation camping at Priest Lake for a week which you began doing in 1977 and which hasn't been all that much fun since 1979.

"Tell me again why we are going camping with your mom and your step dad who you can't stand, and your sister and her boyfriend who I can't stand and your brother's wife who your mom can't stand and both their kids who nobody can stand."

Well, it's for the same reason you also spend a week at Ocean Shores getting sand in every body cavity, not to mention everything you own, with your family; even though you're middle aged, and you may have figured out the stock market and how to manage fifty employees, you still haven't figured out how to tell your family "no" when it comes to attending the annual family vacation.

The problem is, family is important, but not, perhaps, important enough to waste twenty years of vacation on, at a rate of two weeks per year each July.

Now, all this may sound like I'm whining about the arrival of summer, but I'm not. I have learned over the years that a great deal more enjoyment is to be had going with the planning flow than going against it.

Which brings us to the final corollary to the Summer Planning Paradox Rule: If you don't plan ahead, you can plan to do whatever you're going to do — alone, because everybody else has plans.

So, if you'd like to get together with my wife and I for a camping weekend, we'd love to.

How about the third weekend in July, 1998?

I Don't Love Baseball

It begins again, and I dread it.

The deceit, the lying, the faking it.

I tell myself, this year, this year, I am going to be involved, I'm going to care. When the men get together and start talking that man talk, I'm going to have facts, figures, names, and statistics — Lord the statistics, we can't forget those omnipresent statistics — down pat.

But it's futile. And deep in my heart, I know it.

I just don't care about baseball.

And it's not just some sort of mid-life crisis caused by a loss of testosterone or something: I have never cared about baseball.

I feel terrible about this! Isn't there a meeting somewhere I'm supposed to go to where I stand up and say, "My name's Doug, and I think baseball's stupid?"

The last baseball players I cared about were Roy Campanella, Sandy Koufax, and Don Drysdale. That was in 1957. I was in the fifth grade. I also liked PeeWee Reese, primarily because, being the smallest in my class, I related to his name.

Even then I knew I was different.

My friends seemed to know that they were supposed to collect baseball cards. I had to be shown.

I had to take remedial baseball card gathering.

"What do you do with them?" I asked, fanning out the cards, looking in vain for a face or name I knew, while chewing the enormous slab of gum.

"You keep them," came the non-answer, self-evident reply.

What they didn't tell you is that you also have to memorize them if you want to be cool, and learn to spit out the facts on the back of them at every gathering of two or more of your friends.

You also have to learn which ones to treasure and which ones have no value. That, of course, is dependent on how the player played, which is on the back, so if you don't memorize the back you don't know if the front has value.

It's complicated.

Being baseball impaired made me something of a social pariah in 5th grade jock circles, since I couldn't even remember which teams were in the American League and which were in the National League.

(Of course, I also couldn't remember the multiplication tables, which I was supposed to be learning at about the same time, which might tell you something about my attention span.)

It was about that time too, that I learned that a baseball, especially one that has been used a lot and was getting frayed, makes a curious whizzing sound when it comes at your head.

zzzzZZZZZZZZzz.

To me, it was the sound of impending death: zzzzZZZZZZZZzz.

That was also the year I tried out for little league, and mercifully for all concerned, failed.

I believe all fifth grade boys can be divided into two categories: those who view a whizzing, bouncing baseball as an object full of kinetic energy that, if you get in its way, has the power to permanently disfigure and maim you, and those who don't.

I was in the former group. I never saw a baseball coming at me I much cared for.

Now, you may be wondering why, if I didn't like baseball, I tried out for little league.

Me, too. What's worse, I remember wondering it at the time.

We all know that a man's got to do what a man's got to do, but it's easy to forget that a boy's got to do what a boy's got to do. And one of those things is try out for little league baseball, especially when a friend says, "You're trying out, aren't you?"

Uh, huh.

Tryouts were fun.

I'm out in the infield with a bunch of other boys, and the coach is hitting baseballs at us to see who knows how to pick up a grounder. I don't. I could have told him that from the sideline, but instead I'm out there on the baseline with fifty other boys, and he's taking target practice at us.

Crack. zzzzZZZZZZZZzz. Wap. The ball hits Gary Christoffersen's mit as he effortlessly fields the ball hit to him.

Crack. zzzzZZZZZZZZzz. Wap. Mike Taylor makes the team.

Crack. Suddenly I'm thinking: is that ball coming to me?

No, Yes, No, Yes! Yikes! That sucker's moving at the speed of sound! Why did he hit it so hard? ZZZZZZZ. Oh, my god it's bouncing! It's like a pinball and I'm a human bumper. ZZZZZ It's going to hit me!

So I did what I always did: I turned away, ducked my head, and stuck my mit out in the general direction of the speeding ball, and hoped that in the next moment I wouldn't be crippled for life.

zzzzZZZZZZZZzz. It missed me.

It was all I could do to keep from screaming, "I'm alive! I'm alive!"

You can imagine how much fun batting practice was, with someone throwing the ball as hard as they could at an imaginary box six inches in front of me that started just below my head and ended at the only set of knee caps God gave me.

zzzzZZZZZZZZzz. Three pitches, three strikes, no swings.

This just ain't my game.

That was when I knew I wasn't Pee Wee Reese, and I wasn't ever going to be.

Not because I was terribly uncoordinated: heavens no, I was chicken.

But perhaps more important, in spite of all the peer group pressure to the contrary, I just didn't care about baseball.

And I still don't.

In fact the whole season is a little like that baseball coming at me: zzzzZZZZZZZZzz.

Missed me again.

Unwinding

Summer is officially over.

At least according to my biological clock, anyway.

I know this, because the other night I got into our hot tub again. I go there to unwind.

Not that I'm wound all that tight to begin with, you understand.

You see, I don't unwind in the hot tub when it's hot. I've got enough trouble sleeping when it's 90 degrees out. The last thing I need in the summer is to get into a hot tub and crank my body temperature up another ten degrees or so.

So during June, July and August, the old hot tub rarely gets used.

But when fall comes, and cooler temperatures return, one night getting in the hot tub seems like a good idea again, and probably for the same reasons that geese fly south and bears start looking for a place to hibernate and cats suddenly stop shedding, out I go.

I use it a lot after refereeing high school and college volleyball matches. I float around, thinking about the calls I made, and didn't make, where I was on top of the match and where I blew it, and within a few minutes, my whole body and mind has turned to something akin to a rubber band, and whatever I did in the match doesn't matter anymore.

If I stay long enough, I go into cardiac arrest, and nothing matters anymore.

How we each unwind is a pretty individual question.

Some people like to shop. Some do needle point or cross stitch. Some do aerobics. Some like to get drunk and punch out the nearest cop. None of those work for me.

For a lot of people, the answer is sports.

This is okay, except that all too often, what begins as recreation has a way of ending up as a blood sport, and becomes far more serious than, say our jobs, and so unwinding is the last thing that happens.

"Did you unwind playing golf today, Dear?"

"I don't want to talk about it."

"But I thought you said you finally figured out what you were doing wrong with your driving. And putting. And your approaches."

"That was last Saturday, and I said I don't want to talk about it. By the way, I need a new putter. I wrapped mine around a tree."

If you play a sport with your spouse, what should be a way to unwind and have some fun together often has exactly the opposite effect, because we husbands have a way of asking perfectly normal game related questions in a way that comes out sounding all wrong.

"You've got a runner on first, a runner on third, a two and one count to a left handed batter who's hitting right handed with a left handed pitcher and you move off the bag to your _right_? Where did you think he was going to hit that ball? What were you thinking!!!?"

"I was thinking it's time I called Carl Maxey and filed for a divorce."

You know it is time to alter your sports patterns when: A) you find going to work relieves the stress of playing in your co-ed softball league, or B) getting a divorce so you can find a wife who plays second base better than the one you've got starts sounding like a good idea.

My advice is to get a hot tub.

I've observed that how you unwind also changes depending upon your age.

For instance, when you're single and in your early twenties, unwinding is just another word for "party." But then, what isn't?

At 21, unwinding after an exhausting day at work often means meeting everyone else from work who is 21 and exhausted and stressed out at Shenanigans at 5:03, and pounding down a few.

Then moving on to Swackhammers at 7:30 and out to Kelly's at State Line at about 10:00. You shut down Kelly's sometime after one, try to drive home without getting arrested, and after four hours sleep, show up for work looking like Lyle Lovett and start the whole process over again.

Unwinding like that, it's amazing anybody survives their twenties.

By the time you enter your thirties, you should be past all that, but what you're into is anybody's guess.

Some people turn to alcohol to relieve their stress and unwind. (Personally, I've found that too much alcohol can not only unwind me, but actually disassemble me, which is not the same thing. Not altogether bad, you understand, but I've found the putting back together is not worth the tearing down.)

If you have a hot tub, you've probably discovered that a bottle of chablis and 40 minutes of soaking in 104 degree water has the curious effect of dissolving the muscles in your legs.

There's nothing like having legs made of silly putty to make getting out of a hot tub a real challenge.

"Brain to legs. Brain to legs. Come on you guys. I know you're down there somewhere. Let's go. Help me out here. We need to get these kidneys into the house."

Other people eat to relieve their stress, but this only works if you have the metabolism of a blast furnace so you don't add the stress of dieting.

"I've had a tough day at work. Now give me that pizza so I can unwind."

Unwind? Maybe. Lower your stress? After you see what the pizza does to how you look in a swimsuit, I doubt it.

Like a lot of men I know, I've found that a building project is a good way to unwind. This is because a good project takes your mind completely off work, or whatever is stressing you. There's nothing quite like concentrating on not cutting off my fingers with a compound miter saw to make me forget everything else for a while.

Unfortunately, while I'm usually successful in maintaining my concentration on the project, I'm not always successful in preventing my doing bodily harm to myself.

I've come to accept the fact that skinned knuckles and damaged body parts are the price I will pay to unwind during summer.

So, while I will miss the warm weather of summer, I confess I look forward to the cool evenings ahead where from time to time, I will slip into the hot tub and let the stresses in my life just dissolve away.

Along with my legs.

Taking the Kids Camping

It's Friday. And it's summertime.

This unhappy convergence can mean only one thing. That sooner or later, your child will ask you the dreaded question you asked your father: "Can we go camping?"

The answer, of course, is yes. You have no choice. You're a normal parent, spending the better part of your adult life pretending to be your parents parenting you as you parent your children, and since your parents took you camping, you, in turn will have to take your children camping. That's a given.

But before you panic, you have to realize that the camping your child is asking about experiencing is not the camping you enjoyed as a child.

Camping is not the same as it was.

Was when?

Doesn't matter. Was whenever you went camping last. The further back in time that was, the more things have changed.

At one time, I suspect that camping was the general re-creation of the pioneer experience, a time for the handing down of the woodsman's techniques for survival in the wilderness. How to gather wood. How to start a fire.

Today it's apt to be how to aim your satellite dish so you don't miss the All-Star game. Hey! Just because you're out in the woods doesn't mean you be completely uncivilized, does it?

This advancing of camping technology is not a new thing. By the time I was camping as a young boy, the woodsman's techniques my father was passing along to me included how to light a Coleman Lantern without destroying the wick. That's pretty woodsy.

Today, 40 years later, the hissing sound of a Coleman lantern burning still evokes powerful memories of places like Salmon-la-Sac, Sun Lakes and Tawano State Park.

And we never, ever actually cooked anything over an open fire except a marshmallow and the occasional unfortunate wiener. The Coleman stove had replaced the cooking grate in our family.

I was probably in the last generation to go to a forest service campsite and actually go gather wood for a fire; anymore you buy your wood. Or you bring it with you. From the city. (Does that seem a little weird to anybody but me?) I should mention that, being both lazy and larcenous as a child, I tended to gather wood by stealing it from the nearest vulnerable campsite.

The thing is, camping means different things to different people. This, of course leads to a sort of hierarchy amongst campers, or, if you will, a lowerarchy. The fewer creature comforts you take into the woods, the lower on the techno-camping scale you go, and hence, the more macho you are. The more macho you are, the higher up the camper-woodsman-rugged person scale you get to go.

This puts people who camp in motorhomes at the bottom of the camping barrel.

One has to admit that sleeping in an air conditioned comfort in a spacious double bed, zapping your food in a microwave and having a travelling bathroom with a shower is not exactly "camping."

Next to them are the travel trailer and fifth wheel campers, whose conveniences are scoffed at by the people who rough it in those pop up trailers.

They in turn are looked down upon by the waffle stomper types who still insist that camping, by definition, means you spend time in a tent, don't get to sleep well, and smell real bad by the end of the weekend.

Above them come backpackers, who spurn almost all creature comforts and who, consequently, get to sneer at most everyone.

I tried backpacking once. Two friends talked me into hiking into the Enchanted Lakes area above Leavenworth.

And I mean "above."

Rather than taking the trail like all the rest of humanity, we went in the back way, up over a several thousand foot rockfall. "It's shorter," my friends said.

They failed to mention that it was also steeper, and, since we arrived in the middle of the night, in the pitch black, it was also a good way to simply walk right off a 3,000 foot cliff, something I discovered the next morning.

On the plus side, the views were unbelievably spectacular. On the minus side, I couldn't walk normally for a week, and I decided that the entire experience was way too much like work.

Today, of course, we couldn't have taken that trip because we didn't have reservations. Today the woods are so crowded with people who want to get out into them that you have to reserve a space in advance.

The entire notion of booking space out in the wide open spaces because too many people want to go the same place to get away from too many people is just a bit too Kafka-esque for me.

So when your child asks if you can go camping this weekend, you will say yes.

Yes, you will go down to the General Store and drop about three grand on tents and gear.

Yes, you will call the National Camp Reservation System in search of campsite within an eight hour drive that isn't already spoken for.

Yes, you will be happy to pass along to your child the simple joy of the smell of coffee and bacon and eggs cooking over an open campfire, and the woodsy lore of how to light a Coleman stove, and level a motor home.

Yes, you will renew again the spirit of our pioneer forebears.

To which your child will probably reply, "Actually, Dad, what I had in mind was sleeping out in the back yard tonight."

On the other hand, maybe for kids, camping out hasn't changed that much, at all.

The Various Stages of Taking a Vacation

I just got back from vacation.

It was not long enough.

Now, you may take that as evidence of poor planning on my part, but I'm not so sure.

Vacations are like restaurant lunches: sometimes you don't get enough, sometimes you get too much, and sometimes you get exactly the amount you want. It all depends upon how fast you progress through the various and well defined stages of your vacation, and how hungry (figuratively speaking, of course) your psyche is for a break.

There are seven distinct stages to all vacations. Most of these are not very pleasant.

The first stage is Laundry.

This comes after planning and financial counselling and political maneuvering to get to go where you want to go instead of to Disneyland which is where your kids want to go or to your mother-in-law's where your wife wants to go, none of which are really part of the vacation itself.

Laundry might be considered by some of you as a pre-vacation stage, but I contend that your vacation starts when you've left work for the last time, and who does their laundry until the night before they leave?

Next come Pre-Departure Anxiety or PDA.

During PDA, you try to think of everything you forgot, not counting what you think is in the laundry, like your airline tickets, and traveler's checks and your transdermal seasickness patches and kennel reservations for the family dog.

"What do you mean you forgot to get a reservation at Bowserville Estates?"

"No sweat. We leave the dog with the neighbor kids and pay them a buck a day to feed him."

"We don't have any neighbor kids around here."

"Oh."

It is during PDA that people who are afraid to fly start to notice that airplanes all over the world are falling out of the sky at an alarming rate.

Soon however, you fly to your resort destination where your actual vacation is supposed to begin. Your mental image of this event generally includes images of Kathy Lee Gifford looking glamorous and having <u>such</u> a good time.

But first, you must proceed through Post Vacation Departure Stress Syndrome.

This is the stage where you suddenly remember a thousand details about your projects that you forgot to tell the people at work. You can tell who is in Post Vacation Departure Stress Syndrome; they're the ones who periodically sit bolt upright in their lawn chairs and say stuff like, "Oh, God, Oh, God," and look furtively around for a cellular phone. They are also the least tanned ones.

You know the moment when you have crossed from Post Departure Vacation Stress Syndrome to Benign Vacation Vacuousness, the next stage. You sit up, remembering a job you left at the printer's that your client absolutely had to have the day you left that you not only forgot, but you also forgot to tell anyone about, and you say, "Oh, God. Oh, God," and then you sit back in the chair and say, "Ah, screw it. I'm on vacation."

It is only then that you really unwind. This is what you came on vacation for. To be truly away from it all, mentally and physically. This is when your real vacation begins.

It is glorious. It is wonderful.

It is what you work the other fifty weeks of the year for.

This true, relaxed vacation state lasts anywhere from 15 minutes to four hours.

Then you enter the next stage of your vacation, which is Pre-Homeward Stress Syndrome.

This is where you begin thinking about all the things you are going to have to do when you get home. And how you are going to pay for all the T-shirts you are buying, and for that matter, how you are going to carry all the T-shirts home.

During this stage you keep counting and recounting your traveller's checks, and try to recall everywhere you cashed one hoping against hope that you're not down as far as you seem to be, and asking your wife if she has any of them stashed somewhere, and thinking that a couple of lunches and dinners at McDonald's would do you all some good, anyway, all the while wondering if that print job you forgot didn't cost you your job.

People in this stage look pretty much like the people in the Post Departure Stress Syndrome, except that they are tanner, generally.

Pre-Homeward Stress Syndrome gives way to Homeward Departure Anxiety, in which you try to remember which family members you bought trinkets for and which ones you haven't and who at work gave you money for a case of macadamia nuts and who wanted a pineapple and what size, and how you're going to do all that.

It is also, if you are afraid to fly, when you begin to wonder just how a 747 loaded to the gills with people, baggage and pineapples gets off the ground and whether or not there is some previously undiscovered exception to Bernoulli's Law that will cause the wings to loose their lift and make the plane fall out of the sky.

So how long is the right length of time for a vacation?

Well, there are a lot of variables, such as the weather here, the weather there, and whether your kids went with you or not, all of which makes each vacation individual and unique, but I can tell you this: I was gone for ten days, and it wasn't quite long enough.

By about three months.

Although, I have to admit, when anyone asks me how vacation was, I beam that tan smile I now wear and say, "It was great."

Oh, yeah, I said there was seven stages to your vacation, but I only mentioned six. But you know what the last stage is. It's where you really know your vacation is over.

The last stage is doing the laundry.

Getting to Watch Oprah

You know what I love most about getting a three day weekend?

It's not time away from work; I like work.

It's not spending time with my family. I already spend a lot of time with my family.

It's not being able to putter around the house and attending to those little repair jobs that never seem to get done. I sure don't want to waste a day off doing those things.

No. What I love best about having a Monday or a Friday off is getting to join that elite group of people who do that one thing everyday, that one thing that they talk about at dinner, and on the phone and on the sidelines while their kids are out catching pneumonia on the soccer field; that one thing that lets us glimpse the darker, weirder side of the American psyche and somehow come away bonded to each other like we've had a shared religious event – I get to watch Oprah.

And if, by some quirk of fate, I get the day off, and my wife doesn't, I can't wait until she comes home so I can stand there in the kitchen getting dinner ready and say those words that all non-Oprah watching peoples of the world hate: "You should have seen Oprah today."

It's the adult, grownup version of, "I know something you don't."

It doesn't take a brain surgeon to figure out that the world is divided into two separate and distinct classes of peoples: those who by diligence, hard work, perseverance, an accident of fate or divine intervention, have arranged their lives so that they get to watch the Oprah Winfrey Show, and those who just aren't that smart.

Or lucky.

Or both.

It's like the world's biggest club, and you're in or you're out.

And if you're in, you get to talk about it, and if you're out, you get to listen to those who are in.

"You should have seen Oprah today — all her guests were women who married midget male strippers."

Now, I ask you, did anything happen in your life today that even begins to compare with women who married midget male strippers?

No. So you know what? You get to listen.

Now, if the statement is made in the presence of another Oprah watcher, what happens next is pure communication synergy. Like perfectly synched up tape machines, they will replay the whole program for each other, or you, minus commercials.

If you could see the actual show this way it would be better because two or three people talking about an Oprah show will inevitably re-order it and play it back from its most interesting to its least interesting moments.

"Do you remember where the mother who married all three of those brothers told her sister-in-law that she was a slut because she was sleeping with those Hungarian Circus clowns who were joined at the hip, and she said, "I am not, I'm only sleeping with the middle one?" "Yes, and Oprah said…" and so on.

And on. And on.

There are some rules to being an Oprah watcher.

The main thing to remember is, discussing the show is not a game of trivia so much as one of total and immediate recall. The only show that really matters is the one that was on today, or maybe yesterday. It is considered bad form to drag the game into Oprah one-upmanship by saying, "Oh, yeah? Well, I saw the show in 1988 with the battered husbands of the weight lifting transsexuals ... "

It is also against the rules to talk about a show longer than the actual show ran, (or after your listener's eyes glaze over, whichever comes first) and while there is no rule against it, Oprah watchers need to guard against the impression that watching Oprah is as interesting as their own life gets.

Even if it's true.

It is also considered low class to mix a discussion of Oprah with Maury, Geraldo, Joan, or any of the other Oprah wannabes. Even though they are all mining the same vein, ("Women who found their boyfriends in bed with their best friends, shot their friends to death and married their boyfriends anyway — on the next Geraldo") only Oprah should be openly discussed.

This doesn't mean you can't watch the others; just don't tell anybody. It's the difference between discussing what you read in, say Time or Newsweek and the National Enquirer.

You might be wondering why, if watching Oprah is such a treat on my day off, I don't just tape it and watch it later. To me, that is the rough equivalent of taping a football game and watching it later; if it's already over, I don't care anymore. The fun's gone out of it. It's live or not at all.

Because that is what makes her show so good — the immediacy of it all. It's happening now, and when you watch, you're a part of it. I suspect that it is that feeling of participation that is what makes us want to tell about it.

That, plus, how many times do we get to listen to the kind of people she has on her show discuss their relationships and, um, problems? ("Female Attorney Generals who still can't put on pantyhose without running them — on the next Oprah!")

Unless you're in the mental health field, probably not that often.

Which does beg the question: what is it about talk shows that make people who wouldn't confess their problems to you over coffee in the office get up on national television and spill their guts?

Why do guys who stalk women avoid the police but show up

on Oprah? Why would their victims sit there with them?

More importantly, why do we watch?

I think the answer is pretty simple: it's interesting — and it makes us feel normal. Plus it gives one something to talk about when the non-Oprah watcher gets home.

For instance, you should have seen Oprah on Monday. It was about men who date older women, and there was this lady who married her daughter's 18-year-old boyfriend, and the daughter was there, and there was this body builder named Vinny who ...

The Law of Ever-Slower Moving Bodies and Going Skiing

If you are one of the many who will be going skiing this week-end, I have some advice: go alone.

If you don't, if you are going up with your family, and especially if you are going up with more than one family, then tomorrow you will encounter one of nature's most immutable laws.

The law of nature that says, "A group slows down to the square of the number of people in the group."

You may have encountered this slowing phenomena when trying to get your family ready for, say, a wedding. In fact, it is the reason why in most weddings, when the bride should be marching down the center aisle, most of the guests are still finding their way down the side aisles.

The law is particularly strict when it comes to skiers.

If there is just one of you, you get up and you go. If there are two of you, you get up and with a little more time, you go. If there are four of you, you get up an hour earlier, and then you go. If there are eight of you in two families trying to get out of the same condo, somebody should plan on getting up at about 3:30 in the morning, and if there are more than 10 of you, you might as well just go up the night before and sleep in the parking lot.

The rule of slowing human bodies tends to change normal family relationships.

For instance, parents tend to get into good cop/bad cop roles.

"Your father has started warming up the car, so unless you

want to be wearing those Frosted Flakes, I suggest you stop watch-ing cartoons and eat them."

It is not unusual amid the hubbub of people scurrying to lo-cate gloves and goggles to have a child or two go absolutely cata-tonic on the couch.

"Eric, what are you doing?"

"I don't know."

"Do you have all your stuff?"

"I don't know."

"Do you have your gloves?"

"No."

Why don't you go find them?"

"Okay."

As the minutes tick away, and visions of traffic jams going up the mountain and of all the powder snow being chewed up by rampaging snowboarders become more vivid, the group goes into what might be called "Hyperslow."

Hyperslow is when all of the parents each take equipment inventory for each kid, hence a slowing time multiple of the num-ber of parents times the number of kids.

"Boots? Gloves? Goggles? Hat?…Hat? Where's your hat, Eric?"

When you have discovered that the cosmic force that mys-teriously moves ski gear from one place to another has struck, you must invoke the magic words and say the magic chant that will help you locate the missing item, "MAMMA! HAVE YOU SEEN ERIC'S HAT?"

There are a lot of things that you don't want to have to buy on top of the mountain, and right behind five cheeseburgers for your family, is a hat for your absent minded child.

So, you have to decide, is it better to pull mamma off sand-wich making duty to hunt for the hat, or do you stop everybody and do a bag and body search to see if someone hasn't inadvert-ently packed it away into their own stuff.

Either way, the clock keeps ticking.

My daughter recently turned twelve, and this year we have a new ritual in our family called "The doing of the hair." Now, it is the basic male approach to recognize that ski hats are designed to make your hair look like you've been getting shock treatments in a mental institution for about a week, so doing the hair is waste of time.

This is a lost argument, however, on a female over the age of twelve (who might see a boy), and below the age of about forty (who might see one of her friends). Above forty, we're back to that shock treatment look.

And, of course, you can't go skiing with just any hairdo. You need a French braid. The making of which requires about the same number of people as a county road crew.

The final step to being on your way is the herding out the door of everybody. This is when parents resemble nothing so much as well trained sheep dogs. The trick here is to keep the little kids from diving into the nearest snow bank.

It is usually on the way out to the car that the random bladder attack will occur.

"Wait!"

"What is it, Eric?"

"I have to go potty."

"Why didn't you go before, Eric?"

"I forgot."

Now, depending upon how long it's taken you to get to this point, you may actually wonder to yourself just how much long term bladder damage can occur during a two hour car ride. But then you think, no, this kid is going to ski with frost-bitten ears as it is, so the whole parade stops while Eric goes to the bathroom.

It is a little known medical fact that going to the bathroom is a contagious thing, and no sooner will Eric be gone than eight or nine other bladders will suddenly need emptying.

By this time, the bad cop parent will be wondering out loud if just driving off and leaving everybody would teach them all a lesson, and it is then that he will remember that he forgot to get gas or go to the bank yesterday which will necessitate a stop at a gas station and a cash machine, two things that are never in the same place.

Finally of course, you pull out, estimating your time of arrival anywhere from one and a half to three hours later than you wanted to arrive. Usually, it's just late enough to wonder if you should slow down some more and buy a half day ticket.

But at least you're unequivocally, unstoppably on your way.

You know it, because that's the moment when the bad cop parent turns to the good cop parent and asks, "Uh, did you pack my ski hat, by any chance?"

Driving Under Emergency Snow Rules

When it snows, there ought to be a sign somewhere. A big sign like the one on Snoqualmie Pass that blinks and tells you that traction devices are required.

Only our sign would say, "Emergency Snow Traffic Rules Now In Effect."

As soon as it snows, everyone starts using Emergency Snow Traffic Rules automatically. Well, almost everybody.

Snow rules are designed to facilitate the movement of traffic with as little loss of human life as possible.

It is a kind of polite demolition derby and when it snows we're all entered.

Most of the changes have to do with who has the right of way. For instance, anyone blasting their way out of an unplowed side street onto an arterial has the right of way. Anyone coming out of a driveway onto any street has the right of way.

During Snow Rules, stop signs only need to be obeyed when you face them going down hill — when starting again is not likely to be a problem. That is, if you can stop at all.

And you have to remember that people coming up a hill to a stop sign, not only do not have to stop, but are generally encouraged not to stop by everybody behind them who will get stuck if they do.

Knowing who has the right of way can be tricky in some cases. Generally, the rules are designed to facilitate the flow of traffic, therefore, when two cars are meeting in an uncontrolled skid on snow or ice, the car with the least control is said to have the right of way. (Or, if it has already crossed the centerline into oncoming traffic, the wrong of way.)

On the freeway, anyone in a 360 degree spin automatically has the right of way. It's best not to do a 360 if you can help it, but once into one, it is comforting to know that it is everybody else's job to get out of your way.

Under Snow Rules, it is illegal to make a left turn while facing up a hill, which might mean you, and those behind you, have to stop. It is foolish to make a left turn going down a hill, because you might get rear-ended, but if you want to risk it, you can.

Yellow lights are to be totally ignored.

You do have to stop for red lights, although if stopping means you may get stuck, you are allowed to take an immediate left or right turn. It doesn't matter which lane you are in.

If you are traveling up a hill when you encounter a red light, it has to be really, really red for you to stop. Just having been momentarily red is not enough.

The other drivers will understand.

The flip side of that, of course, is that when you get a green light, it does not mean "go." It means, you have to wait to be sure all oncoming traffic has stopped completely and then you can go. In other words, it's got to be really, really green, before you're allowed to go.

Pedestrians never have the right of way under Snow Rules. Never. Not in a crosswalk, not on the sidewalk, never. After all, nobody ever heard of having to dig out a stuck pedestrian, did they?

It is considered bad form to run down pedestrians, however, unless you are totally out of control. It is okay to run down joggers though, because anyone so neurotic about their running that they must run on snow covered streets probably has a pretty well developed death wish anyway.

Under Snow Rules, it is considered a faux pas of major proportions to run into a police car. It is also a ticketable offense.

Under Snow Rules, stupidity is not allowed. This makes driving very difficult for some drivers.

For instance, if you get stuck on a hill, and you have to back down into oncoming traffic, then going up the hill was stupid and you can expect other drivers to be very angry with you, and to demonstrate it with universally understood hand signals.

If you make it without getting stuck, of course, you are daring and admired by all.

If you should get stuck, you can expect no help from anyone, because the stupidity rule applies. Nor are you expected to offer anyone help, unless you can do so without slowing traffic.

Now you might think that lower speed limits would be the rule, but that isn't always the case. Sometimes, you need extra speed to make it up a hill, or through a pile of snow.

Personally, I've found that driving a little like a deranged version of Sterling Moss is just about right.

Personally, I like Snow Rules. That's because I drive under Snow Rules most of the time.

Whether there's any snow or not.

Suddenly Boring Syndrome

It's the eternal question of nature versus nurture. Of the predestined outcome of genetics versus the myriad of environmental influences that shape our personalities.

A question that has plagued mankind for years.

Are people born boring, or do they just become boring after they learn to play golf?

Just kidding.

Actually, golfers tend to fall into two categories: experienced golfers who know by years of hard experience and social rejection that it's very difficult to explain the flight path of a golf ball to somebody who wasn't there, and doesn't care, and make it interesting, and new golfers who haven't learned that yet and come down with SBS: which is medical shorthand for Suddenly Boring Syndrome.

"You should have seen me on the sixteenth tee."

"Yeah?"

"I hit the ball, and it goes up."

"Yeah."

"Then it levels out and I'm thinking it's gonna hook, but it doesn't. It just keeps on going. And then you know what happens?"

"What?"

"It comes down."

"Wow."

"Two hundred twenty-five yards, at least."

"Uh huh."

"Well, you had to see it."

No I didn't. We're talking about your basic Galilean concepts of velocity, inertia and gravity here, and I didn't need to see it.

Now I realize that when you're a beginning golfer, and you hit the ball straight and true for 225 yards for the first time, it is an event. It's like being touched by God, and you want to tell somebody. Everybody.

But isn't that why they built clubhouses?

Experienced golfers just tell you that they had a good round or a bad round, and let it go. They know that behind those glazed eyes and frozen smiles is someone saying to themselves, "I just wanted to know if you had fun — not a stroke by stroke report."

Of course, new golfers aren't the only ones who suddenly come down with SBS.

Sports officials are especially susceptible to it.

I know. I referee volleyball at the high school and college level, and my wife can tell you that there is nothing quite as boring as hearing a call by call replay of a volleyball match.

I have learned that just because she has no interest in hearing about the match I just called, doesn't mean she doesn't love me.

I think.

Suddenly Boring Syndrome has a way of occurring spontaneously among groups of people engaged in the same activity - especially among people who are normally immune from it.

It is for this reason that my wife avoids social situations where three or more of my referee buddies are apt to be together. She knows that the odds are very good that we will all immediately be gripped by a terminal case of Suddenly Boring Syndrome and begin repeating refereeing war stories: "And then in 1983, there was this time I beckoned for serve and my R2 was off talking with the scorekeeper trying to figure out how Ferris got so completely out of rotation and blah blah blah ... "

It goes on for hours. Boring.

Women tend to be universally subject to Suddenly Boring Syndrome after the birth of their first child.

Hey, it's perfectly normal.

Like the new golfer who hits a ball 240 yards, it's like being touched by God and you want to tell somebody about it. And like a group of referees telling war stories, a group of new mothers tend to spiral into oneupsmanship stories that all start, "Well, when the doctor gave me <u>my</u> epidural…" And the next thing you know you're hearing about pushing and breathing and grunting, fainting fathers.

By the time the third and fourth child rolls around, I've noticed the labor and delivery stories tend to be shorter and less graphic.

It's entirely possible for parents to go from a case of SBS with childbirth right into severe SBS with baby.

This is completely understandable if not altogether forgivable.

A first child is so exciting and enchanting that it is hard to keep in mind that the whole world is not dying to know what your baby has done every minute for the past week. Except the baby's grandmother. But that's only because she is probably in the middle of Suddenly Boring Syndrome over the baby herself.

There are, of course many other causes of SBS — a bad boss, a co-worker you either love or hate but can't stop talking about, a divorce is always good for a few weeks of it, even a new car can suddenly trigger a short case of Suddenly Boring Syndrome.

Usually the person with it gets over it for the same reason it bores everybody else; it begins to bore even them. And that's good because then those events in life that seem so extraordinary that you have to talk about them take their rightful place in your history, and in the process make room for the next extraordinary event.

Which could trigger your next case of Suddenly Boring Syndrome.

Now, you're probably wondering if having a case of Suddenly Boring Syndrome is a bad thing. Of course not, perfectly normal. Happens to everybody once in a while.

You just want to be sure you're aware of it, so it doesn't develop into EBS.

Eternally Boring Syndrome.

Buying Snow Skis

It's time.

I have put off the moment for as long as possible, but the deed can be put off no longer. The time has come, and tomorrow, I must act.

A man's got to do what a man's got to do, as my wife would say, reminding me of what my general role in life is.

What I have to do tomorrow is just about the most difficult thing a man can do. It will take great concentration, mental acuity, and physical exertion; it will take great ability and daring and most of my money.

Tomorrow, I am going to buy new skis.

I think. Maybe.

I started this buying process two years ago.

I was on the quad at Schweitzer, and some guy looked at my skis which are getting kind of old and said, "Hey, I used to have pair of those. In fact, those look like my old skis. Did you buy those at the Ski Swap two, three years ago? Whoa! Look at those bindings! I heard the Smithsonian was looking for a working pair of those."

To which his wife said, "Honey, that's not very nice, maybe this gentleman can't afford new skis."

Well, that made me feel better.

If you have ever bought skis before, you know that no where else in the universe, with the possible exception of buying stereo equipment, does style, performance technology, one's personal self-image and sales and advertising B.S. converge so dramatically.

After all, these are not just laminated boards you are buying; they are skis. What you are about to buy is going to say to your fellow skiers volumes about who you are, what you believe in and where — and off what — you ski.

Your skis are your companions in adventure and adversity. When your friends have deserted you, your wife has gone in, and your daughter has rejected you in favor of a bunch of freaked-out looking snowboarders, your skis will still be there, hanging off the bottoms of your feet, ready to do your bidding.

They are also, I might add, the verb in your skiing fashion statement.

So, humiliation fresh in my mind, I came down the mountain and went directly to Lou Lou's.

I went directly to the good skis.

And I went directly into cardiac arrest.

$650! For a pair of skis! Without bindings?

Being a man of decision, I decided I could wait another year.

I figured, what the heck, what were the chances I'd run into Mr. Ski Swap man on the chair again, anyway.

As it happened, I have waited two years, which is better because now my skis are really old, and I am more resolved than ever to replace them.

I went to see Lou Lou again.

Without hesitation, Lou Lou grabbed a ski off the rack. "Zis is the ski you want. Have you heard about zee closed cap monocoque construction? Transfers zee weight from your boots to zee edge in a smooth arc for incredible control. Feel."

He handed me the ski and I flexed it like he was doing.

It felt like a ski to me.

I'm never sure what I'm supposed to feel when I push on a ski like that, but I always make sure I look like I am feeling whatever it is I am supposed to be feeling.

"I see what you mean," I said, not having a clue.

"Feel zis one," he said, handing me another brand.

I flexed that one. It felt the same.

"No comparison," said Lou Lou.

Handing me back the first ski, he said, "Zee way you ski, zis is zee one you want."

He got called away for a phone call, which was good because it gave me a moment to kind of bond with the skis and to study the prices and the different graphics and try to figure out which ski I was willing to pay for.

"What do you think?" I asked my wife who had listened to the whole exchange.

"Did it ever occur to you in all of that, that Lou Lou has never seen you ski?" she asked.

Gee, I hadn't thought of that, I thought to myself. So I said, "Yeah, but except for that part, what do you think?"

"I think you ought to demo a pair before you buy anything," she said.

"Right," I agreed.

The advertising for skis tends to be one size fits all, with all the descriptive brochures saying something like, "This is the perfect ski for the aggressive recreational skier who wants a forgiving ski that carves in the bumps, but is a superb performer in the powder while it delivers great control at ultra-high speeds, during aerial maneuvers, on ice and in crud, and still leaves a lot of room for personal growth."

Is there anybody that doesn't fit?

Translated, what that means is, if you like the looks of this ski, buy it.

But the skis themselves do perform differently.

And the only way to know which one works for you is to try them out. Demo them, as they say in the business. And that's what I am going to do tomorrow.

Checkbook in hand, I am going to separate the hype from the performance. And I am very excited about it.

I have no doubt that one pair of skis tomorrow will fairly beg me to buy them. And I will.

And if I'm really lucky, during the day tomorrow, I may ride up the quad with the guy who ridiculed my old skis, and I, with a brand new, out of the box, pair of skis on my feet will be able to look at his skis and say, "I used to have a pair a skis like those. Did you buy those at the ski swap?"

Experiencing the Joy of Golf For The First Time

As parents, we spend an inordinate amount of time trying to teach our children not to do stupid things.

Don't play in the street. Don't take drugs. Don't talk to strangers. Don't smoke. Don't drink and drive. Don't go out with boys until you're twenty-five. These are all stupid things that we teach our children to avoid.

But part of the problem of doing this job right is there are just so many stupid things you can do, it is almost impossible to educate your child against all of them.

Take playing golf, for instance.

Now, I think we would all agree that playing golf is not one of those things we generally warn our children against doing, but which, especially when you do it for the first time, borders on the criminally stupid.

I went golfing for the first time in my life last summer, and it was such a traumatic event that I am only just now able to talk about it.

I went golfing with my in-laws. I thought they liked me. Now I'm not so sure. I wonder if I offended them somehow, and golf was their way of getting me back. "Want to play golf, Doug? You'll enjoy it. It's *easy*. Even your mother-in-law plays it."

Actually, I had been saving golf for my old age. I figured when I could no longer play volleyball, snow ski, water ski or play Hearts, I'd take up golf.

I may have to reevaluate those plans.

The first stupid thing about golf you notice is the ball is really small.

I'd never noticed how small a golfball was before. And not only that, but the end of the golf club is really small, too. The end of the golf club has lots of strange markings on it designed to help you hit the ball right.

"You want to hit the ball right here," said one of my in-laws, pointing to a spot about midway between several lines etched on the club. Which brings us to stupid thing number two: I'm swinging this club at the itsy-bitsy ball in a highly irregular arc, and I'm supposed to hit it between third and fourth instead of the fifth and sixth lines?

Right. No Sweat. Stand back everyone.

It wasn't until I went to tee off that I noticed another stupid thing about the game. They put the first and the ninth tees right at the clubhouse where everyone gets to watch you.

I didn't think too much about this until another golfer came over and said, "Don't worry about making a fool of yourself teeing off in front of all these people, and don't let the comments of the drunks up there on the porch bother you."

"Thanks a lot," I said. "I won't."

The first time you tee off in your life you notice a couple of things.

First of all, you notice that all of the happy bantering between the golfers suddenly stops.

Birds stop singing.

Waitresses stop serving drinks to drunks who stop laughing so they can watch you.

Cars on the freeway pull over and the people get out to watch you.

It's as if there's a loudspeaker system you can't hear that has said, "Attention, attention everybody. Would everyone please stop what they are doing and look at the first tee where Doug Hurd is about to publicly humiliate himself."

Now, I am a reasonable sandlot athlete. I didn't letter in anything, but I'm not completely uncoordinated. But at that moment, I couldn't even get the ball to stay on top of the tee.

Finally, I teed up to the ball, checked the target lines on the end of the club as if I knew what they meant, stood back and took a couple of practice swings the way I'd seen Jack Nicklaus do on television a thousand times, and then, even as I was beginning to wonder if maybe golf wasn't a huge practical joke played on mankind by a malevolent god, I did my best Fuzzy Zoeller imitation, and sent the ball down the fairway.

I hit a great first shot.

I sort of moseyed back to the cart, swaggering a little. Guess I showed them.

Actually, as it happened, it was my only great shot, and the rest of the game (mercifully played in semi-private) went from the awful to the bizarre.

About twelve strokes into the game, I noticed another stupid thing about golf. The hole you're supposed to putt the ball into is also ridiculously small.

I needed a hole about the size of a trash can to even have a chance.

All of this is not to say that I don't have a talent for the game. I do.

I know this because I made the golfball do some incredible things.

For instance, did you know that if you hold the club just right, you can make the golfball take off 90 degrees from the direction of your swing?

I know; I did it. It hit a tree 90 degrees from where I was aiming (so much for the little lines on the club) and it ricocheted back to the green, coming to rest about ten yards behind where it started.

After everybody got back on their feet, somebody muttered, "You don't see that shot much anymore." After that, all my in-laws lined up in a straight line behind me when I would tee off.

Their theory was this was the safest place to be, not so much because I couldn't make the ball go there, but because if I did, it would have to hit me first.

Actually, I did get in one more great shot.

Well, pretty great. It was the eighth hole, and we were heading back to the clubhouse. The green was way too far away and to the right for me to hit, but I tried anyway.

The ball went long and true.

For a while.

Then it broke left for the clubhouse and more plate glass than I had ever seen in one place before. We all instantly calculated the trajectory and knew we had to get lucky or get out the Visa card.

We got lucky. The ball fell short, landing in the garden below the windows.

It almost killed the gardener, but I figured that was an occupational hazard of his job and he shouldn't have been there in the first place.

With my score in the upper 140s after nine, my father-in-law said he didn't want to play anymore and why didn't we call it a day.

I was all for hanging up the clubs and calling it a whole golf career.

Later that night, I watched an infomercial on TV with Kenny Rogers and some golf pro who has a kit that shows you how to perfect your golf swing and your putting and all that stuff.

It was only $350, and I thought, yeah, that's what I need. I could be good at golf if I got that. Hmmm.

Well, it's like I said: Golf is a stupid game.

BRAIN ROT, MALE MENOPAUSE AND OTHER JOYS OF MIDDLE AGE

Brain Rot

What was the main topic of conversation around your office this week ?

Let me guess.

The Presidential race? Nope.

The Governor not running again? I didn't think so.

Or was it the article in the paper about the medical report that claims men lose brain cells in their frontal lobes three times faster than women?

Bingo!

The article, in case you didn't read it, or if you're a man, you read it and can't remember it, quoted a doctor whose research indicated that men, who are born with larger brains than women, at about age 18, begin losing brain cells three times faster than women, until, at about age 45, men's and women's brains are about the same size. Furthermore, much of this loss comes in the frontal lobe of the brain which is responsible for mental flexibility, planning and attention span.

You older guys want me to repeat that?

I have to tell you this: As I was reading the article, I turned to one of my bosses, the one who is 51 and said, "Did you read this article about mens brains wearing out faster?" And he said, and this is a quote, "I read it but I don't remember what it said."

Uh-oh.

(I don't know if he was joking or not. I was going to ask later, but I forgot.)

Now, did you notice that when this report came out, there was no hue and cry from men's organizations about this research being just another sexist report designed to give bogus biological reasons for stripping men of their dignity, and keeping them locked up in their old age?

No. We are above that.

Of course, you could argue that with our frontal lobes out of commission because of advanced Brain Cell Rot Syndrome, it is beyond our mental prowess to figure out how to do that.

But I choose not to see it that way.

Being almost 50, rather than be affronted or angered by the article, I embraced the report.

It explained so much.

It explained why, in the time it takes me to go from the basement to, say, the kitchen, I can forget what I was going to the kitchen for.

I'm not looking for a show of hands or anything, but how many of you middle aged men frequently find yourself standing in a room saying to yourself, "I came in here for a reason. Now, what _was_ it?"

Me, too.

My wife is always helpful when that happens. I stand there lost for a minute, and she says, "You came in here for something. You're in the kitchen. Did it have anything to do with food?"
(Let us all pray that in the future, when it is the bathroom we find ourselves lost in, the answer always comes to us.)

This Brain Rot thing explains why it is getting harder for me to pay attention to details or to follow the point of a compound sentence that goes on too long. I find this especially embarrassing when I'm the one doing the talking.

It explains why I forget things. Appointments. Anniversaries. My daughter's first name.

Just kidding. I remember my daughter's name.

Ummm...

And it explains so many other things.

You know how when you hear reports of a doctor operating on the wrong knee or removing the wrong foot, or doing a bowel resection when the patient came in for a tonsillectomy, you wonder, how could that happen?

Well, now we know! Brain Rot! If your surgeon is over fifty, he may not have any frontal lobe left.

Actually, I know some surgical nurses and malpractice attorneys, and surgeons without functional frontal lobes are more common than you might think.

Frankly, I'm surprised that the legal profession hasn't jumped all over this one.

"Ladies and gentlemen of the jury, my client is a dedicated, skilled and experienced surgeon whose only problem is, he can't remember body parts anymore. But it is not his fault. He's got frontal lobe brain cell rot. And we will show, beyond any doubt, that the patient knew the doctor was a man before she went into surgery, so she shares in the blame for the fact that she's got new heart valves when what she wanted was a tummy tuck."

Brain Rot! It explains why your boss is getting rigid and inflexible, your husband channel surfs and always orders the same thing when he goes out to eat.

We can't pay attention to anything anymore.

Well, I don't know about you, but I certainly feel better knowing there is a reason for my short attention span, aversion to trip planning and, um, there was something else, but I forget what it was.

Oh, well.

I'll ask my daughter, what's-her-name, when I get home.

The Boat Show

It is a place where a strange rite of passage into real adulthood takes place.

A place where, in our society at least, boys become men, and men decide to become bigger men.

Where the fate of entire families hang in the balance.

An event where some families bond, while others take the first step to becoming un-bonded.

It is the event that can make dropping 25 grand you don't have on something you don't need seem like a good idea.

Boys night out at Deja Vu?

Nope. Worse.

It's The Boat Show. The place where, intuitively, all men realize that the real measure of a man is the size of his boat.

And if you don't have one, you're some sort of social eunuch. This can be very embarrassing, especially in business, where the topic can switch to the size of your boat without any warning:

"Your presentation was superb, and I think the board agrees with me that we should move our $500,000 dollar ad account to your agency. By the way, we should load up the families and go boating some weekend."

"Um, I don't have a boat."

"You don't? Hmmm. That's funny. I thought you did. I know John Robideaux does. Uh, actually, we haven't made a final decision about moving our account. We'll let you know."

Eunuch.

When you go to the boat show, the first rule is, you check reality at the door. This is the stuff of dreams.

Instantly we see ourselves in a boat. We are tanned and fit. In our boat, our pecs bulge and our abs ripple. Baby-oiled young women and white-legged old men cast admiring glances at us.

It's all we can do not to take out our checkbook and buy the first boat we come to.

Now, normally when we men are confronted by large expensive toys, our wives provide an anchor to the real world.

But at The Boat Show, women get into the boat buying thing too.

Young couples stand there, looking into a 14-foot open-bow outboard and share a common vision of loading up the kids, the dog, their best friends and some camping gear and heading out to Kalispel Island on Priest Lake for a weekend of camping like they did when they were kids.

What they don't see is the reality of their three-year-old pitching face first to the floor spilling an open can of pop and a bag of Cheetos the first time dad guns it, and the dog puncturing the upholstery with his claws just before he throws up because he gets seasick instantly.

"We'll become boat-campers," they think, idyllically.

Never mind that A) all the Saturday and Sunday camping spots everywhere on Priest Lake will be gone by Thursday at noon, or that B) you can't get all that stuff into a 14-foot open-bow outboard, anyway.

Can we have a reality check on aisle 3, please?

Welcome to the price/function paradox of boat buying. Which, simply stated is, "The price we think we can afford will not buy the boat that will do what we want it to."

So, almost immediately, we upscale. To help us with this, are the boat salespeople.

"Isn't it a beauty? Fourteen feet of pure fun. Boat show special: just $10,599. How many in your family?"

"Uh, four."

"Really? Then you might want to look at the 16-foot model. It has the advantage of holding four people without sinking. Will you be pulling water skiers?"

"Uh, yeah."

"Well then the 18 is what you really want. And unless you're some kind of eunuch you'll want the new 205 engine, with the skier option package. Get's out of the hole with a skier in nothing flat."

"How much?"

"$23,950. On special."

"Seems reasonable. I certainly want to get out of the hole fast, whatever that means."

"Will you be wanting a trailer with that?"

Now you're on the other side of the paradox: you have a boat that will do what you want, but now you can't afford it.

Fortunately, this is not a problem, because as with all things in life, being unable to afford something is rarely an impediment to buying it.

Now, the nice thing about The Boat Show is that it allows you to do some side-by-side comparison shopping, which is good because if you are a first-time boat buyer, it can be pretty hard to understand why one boat can cost ten thousand dollars more than another that looks about the same.

At the boat show, those reasons become clear. It's not because one has a bigger engine or softer seats. It's far more basic than that.

It's because they know you'll pay it!

"We can buy a Bayliner for 12 thousand or a Cobalt for 22 grand. What do you think?"

"The Cobalt is prettier," your wife says.

"I agree. Let's get it."

Now, the final step in buying a boat is negotiating the price. The way it works is, the dealer sets a price, you ask if he'll take less, he says no and you say okay, and you pay him.

At least that's what happened to us.

But, I should tell you, that was ten years ago and I have no regrets. While it might have been for all the wrong reasons, for us, buying a boat was exactly the right thing to do.

Now you're probably wondering how I have kept from upgrading to a bigger more powerful boat all these years. Well, it's really pretty easy.

When The Boat Show weekend comes, I pile the whole family in the car — and we go skiing.

Name That Dread

Do you think an earthquake is God's way of saying, "Stop complaining!" to the rest of us?

Just wondering.

It certainly has that effect on me.

I mean, a few days ago, the discussion among my clients centered on whether more Boeing jobs would be lost in this area and wouldn't that be terrible, and what if it hurt business, and how awful if the good times we have been experiencing ended.

Since the California earthquake, I personally have been inclined to take the view that things could be worse. That somewhere a force of nature might just be saying, "Hey, you think you got problems? Why don't I level your city in six seconds. Then you'll have problems."

Watching the earthquake coverage on television also tends to make one play the very personal, if slightly neurotic game of "Name That Dread."

If you play Name That Dread with very many people around here, you find that when it comes to natural disasters, we don't dread very much.

Rain in Biblical proportions like they had in the Midwest this summer? A mere inconvenience. A hurricane? Won't happen. How about a Kansas or Oklahoma style tornado that explodes everything in its path? Not likely. And earthquakes? I don't think so.

So what we come up with when we play Name That Dread, are personal dreads, which change with age and the state of our individual and collective mental health.

Just as there is some cosmic rule that says, "Be careful what you call because it just might come," I think there must also be a rule that says, "Take heart in what you dread, because the day will come when you'll dread just the opposite."

When you're young, your dreads are simple.

When you're a fifth grade boy, you dread having to be with girls. Then the opposite occurs, and by seventh grade you dread not being with them.

My seventh grade daughter has expressed a dread of being kissed. I dread the day that changes and she dreads not being kissed.

It's at this age you learn to dread going to the dentist.

Somewhere around 15 you dread having to get a job. Then the opposite occurs and you immediately dread being out of work — a dread that may last the rest of your life.

As a young adult, it's not uncommon to dread getting married. (Our parents, meanwhile, may not dread our wanting to get married, but they may dread our choices. "Why him? Why not Stanley? Stanley's nice." "Because I dread Stanley, Dad.") Of course, we no sooner get married than we get to dread getting divorced, but that doesn't seem to stop anybody. And pretty soon, we get to dread getting married again.

By this time in our lives, we really dread going to the dentist.

Some of our dreads are seasonal. How many of you dread your spouse's Christmas party? Or worse, the summer picnic.

"I'm not wearing a swimsuit in front of all those people." It's small comfort to realize that if the rule of opposites applies, they probably dread seeing you in a swimsuit just as much.

I don't know about you, but I'm at that age where I dread disease. I'm not particular in this. I dread them all. I dread the common cold with the same enthusiasm as prostate cancer.

Along with this comes a dread of visiting the doctor. Because even though you feel okay, you know that if he or she pokes and prods around long enough, or asks enough questions, he will find something wrong.

(Here, the rule of opposites works against you. Would you sooner that he not find it?)

This can lead to a dread of all hospitals, or in my particular case, a dread of being sent to the X-ray department.

And barium. I really dread barium.

When you're old, you still dread heart disease and strokes and what they can do to you. But, again the rule of opposites applies. At some point you may dread surviving them more than dying from them.

When you're old, at least you no longer dread going to the dentist. Instead, you dread your Super Polygrip not holding.

Some dreads are government induced. How many of you do not dread a call from the IRS? "Can we talk?"

Or a report out of Hanford that says, "Okay, okay, we haven't been entirely truthful over the past fifty years about what we've been doing with nuclear radiation, which is why some cows downwind have three heads."

Does this mean we are all neurotic? I don't think so. (I don't know about you, but I dread it when people think I'm neurotic.) I think we're pretty normal.

And that's the point. We're really lucky, because these dreads are all pretty minor when compared to the dread of living with the threat of earthquakes, and the damage they — so terribly indiscriminately — can do.

So when we play, Name That Dread, it's no wonder that people from California — and other parts of the country, for that matter — scoff at us.

"You guys don't have anything to dread."

And they're right.

Of course, the one dread we all have that we don't share with them is the dread that, tired of living with the dread of earthquake, flood, tornado or hurricane, they will all move here.

Now that's something to dread.

Redefining Middle Age

I have discovered a giant void in our language.

You know how economists define the population as middle class, upper middle class, or lower middle class; lower well off, upper lower well off, wealthy, rich, super-rich and Bill Gates?

These definitions have been arrived at because we need to know where we are in life. They are economic mile markers on the highway of life.

Well, I have discovered that there are no such markers for getting old.

Basically, all we have to define the adult years is young, middle aged and old.

And the older I get, the more I am beginning to realize that this will not do. Not at all.

I believe it was Churchill who said, "Some men are born to be old, while others achieve oldness; still others have oldness thrust on them."

Or maybe it was Jack Nicholson who said that.

Anyway, the question that is beginning to loom for us baby boomers is, when are you old?

You know, when do you hit that age when everybody who casually observes you on the street agrees that you are no longer middle aged, but old?

70? 60? 50?

For a man, especially we baby boomers facing 50, this is getting to be an important question because it wasn't that long ago we all considered 50 to be old.

Now, I know that some of you are saying, "Age is just a state of mind." Or "You're only as old as you feel," to which I say, yeah, right.

You've been watching too many Centrum commercials. This is not a great time to be silver. At least, not for me. A great time to be silver is twenty years from now.

Make that 30.

No. The problem is, we don't have enough definitions of the aging process. We go from middle age to geezerhood in one step.

Yesterday I was middle aged, today I'm old.

Is that fair? Heck no.

What we need are some new definitions.

So, I think we could all agree that you are basically "young" until 30; before that, you are a teenager which in adult terms means you don't count.

Young people are allowed, even, really, expected to do stupid things.

"Tell me again why you got a nose ring and married someone you met at the Pearl Jam Concert."

"Well, you know, man, like because, I'm young."

"Of course."

Young is when we are expected to get our first marriage out of the way, abandon the career path our parents went into debt and sent us to college for, and generally waste about a decade "finding ourselves."

After young used to come middle age, but now I propose an intermediate step. Upper young. Maybe "senior young."

You know you're upper young when the rock and roll they play on your favorite radio station no longer sounds like music to you.

After upper young can come junior middle age.

Now, think back: when you were 35-ish, would entering junior middle age have been quite so traumatic as "middle age?"

Of course not. See what I mean? See how much better this would make things?

So then, somewhere around forty (a little younger if you're bald, have had bypass surgery or you have kids in their twenties) you enter regular middle age.

By adding these new age definitions, I think we will have synched up what has actually happened to us, to what we feel has happened to us. I mean, most of us who are forty are just coming to terms with not being twenty anymore.

Now, what is the main problem with middle age?

You've got it: It's not long enough!

You're just getting used to the notion that you are, in fact, middle aged, and that maybe driving a pickup truck with great big fat tires and a chrome bumper and fog lights on top and a stereo system that goes "tunnk, tunnk; tunnk tunnk," and vibrates pedestrians you pass makes you look ridiculous, and suddenly you have to contend with the idea that some people —

like maybe your grandchildren — think you're old.

You? Old?

Well, you're not old.

David Brinkley is old. George Burns is old.

You are merely in "ascendant middle age" — which, let me be clear — is younger than late middle age which comes after early late middle age, but precedes late late middle age.

Now, I'm not there yet, but I think ascendant middle age should begin at about age 54 or after your myocardial infarction, whichever comes first.

And there are a few new rules.

For instance, in ascendant middle age you should dress less for success and more just not to look stupid. This means your Levi 501's are probably out and Dockers are in, and if you think it's cool to wear a grungy flannel shirt tied around your waist and a baseball cap backward like a Curt Cobain wannabe, you're wrong.

It's okay to wear glasses without apologizing, to stop using Grecian Formula 16 where you've got hair and start using sunblock where you don't. And hanging around the pretty young receptionist at work too much is considered bad form.

Now, just like the object of being young is to prepare you for being middle aged, the object of being middle aged is to prepare you for being old without being an old fool.

And the object of inserting more categories between middle age and being old is, with any luck, none of us will ever really be old at all.

And what else could a true baby boomer want?

Choosing the Right Exercise Machines

There is something every wife should know. Sometime in his life, your husband will buy a sports car of some sort. This is called his "Porche period." He will also buy an exercise machine.

This is called his mid-life crisis.

Just a joke. Actually, we buy the car during our mid-life crisis. We buy exercise machines whenever we feel like we are getting old.

Now, as harsh as this may sound, buying an exercise machine has almost nothing to do with you. You may tell him you love him just the way he is in his cholesterol ridden, ever-increasing body, but it won't matter. You see, he's not buying it for you.

At least, not directly.

He's buying it for himself. Or at least, the himself he thinks he ought to be.

It's a man thing.

It happens to all of us.

We're watching the Olympics. We're watching the athletes in their Spandex outfits - especially the skiers and speed skaters, with their bulging thighs and rippling shoulders, and the question occurs to us: I wonder how I would look in one of those outfits?

And it doesn't take long for us to answer. Not very good.

That's why the next day, as we are reading the Wall Street Journal while munching down a Danish and drinking coffee at work, we look at the full page ad for a NordicTrack and begin thinking to ourselves, "You know, I should probably have one of those."

This is really stupid.

What we really mean, of course, is that we should have the body that such machines promise.

One ad for an exercise machine had the headline, "Have the body you had at 25." That gets right to the heart of where we baby boomers live, doesn't it? Why don't they just say, "Middle age not all it's cracked up to be? Old age looming in your future? Feeling a little fat? Don't grow old. Buy our machine. Be the stud you were at 25 again. Just send $3,000 dollars to Peter Pan Appliances, and we'll make you forever young."

(Actually, I think it misses the mark: by 25, most of our bodies were in a serious state of neglect, disrepair and decline. Show us a machine that promises the body we had at 18 and I guarantee we'll buy it.)

And if the Olympics weren't enough to motivate us onto a contraption like a NordicTrack, there is always the SoloFlex or SoloFlex wannabe infomercial.

In these, for a half hour we get to watch what will happen to us if we buy a SoloFlex.

Now, as a marketer, I'm here to tell you, in the name category, SoloFlex wins, hands down. If you are a young man, you almost have to buy it just on the strength of the name.

Solo: One man, alone, doing what a man's got to do. Nobody to help. Just Spartan discipline, sweat, and sheer force of will. And flex: The very essence of manly, muscular activity. To a man, the name translates to, "Are you ever going to be sexy if you buy this thing."

What the name doesn't tell you is that you lift against a series of rubber bands instead of good, old fashioned weights. This is okay, however, because it adds an element of risk to the workout.

"Gee Doug, How'd you break your nose?"

"Well I was doing curls on my SoloFlex when the rubber bands broke and I smashed the bar into my face."

Now, when you're watching these, you have to remember the first rule of infomercials which is, it doesn't matter what they're selling, you're never going to look that way.

This rule applies across the board by the way. If you're a woman, you can buy all the make up you want and apply it with a trowel, and you still won't look like Victoria Principal when you're done.

And we men are never going to have the body of the guy in the SoloFlex commercial, which he probably got by lifting free weights.

But we tend to forget that, don't we?

We also tend to overlook the blindingly obvious fact that this thing is a machine. It fills a whole room.

Now if you are a single man, living alone and your want your SoloFlex in your living room, who cares?

But when you get married, I'm here to tell you, your wife cares. It doesn't matter what exercise machine you buy or where you put it; she wants it somewhere else.

"Look, it folds up and goes under the bed."

"Get it out of here."

"It keeps my muscles toned, reduces stress, increases my cardiovascular fitness and lowers my HDL cholesterol levels to 173."

"Get it out of here."

"Honey, I'll die without this machine."

"Then I'll miss you. Get it out of here."

The other blindingly obvious thing we tend to forget is, the first word of workout is "work" which is what we spend most of our life avoiding and why most of us don't workout in the first place. (That, plus, a good workout can cut right into your beer drinking time.)

And that fact isn't going to change, no matter what kind of machine we buy.

But that's pretty easy to overlook as we contemplate our sagging pectorals and non-existent biceps, as we watch some young guy with a body we never had do bench presses on a machine that promises, if not eternal youth, then at least a respectable chest.

The whole thing makes me wonder, do you think that in — I don't know, twenty years — the speed skaters who won medals this year will be sitting front of their TVs watching infomercials on the latest exercise machines and be thinking, "You know, I ought to get one of those things."

I sure hope so.

What Have I Done?

I first asked the question 30 years ago.

It was August of 1964. I had graduated from high school a few months before, and I was on the first day of a planned one-year trip to Europe and maybe beyond — maybe around the world, for all I knew.

While the rest of my friends had studied and planned for college, I had read numerous, well ... two articles about how some young vagabonds were hitchhiking around Europe, singing folk songs for meals and living a great adventure while seeing the world.

Singing folk songs for meals? You mean you didn't even need money?

That was for me. I didn't have any money. I couldn't sing, either, but that hadn't ever stopped me before.

Now, you have to remember that this was a time when every self-respecting teenager knew three guitar chords and all the words to all the songs of every Peter, Paul and Mary, Limeliters, Kingston Trio and Chad Mitchell Trio album ever made. And the really hip ones even tracked this guy named Bob Dylan, and singing for meals seemed at least plausible.

So there I was, just eighteen, just one day into my great adventure, hitchhiking from Seattle to New York to fly to Europe, laying in a sleeping bag somewhere under the vast and starry Montana sky, when the enormity of what I had set in motion struck me.

And I asked life's big question: What have I done?

Now, this is not the same as the job interview question, what have I <u>done</u>? Which is what you ask, rhetorically, as you try to figure out how to make zero job experience sound like at least something.

Nor is it the same as the question, "Why did I do that?" Which is what you ask when your car is dead because you left the lights on last night, and you've got the most important presentation of your life in 15 minutes.

No. Those are questions for life's temporary setbacks.

We're talking about the question all adults ask themselves when they've done something that appears to be really stupid. You know, taking the path less travelled in the yellowed wood only to find it was a really dumb thing to do and now you are hopelessly lost.

With any luck of course, you won't have to make those kinds of decisions too often.

After my trip to Europe, which turned out great, by the way, the next time I had to ask the question I was in my bunk during the first night of basic training in the Army.

I spent the whole night sobbing, "What have I done, oh Lord, what have I done?"

(Going to Europe I was just homesick; in the Army I was homesick and I thought I might just die. A most unpleasant combination.)

I have discovered that a lot of people ask the question when they leave a good job for a bad one.

Now, maybe you're thinking, I thought I was the only one who made a bad job choice.

No way.

See if this sounds familiar:

You had an okay job, but you wanted a better job, and so you quietly looked around, and when another opportunity came along, you carefully weighed out all the pro's and con's and after sleepless nights and talking with your spouse, you finally decided that you couldn't possibly pass up this opportunity, and inside of one week (and if this has happened to you, you are nodding agreement, because it always happens inside of one week or not at all) you are sitting in a meeting with a boss who has gone from charming to impossible right before your very eyes, and while your boss is ranting about something, you pull back to that private space everybody has right behind the focal point of their eyeballs, and you asked yourself, "What have I done?"

Right?

We all do it.

The question is usually less about why you burned the bridge you just crossed as it is about what motivated you to cross that bridge in the first place.

And by the time you ask it, it's all academic.

The only thing left is the question that inevitably follows, which is, what are you going to do about it?

If it's a job you're talking about, the answer to that question depends upon what you need more, your pride or your paycheck.

Paycheck!

I don't know about you, but when the equation ratchets up from pride to happiness or a paycheck, I'll almost always opt for happiness.

Of course, it's hard to be happy without a job, especially if you are wondering what you have done.

Now, finding yourself in a bad job is not the worst thing that can happen to you to make you ask the question.

We all know of somebody who asked themselves the question right after they got married.

"What do you mean you have fifty thousand dollars in unsecured debts that I am now responsible for?"

"What children from what prior marriage?"

"What do you mean you don't want to work anymore?"

"Your mother is going to stay with us for how long?"

What have I done?

And if some people ask the question after they get married, it's probably some sort of poetic justice that others ask it after they've gotten divorced.

There's nothing quite like watching your new wife get fat and ugly and your ex-wife get thin and beautiful to make you wonder, "What have I done?"

In fact, I know some ex-wives whose sole purpose in life is now to make their ex-husbands ask that question.

So, if you have made a life-type decision that appears to have been really, colossally stupid, take heart, everyone around you has done the same thing at some time or another.

And who knows, maybe if you live long enough, you'll get to that point where you ask the question, "What have I done?" and you'll know the answer is,

What difference does it make?

Obeying Life's Unwritten Rules

Which is worse, committing a felony, or breaking one of life's many unwritten rules?

I think we would all agree that breaking an unwritten rule is the more serious crime.

After all, if you commit a felony, you get to get a lawyer who, in the American tradition of providing you the best possible defense, will say anything to any judge or any jury on your behalf.

But when you break an unwritten rule and someone catches you, it's a done deal. Bam. You're guilty. And there's no lawyer in sight to say to anyone present, "Excuse me, but my client has been gorging on Twinkies most of his life, which, as we all know, leads to diminished mental capacity, so he can't be held responsible for not abiding by the unwritten rule that says when you ask your biggest client to approve a million dollar ad campaign you have to wear a suit and tie, instead of jeans and a pink Hawaiian shirt."

Business is fraught with unwritten rules, of course.

Rules like, at a business lunch, never order anything you have to eat with your fingers. That's a good unwritten rule.

There's nothing quite like having a pile of chicken bones or ribs spilling off your plate and barbecue sauce from one ear to the other to inspire business confidence.

Dress codes used to be a major part of the unwritten rules of business with suits and ties being the rule, but some of those are changing. For instance, we now have an unwritten rule that it's okay to wear jeans on Friday.

In advertising, if you always wear a suit and tie, your clients may think you're wound a little too tight to be really creative, and hence, to create great advertising. This in turn, creates what might be called an unwritten paradox, because clients rarely let you do great advertising anyway.

But you've got to be careful, because there are jeans and there are grubbies, so the unwritten rule to the new unwritten rule is you get to be in jeans, but you'd better not be grubby.

It can be confusing.

Of course, the unwritten rules of business are not half as confusing as the unwritten rules of marriage.

That's because in business there is a whole framework of rules that are written down to which the unwritten rules are added, while in marriage, none of the rules are written down, except the basics which are to love, honor, cherish and obey, but those don't give you any guidance at all when it comes to figuring out whose job it is to unload the dishwasher.

So you have to sort of figure out the unwritten rules as you go.

This can be very stressful, and many marriages don't survive the process.

The first unwritten rule all husbands learn is, if you're going to be late from work, call.

You can go out for a beer after work if you want, but call. It has to do with getting dinner ready and being stood up and stuff.

You call about twice and that rule evolves into unwritten rule number two which is, "Don't be late, period."

Some of the unwritten rules arise from simple need. Because both my wife and I work we have evolved an unwritten rule around our house which says, "If you wear it, you iron it."

Which is why my shirts have that slept in look about half the time, and which follows its corollary rule which is, "If you wear it, you wash it."

Which is why sometimes my clothes also smell funny.

It works for us.

There is no law that says that an unwritten rule has to be unspoken as well.

This allows parents the legal authority to gather their children together for a family meeting and announce, "There's going to be a few new rules around here," and then proceed to announce that henceforth, rooms will be picked up, and homework and chores will be done before there's any television or telephoning or playing with friends.

Right.

We parents do this, forgetting that there is another unwritten rule that says that children universally ignore such pronouncements.

Children formulate their own unwritten rules — and change them — at the speed of light.

The mother of all their unwritten rules is, parents should never embarrass or humiliate their child. Unfortunately, a parent can never know, from day to day (or even moment to moment, for that matter) exactly what parental behavior will be embarrassing to their child.

Sometimes just showing up to watch, say, a little league practice is a major offense.

"What are you doing here?"

"I thought I'd come watch you practice."

"Why?"

"Last time you were mad at me because I didn't show up."

"That was last week. Will you stop mothering me."

"I'm your father."

"SEE?"

Like I said, it's confusing.

So what's to be done?

At the risk of sounding like a politician who wants to write one more law onto the books to solve some perceived social ill, I think we need one more unwritten rule: that we should ignore violations of unwritten rules.

Of course, maybe that's already an unwritten rule.

Fear of Heart Attacks

There are two words that strike terror into every red blooded, meat eating, beer swilling, sedentary, middle aged American male: Support Payments.

Ha! Just kidding.

No: the two words that cause men's ears to perk up around

here are: Heart Disease.

We can be having a typical male type conversation about whether or not Michael Jordan is the best basketball player who ever lived or ever will live, and we can be in a heated game of oneupsmanship wherein someone recalls and describes with great detail, including game, opponent, quarter, score, and time left on the shot clock, the most astounding basketball play ever, to which someone else says "Oh yeah" and describes a play by someone else that was even more astounding, to which yet another person says, "Oh yeah," and recalls yet another play that was even better, and someone says almost inaudibly, "Did you see this article about heart disease?" and every male in the place will forget about Michael Jordan and say, "No, what? Heart disease? What? Something new? What? Read it!"

You see, we know that we all have heart disease.

Oh yeah, we go to the doctor, and he listens to our heart through a stethoscope, an instrument of such precision that it hasn't changed appreciably in a hundred years, and he tells us we're okay; but we know that out there, somewhere above 140 beats per minute, a myocardial infarction is just waiting to happen.

So, somewhere about the age of thirty, we men all get one main, over arching goal in life, which is never to see the inside of the Heart Institute next to Sacred Heart while strapped to a gurney.

Often, this awareness that your heart might just stop comes from a significant event in your life. Like somebody you know having a heart attack.

Or having one yourself.

Or thinking you're having one.

I once had chest pains while jogging, so rather than discover that my heart was a mess lying face down on the sidewalk in running shorts and Nike's, my doctor scheduled a stress EKG.

That's fun. They shave parts of you, attach electrodes to the shaved parts, get the paddles ready in case your heart decides to stop, and then try to induce a heart attack.

"What happens if you can't get it started again?" I asked.

"Well, we'll know that your chest pain wasn't caused by the stuffed green pepper you had for lunch that day, won't we?" said my doctor.

That was comforting.

So we read about what causes heart disease.

And we adjust accordingly. Less red meat. More fish. (Wait a minute: doesn't some fish have high levels of lead? And what if the salmon I'm eating swam past Hanford? It's kind of a Day-Glo pink. Forget about it, that's a different disease.)

Stop smoking. Be obnoxious to people who do. "Excuse me, but would you put that out? Your smoke is doing damage to my heart valves, and I don't have any spares."

And just when you think you've got it all nailed down, and that you have eliminated heart disease from possibly striking you, the medical community issues one of their periodic "We know that we told you what we knew, but it may turn out that we didn't know what we thought we knew, after all," statements.

Like that there is something in French red wine that prevents heart attacks. "Okay. If I have to add a glass of expensive cabernet to my diet to stay alive, I can do that."

Or that maybe it's iron in your blood that <u>causes</u> heart attacks.

"What! You mean that for the 15 years I've been taking One-A-Day with Iron Vitamins, I have been <u>increasing</u> my risk of heart attack?"

"Umm, so it would appear. Yes."

So now, in order to get my ferritin levels down from their death defying levels, I have to visit the Blood Bank three times a year, and leave a deposit.

Assuming they're open, of course.

And is there a connection between heart attacks and baldness — or is it just a coincidence that fat, balding men have their hearts stop a lot? This is most distressing because I can drink red wine, but I can't seem to make hair stop falling out.

The baldness thing might also be connected to testosterone levels — too much? I doubt that. Too little? I don't want to think about it.

But I don't want a heart attack, either.

And now, after stocking up on red wine and donating blood, buying a lifetime's supply of Rogaine and wondering if worrying about a heart attack can alter my testosterone levels and bring one on, a new study suggests that maybe heart disease is caused by a bacteria. And if so, it might be possible to prevent heart disease like you prevent measles — with a shot!

(I'll bet that's giving the long range planners at The Heart Institute — assuming they have any — fits. "Well, we could change the sign over the door and call it the Prostate Institute.")

Personally, I'm not sure what to make of all this new medical information. It's all terribly confusing.

I think I'll try to sort it out over lunch today. Over a big Chapter 11 steak with a baked potato and sour cream.

But what if it turns out it's the sour cream that actually causes heart attacks?

With any luck, by the time they discover that, I'll be gone.

The Graying of America

There is a serious problem in America today.

It's a problem we face both collectively as a nation, and as individuals.

It is a problem we must come to grips with if we Americans are to lead the world into the next millennium.

It is a problem that strikes to the core of our very identity.

It's called, "The Graying of America," and it refers to the myriad of problems caused by — and this is difficult for me to say — the aging of the baby boomers.

(I should tell you that this conjures up an image of a couple of geezers in a nursing home singing, "What a drag it is growing old ... oops, I lost my teeth.")

Well, I know how I'm dealing with this aging thing; I'm in denial.

It wasn't that long ago that we had the debate about when middle age began.

So I'm not about to concede to old age. To getting gray.

Now, as it happens, I don't have any gray hair. Well, not much. I've got a hairline and a bald spot that looks like I made God mad somewhere in the past, but gray? Nothing I can't pluck out with a good set of tweezers.

And like most men, I'm holding tenaciously onto the basic male viewpoint that I haven't really aged at all since I was 23. Okay, 27.

Everyday we get up and chant our Peter Pan — baby boomer mantra: I'm not growing old, I'm not growing old.

And then one day, we make a mistake and look into the little concave mirror our wife uses to put on her eyeliner that magnifies her face about six times so she doesn't poke her eye out, and we realize that close up, our skin looks like the outside of a bad orange with something left over from the Exxon Valdez clogging the pores and we've got a serious case of varicose veins of the nose, (which seems, curiously, larger than it used to be) and that the crows feet around our eyes don't look like crow's feet so much as a view of the Mississippi Delta from space, and that our face is beginning to get those blotchy spots that look like freckles treated with Ortho-Grow that grandfather had all over his face when he was in his seventies and nearly dead, and in the middle of our mantra we realize, my God, I <u>am</u> growing old.

They ought to have a little warning sign on those mirrors that says, "Caution: facial wrinkles may appear bigger, deeper and more pronounced than in real life."

Now, the good news is, for anybody else to see what you see in that little magnifying mirror, they'd have to have the visual acuity of a bald eagle, so it's doubtful that anyone else, save perhaps your spouse, will see the wreckage your face is becoming.

But the bad news is, you know you've got wrinkles.

And wrinkles, like emphysema, only gets worse, denial or no denial.

Fortunately, this reality check only lasts a moment. We look away from the magnifying mirror into the regular mirror and, with that interesting selective vision we men are blessed with, suck in our gut and conclude, "Yep, not a day over 27."

Ommm. I am not growing old. I am not growing old.

Still, it's about this time that we begin to think about staying out of the sun, and that maybe the last few years in the tanning booth haven't been such a hot idea.

Still, the graying of America is not as bad as it could be.

At least we're graying.

When I was a kid, it seemed to me we went through the bluing of America. It seemed like about half of the mothers of my friends went from gray hair to blue. Some even went all the way to light purple, but they were in a minority.

And if they really wanted to be harsh, they could have called it the balding and fatting of America. Or they could pick on those little age lines. The wrinkling of America.

All of this aging poses serious etiquette problems.

For instance, does anyone really know if you are supposed to notice that someone who used to be gray, isn't any longer? "Gee, I like your hair — is that shoe polish you're using? You look ten years younger. Really stupid, and like you're deep in your mid-life crisis, but ten years younger, nevertheless."

Or is it more polite just not to notice? I don't know.

I'm not growing old. I'm not growing old.

Television advertising isn't helping any this. I noticed recently they now have Grecian Formula 16 for your beard. (Take the gray out! Take the years off!)

Hey! What ever happened to the quaint notion that a man becomes distinguished as he ages?

Personally, I'm beginning to think that was propaganda to hold up fragile male egos. Certainly some men get to look distinguished, but most of us, I fear, will just wind up looking old.

And when I look at my craters of the moon face in that magnifying mirror, I see a vision of my future face, and it does not make me happy.

Spending my old age looking like Willy Nelson's younger and slightly anorexic brother does not thrill me. "Ridden hard and put away wet," is the phrase that leaps to mind when look in that mirror.

And it probably thrills my wife even less.

Now understand, I'm not especially bummed about being old. I just don't want to look old.

One alternative would be to smear on copious quantities of one of those new Alpha-Hydroxy based creams with names like Age Defying Complex — a sort of industrial strength Oil of Olay, guaranteed to make my skin softer, suppler, younger.

But then I'd have to go to bed with my face covered with that goo, and when it comes right down to it, I'm too old for that.

I think instead, I'll just throw away the magnifying mirror.

Male Menopause

It was Sunday night.

I was reading the Sunday paper after a good day at the lake.

You know how that works: five days a week you read the paper in the morning to get ready for the day, but on Sunday night, you are just sort of catching up on the world, making sure there wasn't anything earth shattering that you should know about before you go back to work on Monday, like O.J. saying, "Okay, okay, I did it. Geez you guys," or something.

In short, it is not the time you want to read about upsetting subjects. Rather, you want to just cruise through, confirm that all is well with the world, and head off to bed.

But this Sunday night, it was not to be.

Because there, on the page following the pictures of the newly married couples and the couples who have made it to fifty or sixty years together was an article about ... male menopause.

Aaagh!

Now, I don't know how other men feel, but if I never heard the words "male menopause" used again it would be too soon.

Male menopause fits right up there with words like "enlarged prostate" and "kidney stones" as words I don't need to hear.

Not that I'm in denial or anything.

I mean, what happened to mid-life crisis?

That I can deal with. The term mid-life crisis has panache, a certain elan. It conjures a non-lethal slide into the wall in the Indy 500 of life, something you correct out of by using skill and daring and luck.

Look at the words: Crisis. As in "crisis management." Hey, we men can handle that! That's how we have spent our whole working life, right? Crisis management describes everything from how we parent to how we take family vacations.

And "mid-life." That's okay. I can live with being mid-life. Mid-life means I get to live to a hundred, give or take a few years.

And the words together suggest a beginning and an end. "He had his mid-life crisis and now it's over. And except for the fact that he's left his family and become a priest, nothing much has changed."

But menopause. Male menopause.

Now that's something else.

The very words suggest something altogether different.

A crisis is external; menopause is internal. And worse, inexorable.

Like the bumper sticker: menopause happens.

A crisis has a beginning, a middle and an end; menopause is hormones that get out of whack and never get back in whack. Or hormones that go away and just never come back.

I don't want to read this, I thought, as I read on.

I was right.

"Menopause manifests itself in a thousand ways," the author wrote.

I knew it! A thousand ways! I've probably already got it. He said it starts about the time a man turns 45 and I'm already eons past that dreaded mile marker.

Now, I should tell you that I am descended from a long line of hypochondriacs, and it's not unusual for me to begin manifesting the symptoms of whatever the latest disease is I've been reading about.

"Honey, I've been reading about this and I think maybe I've got something wrong with my head, a brain tumor or something. I can't see and my head hurts."

"Try opening your eyes."

"Oh, that's better."

"And I suspect your third glass of merlot last night has more to do with your head hurting than a tumor."

"You do? Hmmm."

So I know I've got to be careful.

The writer suggested that he was at risk because he came from a long line of menopausal men.

Did I?

What difference did it make? He said it happens to us all.

Now, nobody ever said life was fair, but you couldn't help but read a little of the article and realize that male menopause and female menopause are not created equal.

In the first place, when women hit menopause they know the trade off is their periods (known as "the curse" in some circles) are coming to an end. Men have no such offsetting internal benefit that might be looked upon as a silver lining.

On the other hand, according to the article, men who go through male menopause, get a tan, start working out and get in shape, buy a convertible and get a new, younger wife, which might cause the more cynical among us to ask, so what's the problem?

Not me, of course.

Still, how many women who go through menopause and get a new 19 year old husband out of the deal?

By the time I finished the article, I was thoroughly depressed.

Death, taxes and now, menopause.

I wondered, for a moment, what the odds of survival were if a couple went through menopause at the same time. Probably not very good.

"Hot flashes? You think hot flashes are a problem? I'm in clinical depression!"

I wondered if I was already menopausal and that was why I didn't want a pickup truck with huge tires, a rack of lights on the top and a stereo system that operated best right at the pain threshold.

The fact that I had never wanted one of those didn't occur to me right then.

I put the Sunday paper down, gathered up all my testosterone and limped off to bed.

By morning I was feeling better.

It was a great day.

I decided that I probably wasn't menopausal after all.

Not me, I thought, as I checked out my weekend tanning effort in the mirror, inspected my bald spot for signs of growth and packed my bag for a noon workout at Sta-Fit, and wondered how I would look in a Miata or a Corvette.

Still, I thought, maybe I should make some changes in my life.

To begin with, I think I'll stop reading the Sunday paper.

BLOOMSDAY, COACHING KIDS AND TRUCKS CALLED TACOMA

A Truck Called "Tacoma?"

I am watching television.

The truck ad comes on. The camera tilts at a crazy angle, making the little truck look alternately like it's zooming up and then down the world's steepest road. Then it's bouncing through the dessert, being driven in that wonderful, irresponsible way they drive all trucks in television commercials that makes the act of destroying a brand new truck by driving stupid look like a perfectly rational thing to do.

In short, it's a man's commercial: a little light on the logic and heavy on the testosterone.

And I'm really into it. I'm thinking maybe I should own a truck again and drive like the maniacs on TV.

And then the announcer says, "...the new Tacoma from Toyota..."

And I say, What? They named a pickup truck a Tacoma?

Did I hear that right?

Yes. That's weird. Have you ever been to Tacoma?

Now, being in the business where occasionally we are called upon to name products, I know that naming a new product isn't easy. And naming a new car or truck would be really hard because there aren't really any rules.

For instance, some car names mean something. On the surface, at least, the name has some logic to it.

"We're going to call this new Ford an Explorer."

"Why will we do that?"

"Because 'Blazer' is already taken, 'Pathfinder' which means the same thing sounds kind of wimpy, and besides the name will look good in print on the back of a National Geographic."

Maybe that was the case with Tacoma.

"Okay, what do we know about this truck?"

"Well, it's not very big, it's ugly and it smells."

"Well, in that case, we'll call it the Tacoma."

"Wow, that's good, boss. Maybe we could call the stripped down model the Puyallup."

Of course, maybe they just looked at maps and names of places until one jumped out at them, purely on the strength of the sound of it.

Sometimes, that works great. Chrysler New Yorker; Buick Riviera, and the one I like best, Bonneville.

Bonneville! The very name suggests great stretches of salt flats where drivers with names like Craig Breedlove drive cars with military surplus jet engines and go 500 miles an hour until their tires blow apart from too much centrifugal force and they die in a giant fireball.

Bonneville. It just has a ring to it.

Of course if you're from Utah, Bonneville may sound like Tacoma, if you know what I mean.

Other car names imply something or try to define the car. Land Rover. "I want a car that allows me to rove about." (It's a minor semantic point, but don't bandits 'rove'? I wonder if that came up in any of the focus group discussions.) Escort. Suburban. Voyager.

I drive a Voyager.

For some reason, the name Voyager has always had the ring of Star Trek to me. Maybe because of the Voyager satellites. Or it may have something to do with the fact that when I punch it from two blocks away trying to get through a yellow light, my daughter does her Scotty impression from the back seat.

"Captain, I canna hold her much longer!"

But no where is it written that the name of a product — especially a car — has to actually mean something. The paradox is that often the name will come to mean what the car is.

I was clear out of high school before I learned that an impala was an African antelope before it was a '57 Chevrolet. I think I actually had the fleeting thought, "Wow, they named an animal after a Chevy. That's cool."

But that's also why cars can have names like Eclipse, Dart, Ciera, Achieva, Supreme, Toronado, Metro, Civic, Accord, Tempo and Grand Am.

Names that sort of mean something, but not really.

Further complicating naming things is that in a lot of cases, you don't really want a name so much as a designation. In the car business, these turn into numbers and letters.

Hence the I-30; or, if you're a dyslexic German, you put the i at the end: 320i. There's the 626, 450 SL, GLC, SST, 442, Si, SX, DX, LX, SE, 240Z, 240ZX, LSMFT, RX7, F-100 and the best of all, the GTO, which stands for Gran Turismo Ophthalmology.

Still I've sat in enough of these meetings where the client has the nasty habit of asking the question, "Yes, but what does it mean?" enough to be amazed at some car names.

I mean, how did "Probe" get through? Have none of these people ever had a physical examination?

And the one I always wonder about is the Ford Taurus.

Taurus? Isn't the Taurus a bull? And don't bulls gore people once in a while? And isn't bull the universal symbol for, well, what you expect to get when you step into a car dealership? And get gored?

Actually, now that I think about it, I guess it makes a lot of sense.

I know that ultimately, if it is done right, the product will come to mean the name, instead of the other way around. So the name doesn't really mean anything.

Still, I don't think I could drive around in a truck called a Tacoma.

That's a bit too much Taurus for me.

Mother Ducking A Team Of Teenage Volleyball Players

Some years ago, Gail Sheehy wrote a best seller called <u>Passages</u>, where she held that just as children pass through normal, predictable phases like the terrible twos and rebellious teenage years, we adults also go through predictable phases of adulthood — leaving home, early adulthood, and so on.

However, it has come to my attention that she may have forgotten one.

The coaching phase.

Now, granted, not everybody goes through this phase.

I suspect this is because of the popularity of the Lamaze method of child birth, where the partner is called a "coach," and whose primary job is to tell the woman he loves, who is strapped to a table and in agony, to breathe — an instruction that seems superfluous at best and detrimental to the relationship at worst. And in any case, doesn't have anything to do with real coaching, which involves a team of hormonally imbalanced teenagers.

If you want to see what coaching children's sports is all about, I suggest a better role model is to watch the mother ducks with their ducklings at Manito Park.

Because if you coach, sooner or later, you will take your team on the road to a national festival or championship or tournament or something that will take seven days out of your life and require that you all stay in a motel together, during which time, you will resemble nothing so much as a large, human shaped mother duck.

Danger! Quack! Stay close! Quack! Where's Courtney? Quack!

I know. I just traveled to Orlando, Florida and back with my daughter's volleyball team — nine 14-year-olds whose primary interest at the national volleyball championships seemed to be finding boys.

Quack!

Now, I should say that I had great parental help along, and that we parents all agreed that off-court, the girls were <u>not</u> my responsibility. Still, being coach carries with it a level of authority you never really get to shed.

It starts on the airplane.

"Can I sit next to Kelsey? Alicia just threw up."

"Did you tell Alicia's dad?"

"He's asleep."

Quack!

Getting them through the new Denver airport was fun.

"We are at gate B187; we have to get to D16 in four minutes. Where's Courtney? Let's go."

Quack Quack!

"Can I go to the bathroom?"

"Coach, I can't find my ticket."

Quack!

Now, I have traveled with this group before, and in the past when we hit the hotel, they found, in this order, all the pop machines, the ice machines, the pool and the hot tub room, if there was one.

Since they tuned 14 however, a new target has been coming up on their radar screen: boys.

It's amazing. This group, that sometimes can't organize a trip to the bathroom, suddenly started functioning with military precision.

"Command and Control, this is Red Dog One. We have confirmed seven — repeat — seven buff bogeys around the hotel pool. Pass the word the pool is a target-rich environment."

"Roger, Red Dog One. We copy you on that. Switch to bikinis and engage the targets at your discretion."

I came down to find all nine of my players along with three 15-year-old boys visiting from England sitting in the hotel hot tub that was just big enough to hold eight.

And it didn't help my anxiety level any knowing that three

of my nine were medically certified as boy-crazy.

Quack!

It was turning into a good trip for the girls, and we hadn't even seen a volleyball court yet.

The boys thought they had died and gone to Heaven.

We were only one of three volleyball teams staying at this particular hotel, and as near as I could tell, the boys had made pool contact with all three. When one team would go off to play, they would just float over to another one.

I don't think any of them ever saw the Magic Kingdom.

Or cared.

Eventually, of course, we did actually play some volleyball.

But not before the daily ritual known as "The doing of the hair."

There I am before the first match, adrenaline starting to flow, trying to get my players pumped for national competition. They, however, have a higher priority — French braiding each other's hair.

Quack!

Well, it's important that everybody's hair look the same.

That's okay: I'm adaptable. The next day I lay down a new rule. Hair done <u>before</u> we leave the hotel. I'm sorry if that means you have to get up at 5 a.m.

Now, every coach of seventh and eighth grade girl athletes will tell you that he really has two teams. One that plays perfectly and can make no mistakes, and its evil twin that plays like it's got a flatline EKG and has never seen the game before.

One never knows which team will take the court. Or for that matter, when they will change from one team to the other while on the court.

Quack!

As we had all year, we saw both in Florida.

Was it all worth it? Is the coaching phase of adulthood worth the anxiety that comes with it?

The answer, I think, lies with the ducks at Manito.

Because when the little ducks are learning to fly, they are awkward and they crash and burn a lot.

But when they finally get it right, watching a young duckling take to the air is truly a thing of beauty.

And somewhere, there is a mother duck watching, who is very proud.

Quack!

Tatooing On Your Makeup

I work in advertising. A good portion of my job is to write advertising that interrupts your consciousness, piques your interest and compels you to read the rest of the ad, where my sterling prose will convince you to buy whatever it is my client of the moment happens to want to sell.

Now, it's my personal belief that the best two headlines to stop you dead in your tracks and get you to read the rest of my ad are, "Great Sex," and, "Free Beer." I try not to be bothered by the fact that neither of those headlines have anything to do with what my clients sell.

And now there's another. And I didn't even write it.

I saw it in a small ad in the paper a couple of weeks ago. I was on my way from Ann Landers to Calvin and Hobbes when it stopped me cold.

"Permanent Cosmetics," it said. Below the headline was a photo of a lovely lady, and below that was the sub-headline, "Wake up with your makeup on!"

Huh?, I thought, not getting it.

You mean, like, if you shut down the P.I. some night and you wake up in a strange room, you still have your makeup on so you don't scare whoever is next to you? Like that? And in that situation, shouldn't you be more concerned about how you smell than how you look? And who you're with?

I read on. "At About Faces, we take away that concern by applying permanent eyebrows, eyeliner and lip color."

I was still confused, trying to reconcile what I know about cosmetics (which is next to nothing) into the notion of *permanent* cosmetics, and how that would happen, when the neural clusters somewhere deep in my cerebral cortex made all the right connections, and like a slot machine coming up with three cherries rang out: Tatoo!

This ad is about tattooing! Your face!

And then I thought (and this is a quote), "Ooo, yuk."

I looked back at the picture of the lady.

The photo looked like one of those glamour makeover photos. The kind where they make normal looking young ladies look "glamorous."

They do this by applying enough lipstick and makeup to make even KREM TV reporters envious, covering all the zits, filling in all the wrinkles, and then draping a feathered boa over the bare shoulders and shooting the whole thing through a filter that softens and fuzzies up what can't be covered with Max Factor technology, generally making the person in the picture look very glamorous.

Sort of like they'd look if Cindy Crawford was born with their face, if you know what I mean. Which is great, except for the fact that in the glamour photo, people don't look at all like they do in real life, which is more or less what they're buying.

I looked at the photo closely.

"Stylish" was one word that came to mind. Another was "done."

Nicely done, but done, nevertheless. Done like you were going to a dinner at the Spokane Club.

I wondered, is that face tattooed on?

Hmmm. Her eyebrows had that disconnected-from-the-facial-structure Connie Chung look; kind of removed from where God thought they would look best and re-applied about an inch higher on the forehead.

Again, not unattractive, but not exactly normal, either.

Are those eyebrows tattooed on? Does she wake up looking

like that? And then I wondered, does Connie Chung?

I went back to the ad.

It said that permanent make up was an art and that skill and experience meant everything. It then went on to say that the lady in the picture, the one with the free-floating eyebrows, was a pioneer in the field.

Time out.

A pioneer in a field where experience means everything?

Isn't that an oxymoron? Like airline food, or military intelligence, or government service?

Doesn't that beg some questions, like whose face did she train on?

Is there some lady out there who permanently looks like Liz Taylor did in Cleopatra? "Hmm, I've got to work on the eyeliner thing. Maybe a smaller needle."

And who decides how much is enough?

Makeup, after all is a subjective sort of thing. Your beauty really is in the eye of the beholder, even if the makeup sits on your face. One person's just right is another person's too much.

"With all that make up on, your wife looks like a brazen hussy!"

"Yeah, I know, Mom. Isn't it great?"

It may have just been a coincidence, but the day I saw the "tatoo your face" ad, I also saw a beautician who had these purple slashes of makeup on her cheekbones where a little blush is supposed to be.

She looked like a blonde Pocahontas in war paint.

It made me want to call someone for help.

"911? We need a Mary Kay consultant dispatched to 29th and Grand right away. Oh yeah, this one's a real mess. This is a two-pink-Cadillac job we have here. We need all the help we can get."

I mean, how do you know the person who is tattooing your eyebrows to a new part of your face isn't visually impaired? Or uncoordinated?

"Uh-oh. Got the arch too high. Oh, well. You look good sort of perpetually surprised."

What if her idea of good make up is the same as the war paint lady's?

And what if you marry a man who likes a scrubbed clean look in the morning?

There is something very weird about it all.

Oh well. I'm just glad that men wouldn't do anything as weird as that. Except for a hair transplant, which isn't <u>that</u> weird.

Not that weird at all.

Why are you staring at my forehead?

The 10 Steps of Doing Bloomsday

It is Friday morning.

That means, if you are running Bloomsday, you should be entering step five of the Bloomsday experience: Acquiescence.

As all experienced Bloomies know, there are at least 10 distinct steps or phases in the Bloomsday experience. And that's for those who aren't particularly neurotic about their running.

The first Bloomsday step is self-doubt. This is where you look deep into your soul and ask: Can I do it?

This is where you should be asking something far more prosaic, like, why would you want to? But only people who have done Bloomsday a couple of times get around to that more obvious question.

It is during this phase that a phenomena called the Nike reflection takes place. During the Nike reflection, you look at the Nike ads where they have these incredibly lean and lithe and athletic athlete-model types running across mountains and deserts and ghettos, and you see your reflection!

You become that lean, lithe, athletic model. "Yes!" you say. "I'll just do it!"

This can be very bad for your knees.

Having had your Nike moment, you now move on to the

pre-training step.

Pre-training is where you strut your newly found Nike/runner/ego/self around, and say stuff like, "I'm going to do Bloomsday!" while you also say, not necessarily out loud, "And I'm going to start training, um, next week."

It's my personal belief that it's the "next week" part of that statement that is the reason most of us don't look like the model/athletes in the Nike ads.

Bloomsday being on the first Sunday in May, it is not at all unusual for Pre-training to last until April 23rd or so.

Naturally, the next step is training. Training is wonderful because it is the time when you get in touch with your body. In fact, if you're like most of us, you'll have intimate conversations with parts of your body you never even knew existed.

You're out there, running along, feeling the wind in your face and the sun on your back and feeling truly alive, and your knees are screaming, "What the hell are you doing? You take me to see Alex Verhoogan, this minute!" And your spleen, speaking on behalf of all your gut is asking "Hey! What's all this bouncing around stuff," while your heart and lungs start sending emergency messages that sound a lot like, "Attention! Attention! We are approaching complete system failure. Shutting down all systems starting now."

This gives way to step four which is self-loathing for not having the will power to start the training phase earlier. During self-loathing, those of us over forty actually calculate the odds that we won't survive the entire race.

After self-loathing comes acquiescence. This is where we come to peace with the nearness of the race, the limitations of our bodies and accept the fact that we are what we are, and what we are will have to do.

And, the Nike ads notwithstanding, that we probably won't win the race.

That's where you should be now.

It's not all bad, though. During acquiescence carbo-loading takes place. The motto here is, "Eat pasta, drink and be merry for tomorrow we eat pasta, drink and be merry, for the next day we run and want to die."

During acquiescence, women go into pre-race planning while men do some serious expectation downsizing.

Pre-race planning is not about your race plan, but about the nuts and bolts of getting there. Like thinking about where you're going to park.

"Park?" we men say, somewhat incredulous that anyone would waste a moment of carbo-loading time to even think about it.

"There will be 50,000 people all jamming into the same five block area downtown at the same moment. Don't you think that might cause a parking problem?" our wives ask.

"Hmmm," we reply, not wanting to admit that, frankly, we hadn't thought about that.

Nor had we thought about what we were going to do with the extra clothing we would want to shed during the race, and where, exactly we said we'd meet all our friends who were also in the race and what to do about a potty stop, which, given the excessive carbo-loading and morning coffee drinking was going to be an important question before the race ended.

Step seven is the actual race itself, during which you discover that for many runners, Bloomsday has little to do with any actual running. It has everything to do with being there, and being a part of it.

Whatever that "it" actually is. This may make you re-think your training regimen, such as it was. A lot of people at the start realize they should have spent more time training by running in a crowded elevator in the Seafirst Building.

Personally, I think not getting kicked in the groin by following too close to someone in front of me and not tripping and getting trampled to death by everyone behind constitutes a successful start.

Finishing alive constitutes a successful finish.

Step eight in the race is "The Wearing of the Shirt." It is this step that separates those who ran from those who watched. It is your badge of accomplishment.

It says "I did it."

Like those people in the Nike ads. Sort of.

The shirt also says ask me about my time.

It is here that you discover the Bloomsday Paradox, which is, with 50,000 participants, your time means nothing, but without your time, the race means nothing.

Almost immediately, that puts you into Step nine, which is time talk.

You know your time means nothing what with all the people and the walking through Peaceful Valley and all, and yet, you ask everyone you see, "How'd you do?" gloating secretly when your time is lower and making excuses when it's not.

This step continues at least through the next day when you scan the paper to see the race results.

The final step is closure.

This is where, when you finally no longer need massive doses of Ibuprofen to get through the day without grunting every time you move, you see a Nike ad, and you imagine yourself like the model: lithe, athletic, and fit, and you know that if you started now, that by next May, you would be really ready — not just sort of ready like you were this year, and you think, hmmm.

And then, "I think next year I'll go fishing instead."

Coaching A Team of Girls

The call will come when you are at home.

It will come in the evening, when you are relaxed; when your guard is down. Maybe the people will know that you enjoy a glass of wine or two with dinner, and so your judgment will be a little clouded, your intellectual acuity not at its usual razor sharp edge.

Most likely, they will call right after you have just watched something mindless on television, like "Baywatch" (the one show that really improves if you turn the sound off) so they know your mind will be focused on other things.

It is then that they will spring their trap. "There's this team of kids, see, and we thought you'd make a good coach."

"Me?" you respond with all due modesty as the hook sets itself back by your second molar.

"Yeah, your name keeps coming up. You'd be great," they say, letting out a little line.

Now, when that happens to you, and visions of yourself as a modern-day Knute Rockne or Vince Lombardi or Pat Riley to a bunch of 11-year-olds begins to dance through your head, it's pretty hard to say no.

It's also pretty hard to remember to ask the person calling the obvious question, which is, "Why don't you do it?" To which the probable answer would be, "Because I'm not a fool."

But before you say yes, and they reel you in, there are a few things you should know about coaching kids.

The first is that your primary qualification might just be that you are alive without an actively debilitating case of emphysema, as opposed to any particular knowledge of the sport you're being asked to coach.

I know. I coach a girl's volleyball team, and my two main qualifications are that 1) I'm not dead, and, 2) I said I'd do it.

You should also know, if you coach a girls team like I do, the younger they are, the higher and louder they can, and do, scream.

And they scream all the time. If your team is below the age of twelve, my advice is get a set of ear plugs. Just because you're giving up your time doesn't mean you should have to give up your hearing, too.

If you accept, the first thing you have to do as a coach is learn to talk coach-ese. This means starting every sentence with "Okay, listen up!"

You will also have to learn that your players may have a different intensity from yours. For instance, after explaining a crucial defensive strategy and asking if there are any questions, no doubt one of your kids will ask, "Well, um, like, will we have to wear those shorts that are really ugly?"

Somewhere along the way, you will have to invent your

coach-persona. Or personas. Being schizophrenic and developing multiple personalities might be an occupational hazard when it comes to coaching kids. Except for the cost of your anti-psychotic drugs, however, it can be a real advantage.

You can be the drill sergeant. "Drop and give me ten, you worthless scumbags."

You can be Mr. Rogers. "Okay, now we're going to pass the ball to the person up front we call the setter."

You can be the coach intellectual. "In passing the volleyball, we take energy out of the ball by meeting it with our forearms, making what we call a platform from which the ball ricochets...blah, blah blah."

I'm here to tell you, that one doesn't work. At least not with 12-year-olds.

Your coach-persona may be the same person you are when you're not a coach, but unless you coach professionally, that's unlikely.

That's because there is nothing quite like watching a bunch of sixth and seventh graders go into a game and forget weeks of what you thought they had learned in practice. This, in turn, makes you "go ballistic," as we coaches like to say, and go from being Mr. Nice guy to Mr. Raving Lunatic.

It is here that we novice coaches ask really stupid questions.

"Why did you do that?"

If the kids weren't terrified of our Jekyll-Hyde transformation, and already on the verge of tears, they should say, "Gee coach, I don't know. Letting the other team score the winning point seemed like a good idea at the time, but I guess that was a mistake, huh?"

Coaches above the novice rank give history lessons. "Allyson, that was your ball." Chances are if it dropped at her feet, she probably knows that already.

Which brings you face to face with the central paradox of coaching, and for that matter, of all sports. If we're supposed to be having fun out here, why are the coaches yelling all the time?

Part of it is because we don't know any better, and part of it is because we know that, like it or not, there is this thing at the end of the game called winning or losing, and it's a lot more fun to win than to lose.

And as coaches, we know that when the team comes in second, it will be little comfort for them to know that someone else may have come in 10th.

So it's easy to forget that what they are learning, and the environment in which they are learning it, will have far longer-lasting effects than any win-loss record.

So we impose discipline. We critique. We cajole, we nurture, we threaten, we beg, we explain and re-explain and demonstrate and re-demonstrate, and we live with the curious belief that if we can just find the right combination of words and actions, we can magically teach 12-year-olds in a few weeks what it took us years to learn.

So before you say yes to that coaching job, you should know it can be a very frustrating experience.

On the other hand, every once in a while, right out of the blue, out there on their own, your kids will do something absolutely, perfectly, right.

And it is magic.

So, tonight, if you get the call, and someone tells you they think you'd make a good coach, and you feel that hook set and they start to reel you in, what's my advice?

Assuming you can keep it fun and you like having multiple personalities, I'd say go for it.

Adding Descriptive Titles to Our Names

Does your name mean anything?

I didn't know mine did until about fourth grade when my next door neighbor, Ann Schaefer, showed up with a book of names and their meanings.

"Douglas means 'black heart'," she said, with some perverse joy at the fact that my name had a less than completely desirable meaning.

Anne was almost two years younger than I, had already skipped one grade, was closing on skipping a second and was clearly my intellectual superior.

"What does Anne mean?" I asked as I took the book from her and began looking for her name.

"They're in alphabetical order," she said, helping me out, and then told me what her name meant, which I forget now, but was something like, "smart and pure as the driven snow."

I was hoping it would mean "insufferable little snot."

Now, the reason I brought that little story up is because it has occurred to me that part of the reason our society is in such a mess is because we don't get to add descriptors to our names that help us recognize each other's achievements, accomplishments or attributes like some other societies do.

Imagine how much better things would be if by virtue of a title, we knew better who we were dealing with.

The early Romans and Greeks had descriptors: Pliny the Elder. Or was it Pliny the Younger? Probably both.

And when they introduced Richard the Lionhearted, do you think there was any doubt that this was a guy you probably didn't want to mess with?

We need something like that, to help us sort out our pecking order and make sure that we pay respect to each other's accomplishments.

And this should start in childhood:

"Children, we have a new friend joining us in daycare. Everybody, meet Amanda the Spoiled. Amanda, this is Susie the Shy, Robert the Unintelligible and over there is Alex the Hyperactive. Alex, get down from the light fixture please."

Later on, as we grow and develop toward adulthood, the old descriptors would fall away and new ones could be added.

"Hey, did you hear that Lisa the Beautiful is going out with Gabe the Self-Centered?"

"Really? When did she break up with Alex the Incorrigible?"

"And did you hear that Marcia the Rabid and Johnny the Obsequious both got into Law School?"

Now, this would not be the same as a pet name, although there might be some crossover.

I have a friend who used to refer to his wife as "Thunder Thighs." "Let's go, Thunder Thighs," he would say affectionately.

They're not married anymore. Which might say something about choosing pet names. Or letting your thighs get too big.

But we're not talking about pet names — we're talking about recognizing attributes and accomplishments.

And sometimes, you just can't reduce that to a one-word descriptor, although sometimes it's tempting. This is an aside, but when you see the movie title, "Dumb and Dumber," do our county commissioners come to mind? Maybe it's just me.

No. Sometimes you need a whole phrase to capture the essence of a person. The Plains Indians knew this. I mean, "Dances with Wolves" was the name they gave a guy who, well, danced with wolves.

We need to do that.

It would make our relationships so much clearer.

A teacher might be honored as, "She Who Shapes Young Minds;" a doctor as "Healer of Men;" community college presidents as "He Who is Both Overpaid and Incompetent."

I mean, wouldn't that be better? Wouldn't it be better if you heard in court, "All rise. Court is now in session. Judge She Who Sues for Libel When She Doesn't Like What's Written in the Paper, presiding."

And our police chief. Mangan. What does "Mangan" tell you?

Nothing.

On the other hand, if, He Who Goes Ballistic When Flipped Off By Punks," was his name, he might not have <u>been</u> flipped off by punks. I mean, did you ever hear of anybody ever flipping off Richard the Lionhearted?

And living?

I rest my case.

But it's not just for public figures. This works for everyone, at all levels.

I mean, who among us hasn't had a boss at one time or another who should be renamed, "He Who Does No Work?"

It's "Dances with Wolves" updated to corporate America.

"I think everybody in the meeting knows each other. We have Made of Cow Dung from marketing, Fiddles With the Truth from PR, Eats Small Children from Human Resources, Can't see Past the Beans from Accounting and Has No Shame from Legal. The president, Man Without A Clue, will be joining us later."

Now, I admit, there are some things that need to be worked out here, like are your names cumulative — I mean, do they just keep adding up over time, or are they like traffic tickets, where after three years you get to drop them from your record?

And if you get married, do you take your spouses name? ("I now pronounce you Mrs. Doesn't Do Dishes") or do you merge them or hyphenate them ("I now pronounce you Susan Attacks like a Jackal-Doesn't Do Dishes").

Today as you go about your business, just think about the descriptive names the people you deal with might have, and see for yourself if this idea doesn't have merit.

And if it does, maybe we could get a powerful politician on our side.

Someone like the Senator from Oregon, whatshisname?

Senator Shoves Tongue In Everyone's Mouth.

Hmmm. Maybe not.

Address Discrimination

Stop at any four-way stop sign near the edge of town these days, and you will be presented with housing development signs that are irrefutable evidence that there is a new social evil creeping across the land. And I am embarrassed to admit that some members of my profession — advertising and marketing — share in its insidious spread.

It is an evil that separates the have's from the have-not's; that selectively stratifies and snobifies our society and clearly discriminates against a large and innocent majority.

I am speaking of address discrimination. Address discrimination is when you get to say that you live in a place with a name instead of on a mere street.

When somebody asks where you live, do you have to say, "I live on the five hundred block of East Heroy?" or, "I live on 27th?" Or do you get to say "I live in Quail Run."

"Quail Run." The very name suggests not houses, but manors. Houses are for people who live on streets with numbers.

I know. I used to live on 17th. 17th is a nice street. Not as nice as, say, 27th or 44th or 62nd, but nice all the same.

Still, when I would tell people I lived on 17th, I could see they were calculating how far above 12th I was, which for a while there a few years back, was the scene of numerous drive-by shootings, family killings and other criminal goings-on. One guy actually buried his wife out in the back yard.

That sort of calculation doesn't happen when you tell people you live in Quail Run.

Being in advertising, and knowing that someone, somewhere has to think up these names, I wonder what they were thinking when they came up with some of them.

For instance, what names did they reject before they settled on Quail Run? Quail Walk? Pidgeon Run? Seagull Hollow?

And where are the quail in Quail Run?

Ask a real estate agent that, sometime. "Actually, you see, there aren't any. We killed them all putting up these houses."

And what about "Inverness?" What a great name. It conjures craggy wind-swept cliffs with waves crashing below. A development inspired by the Scottish seacoast at it's most rugged and beautiful?

Not exactly. Actually, it's a piece of scrubland on the side of Brown Mountain nobody wanted until now. Still, doesn't

"Inverness" sound better than "17th?"

This address discrimination has been going on for several decades now, of course. This gives us a perspective on how well the names hold up. Some names probably sound pretty good when they're thought up, but sound pretty dorky a few years down the line.

I remember being told by a friend that she lived in the Ponderosa.

"You're kidding, of course." I replied. "With Hoss and Little Joe?"

She didn't think that was funny at all. "The ponderosa is a kind of pine tree, indigenous to the area," she explained.

"Right," I said. "Say 'hi' to Pa Cartwright for me."

It could have been worse, I suppose. She might have lived in Sherwood Forest. On Friar Tuck Lane. Or in a place called Ivanhoe.

The fact is, some development names are just better than others. I suspect those are the ones thought up by the advertising professionals instead of the builder's family sitting around the kitchen table.

For instance, compare Glennaire with Devon Ridge. Not knowing anything about either of them, which one would you assume was higher up the economic food chain?

Right. Glennaire sounds like something a builder named Glen came up with. "Devon" on the other hand, sounds very classy. Slightly British. And Ridge invokes the high ground, both metaphorically and militarily speaking.

Some places just come out and claim the high ground outright.

Highland Park.

What a name! It's the high, high ground. It's a park. Homes there don't have lawns — they have grounds. The name says it all.

Some street names have the cachet of development names. High Drive, for instance. Twenty years ago when I first moved to

Spokane, I thought the appropriate response to hearing that someone lived on High Drive was to suck in a bunch of air like toking on a joint and say, "Me, too."

Rockwood Boulevard has that classy ring to it too, although now, thanks to the Rockwood clinic, the name Rockwood conjures up images of faulty heart valves and spastic colons about as often as stately old homes.

The conceit of housing development names is there is the unspoken assumption that by virtue of their named existence, you, the outsider, will (or should) know where they are, and, by extension, know what it takes to live there.

As opposed to mere street addresses, which are little more than map coordinates.

Sounds like discrimination to me.

So, what's to be done?

Well it's unlikely that developers are going to stop naming their developments any time soon.

(Would you buy a house in a place known as "the nameless development eight miles from Francis on Indian Trail Road?" Not likely.)

So, I suggest we retroactively name all the neighborhoods in town.

There are lots of good names that aren't taken. Southwoods, for instance. That's a good one. That could be the area below Northwoods.

And how about Sunset Ridge. West 1st could become War-Zone Acres.

Down on 12th they could become "Drive-by Estates" Hmmm. Maybe not. I admit its an idea that needs some work.

But you see the potential. When someone asks where you live, you could say, I live in Devonshire-On-the-High-Ridge-Near-The-Quail-Run-Park."

And when they say where's that, you can answer, "17th and Freya."

Dining on the Street

I think we, and by we, I mean the city of Spokane, have officially made it to the big time.

I say this because all of the really great cities of the world — Paris, Rome, Spokane — all of these cities share a common characteristic that sets them apart from the lesser cities, like Post Falls: sidewalk dining.

Sidewalk dining!

The very words evoke the sounds of distant accordion music wafting on the breeze, and lovers walking hand in hand.

With Sidewalk Dining, Spokane Falls Boulevard takes its rightful place along side The Champs Elysees. It's like we're all in Gigi, and any moment Maurice Chevalier will show up singing "Thank Heaven For Little Girls" as we dribble pizza sauce down our chin.

Now, before we get all warm and runny inside and engage in an orgy of self-congratulation about this outside dining thing, you need to know that sidewalk dining, while catapulting us into ranks of the truly sophisticated, also has its down side.

Like all things in nature, there is a yin and yang to sidewalk dining.

First of all, we should define our terms here. Sidewalk dining is not eating inside under a glass on what <u>used</u> to be the sidewalk but now is just an extended part of a restaurant like at Cyrus O'Leary's or Rocky Rococco.

Nor is it eating at one of the rolling hot dog stands that have sprung up all over.

To qualify as outdoor dining, you must be at a table, preferably with a colorful umbrella, outdoors, on the sidewalk. If the table is white and in the glare of the sun so it makes you almost blind, that's even better.

One of the yins of outdoor dining is you get to eat outside. The yang of that is, everybody outside gets to see you eat.

There are lots of things humans do that are beautiful and poetic, but in most cases, eating isn't one of them. Now, inside tucked into a restaurant where everybody is eating, this is no big deal, but outside, where you sort of inflict your table manners on innocent bystanders, it's an altogether different story.

I mean, do you really want to be having a lunch in front of Domini's and try to get your mouth around one of those sandwiches where the whole world can see you? Especially across from a construction site?

"Attention, attention please. We have a roast beef on rye alert at Domini's. The young lady in the blue dress, at the table by the door, the one with the mayo up by her ear, is about to attempt a full top to bottom center bite. Holy Moly! She did it and with room to spare! That lady's got the elastic jaw of a boa constrictor. Let's give her a big round of applause, boys!"

Another yin to the yang of being outside is, what do you do when you're having lunch and people you know walk by?

Inside there's the tacit understanding that you're all, well, inside. But outside, one of you is inside/outside and the other is outside/outside, as it were.

The entire scene fairly screams, "I'm sitting in a posh restaurant outside, sipping a petit sarah and having smoked salmon fettucine and you're carrying a Big Mac back to your desk in a bag."

Now who do you think has the power in this little social equation?

This can be especially awkward when it is your boss who has the Big Mac.

Just a point of etiquette here; restaurant owners consider it bad form for outside diners to invite brown-baggers passing by to join them, or to pass out the free bread sticks and salad to friends passing by and then have the gall to ask for more.

And there is always the risk that if you are having lunch alone in one of those places, they will put you outside — precisely where you don't want to be.

The other day this happened to one of my co-workers.

Not only was he alone, but there wasn't even anyone else in the outdoor section, so he was really alone. It was like they had banished him to the restaurant equivalent of Siberia.

Of course, it didn't help his ego any that just about everybody he knew walked by and pointed all that out to him.

"What's the deal, Dennis? Have they seen you eat or something? Do they always seat you where they can just hose down the area around your table?"

We were so funny.

Some outside places are just plain bad for your health. If you're outside at Street Music on Howard across from PayLess when the buses come, you could die from an overdose of diesel fumes, not to mention second-hand cigarette smoke from people waiting for the bus.

And some of the places have metal picket fences around them, like the Olive Garden and Rock City.

If you happen to be watching a pretty girl cross the street instead of watching where you're going and you stumble into one of those fences, you're at serious risk of puncturing your spleen not to mention humiliating yourself as you pitch yourself face-first into someone's lasagna.

"Terribly sorry. I'll just lift myself off this spike and be on my way. Could I borrow your napkin? I seem to be bleeding. Nothing serious. Just a flesh wound."

Those fenced-in areas have all the ambiance of a cross between New Orleans' French Quarter and the Geiger Corrections Center.

Eating in one of those place makes me feel like I'm in a zoo and I'm the animal. To be complete, they need to hang a sign on the fence that says, "Please don't feed the diners."

But that's okay. If people want to eat their lunches and dinners with exhaust fumes, car noises, skateboarders screaming by and panhandlers ("Are you gonna finish that pizza, man?") then I say great.

Have at it.

But, I know what I look like eating a Domini's sandwich or the spaghetti they serve at the Olive Garden. And I don't think I should inflict that on passing pedestrians.

So, I'll be right down the street, having lunch at the hot dog stand in front of the Seafirst Building.

Or at my desk, munching down a Big Mac.

Seven Habits of Highly Effective People

First, all we wanted to do in America was win friends and influence people.

If we did that, all would be well. We could do that through the power of positive thinking, we were told.

Then a book told us that as people, we played games.

Well, that made sense, I suppose. If you "won" friends (instead of, say, earning them, like merit badges) you must have been playing some kind of game. We all played games according to the self-help book, <u>Games People Play</u>. In fact, life was a game. (Some of us, in the '60s kept calling to the referee of life "Time out!" but he wasn't listening.)

After games came <u>I'm OK; You're OK</u>, except that if you read it, you know that what the author really meant was, "I'm OK and You're Probably Pretty Screwed Up," which was why you were reading the book in the first place.

Then there were the business books: There was the <u>One Minute Manager</u> (who were they kidding?) and we all went in search of excellence, then we went beyond excellence, and finally went in search of chaos, which, if you have anything to do with any of the major companies around here, you didn't have to look far to find.

That's when I went in search of another Elmore Leonard mystery.

But now, the self-help book people have raised the ante.

For those of us who are still trying to evolve to a higher state of being, the new goal is to become "highly effective."

Highly effective at what, you might well ask.

At everything, seems to be the answer.

You mean, it's not enough just to be okay?

Not any more.

But that's the bad news. The good news is, to be highly effective, we only need to have seven habits.

Now, before those of you out there get all excited, saying, "Wow, man, that's cool! I've got lots of habits: I smoke, I drink, I slurp my coffee, my first wife said I had a bad habit of leaving my underwear on the floor…"

Those are not the habits the latest self-help book is talking about.

We are talking about good habits. And not the good habits your mother tried to teach you when you were growing up. Make your bed. Stand up straight.

No. These are the habits explained in great detail in the book, "The Seven Habits of Highly Effective People," which you've probably seen sitting around on people's desks and in book stores and things, and you've wondered what those habits are and how many of them you have.

The answer is, probably not very many, unless, of course, you're already highly effective. At everything.

So what are the seven habits of highly effective people? I think I can tell you those without giving away the plot of the book. They are (1) be proactive; (2) begin with the end in mind; (3) put first things first; (4) think win/win; (5) seek first to understand, then to be understood; (6) synergize (yes, you heard right, there is a habit called synergizing); and (7) sharpen the saw.

Sharpen the saw?

Now, how many times has your boss pulled you in and praised you by saying, "You have a nice habit of synergizing. I like that. Plus, you keep a sharp saw. That's good, too."

Not very often, I'd guess.

So you know, even at a quick glance, that you'd better buy the book.

Now, there are some habits that the author doesn't mention. Like for instance, I've noticed that the highly effective people I know have a habit of making a lot more money than I. And they also have a habit of always being in a meeting when you want to talk to them. Plus, they tend to be real opinionated.

So there are some habits that aren't covered.

Personally, I suspect that this is because the author, who has clearly hit the mother lode of self-help here is already at work on a sequel: It will be titled something like: "Seven More Habits of Highly Effective People I Forgot to Tell You About," or "The 14 Annoying Things Highly Effective People Never Do," or, "Don't Be Stupid, And Other Habits Your Kindergarten Teacher Never Taught You."

Now, you would think that walking around with a book like Seven Habits would be like an admission of guilt — that it would be like telling the world that you need to read the book because you are not highly effective and you don't have those seven habits and you are somehow lacking as a human being.

I mean, why don't you just wear a sign that says "I'm 0 for 7: totally ineffective." Or, "I'm 5 for seven: moderately effective."

But it doesn't work that way, does it? That's the paradox of self-help books.

Instead of guilt by association, we get the benefit of non-guilt by association, i.e., the fact that I am reading the book means I am perceived to be more effective. At least more effective than someone who has not read the book.

Never mind the fact that I have none of the seven habits.

And there is the second paradox of self-help books. Those who read them probably don't need them. And those of us who do need them are probably incapable of change.

So, should you buy this book?

Yes. Definitely.

And you want to keep it out where people can see it. That way, people will know you are now among the highly effective.

I've been thinking about reading it, but I don't know.

Reading that sort of book can become a habit.

Cheating on Ethics Questions

The headline read, "More Americans failing ethics test."

"Well that's real nice," I thought. We Americans can't do science, we can't do math, our geography knowledge stinks and now we are failing ethics.

The article in the paper said a new Money Magazine survey has found that we Americans are less ethical than we used to be.

Less ethical? Us? Americans?

The country that produced the savings and loan scandal, hordes of government lobbyists, the entire nuclear industry (with all its honesty and integrity), advertising agencies and Michael Milken, not to mention the Menendez brothers and Leslie Abramson and, for that matter, elected Bill Clinton President — us unethical?

How can that be?

Personally, I suspect it is a flawed survey. I suspect that the questions didn't give the surveyee's nearly enough information.

Because ethics don't live in a vacuum, like the square root of four does.

Ethics exist in real life, real time, real space, and like everything else that does that, they tend to be situational.

I mean, for instance, the story said the survey reported that a third of us would cheat on our taxes.

Only a third? Where'd they do this survey? In a seminary?

Does this count those who don't even pay any taxes? And what about those who treat their deductions, as the accountants like to say, "aggressively?" Is that cheating? Or do you have to get all the way to "creative" with your expenses before it's cheating?

It seems to me, they asked the wrong question. According to the paper, they asked if you would report $2000 in cash income on your tax return.

The answer is not yes or no, but, "that depends." Where did the money come from? A rich uncle? A Tupperware party? A garage sale? A Zip Trip holdup?

How can you answer if you don't know?

Of course, the real question is what's a question about the IRS and paying taxes got to do with ethics, anyway?

Survival, possibly. Your IQ? Maybe. Common sense? Certainly. But ethics? I don't think so.

Unless, of course, the question was phrased "If the government of the United States spent every tax dollar wisely, and government waste and malfeasance was zero, and special interest groups had no influence in Washington, and all taxes were fair, would you cheat on your taxes?"

Ah…No.

But I doubt the question was posed like that.

Like I said. Flawed survey.

Apparently the survey concluded that 24 percent of us would not tell a waiter if we noticed we had been undercharged for a meal.

But again, not enough information is presented.

Do they tell you if the waiter has to make up the loss from his own pocket? Did he get your order right? Was he obsequious without being fawning?

And what about the global ethical questions? Is this a mom and pop restaurant, owned by, say, a struggling former neurosurgeon, or a restaurant owned by a multi-national corporation with operations in third world countries where the oppressed masses struggle against the tyranny of history and the tide of change, and dining and dashing can be seen as not just ethical, but the only moral course to follow?

Not to mention, was the food good?

I mean, an ethical test isn't like the SAT where the answer is right or wrong. There are mitigating circumstances.

Twenty-three percent of the respondents said they would commit a crime to get 10 million dollars if they knew they wouldn't get caught.

Uh, huh. I know what you're wondering. What crime?

Well the article didn't say, but it begs the question what crime might you commit for 10 million dollars if you knew you would get away with it?

Murder?

Nope.

Blackmail?

Nope.

Embezzlement?

Nope.

Insider stock trading?

Hmmmm.

Those of you who are ethically challenged are thinking to yourself, "If I don't get caught, what difference does it make?"

One of my colleagues allowed as how it is illegal to run naked through Riverfront Park; but for 10 million bucks, he'd be out the door in a flash, so to speak.

For 10 million dollars, I'd be right behind him.

Remember, this is a test for ethics, not moral turpitude.

We have ethics in advertising. It's morals we lack.

Maybe the Money Magazine survey is right, maybe we are letting our ethics erode away in America.

On the other hand, think about this. If a survey on ethics says 45% of the respondents are dishonest enough to cheat on their taxes and 24 percent would stiff a waiter and 23 percent would commit a crime for 10 million dollars, why should we believe that any of them are telling the truth?

Current House Deficiency Disorder

Our family is in the grips of one of the most insidious diseases of modern times.

I've been through flare ups of it in our family before, so I should have seen it coming, but I didn't. At least, I didn't think it would be this bad.

We had a serious bout of it about a year ago, but nothing

much came of it, and I thought we were over it.

Cured. But, like with so many diseases today, you never get cured. You just don't have an active case of it.

But now it's back, and both my wife and I have it. Even my daughter has a touch of it. And when that happens, you just have to ride the thing out and hope the damage isn't too bad.

You've probably guessed by now we're dealing with a serious outbreak of Current House Deficiency Disorder.

Current House Deficiency Disorder (or CHDD) is the fuel that drives the real estate market.

Doctors will tell you that CHDD usually develops from a case of Non-specific Rental Unit Malaise, which attacks the central nervous system by planting the notion in your brain that if you are renting instead of buying a home, you're stupid.

This is not always the case, but once that noxious weed has taken root in your brain, it's almost impossible to root out.

So you buy a house.

And you think, well, that's that.

Wrong. When it comes to home buying, that is never that. Because what you have really done is upgrade from Non-Specific Rental Unit Malaise to its more virulent cousin, Current House Deficiency Disorder, which you never get rid of.

Sometimes an attack of CHDD comes quietly.

You think you're happy where you live (not paying rent and all), and you hear your wife say to someone, "... what I'd really like is a family room, but for now this is okay ... "

Family room? For now? And you think, I thought we liked this house. I mean, we went into debt for thirty years to live here, didn't we?

Yes, but welcome to the world of CHDD: your house — every house — has deficiencies. And like it or not, seeking a house that doesn't have deficiencies will now be a life-long project.

Now, you might think that remodeling or finishing a basement would prevent CHDD, but it doesn't — that's an old wives tale.

"Why do you want to move? We just spent all that money finishing off the basement."

"Yes, but if mother comes to live with us, she won't be able to get up and down the stairs."

"Your mother is coming to live with us?"

Sometimes the onset of Current House Deficiency Disorder is anything but subtle. You are looking out your living room window, over the house across the street up to the new houses being built on, say, Five Mile Prairie or up in Painted Hills or Northwoods or Brown Mountain, and you think, "This house sucks."

For reasons not entirely clear to medical science, a house deficiency — in this case the lack of a view — that hitherto before didn't matter, suddenly does.

Personally, I've found that when an attack of CHDD occurs in my wife, it is best not to argue about it. There will be plenty of time for that when she finds a house she wants that we can't afford.

CHDD can be triggered by external changes, of course. Adding or deleting children to the family being the most obvious example.

The paradox here is when you're young and your family is growing and you need the space, you can't afford it. And when you can finally afford a bigger home, your kids are leaving home and you don't need one.

Of course, that doesn't stop anyone, which is why a lot of older people live in homes that are too big for them.

In that situation, you shouldn't be too quick to sell, because the chances are good that half of your children will get divorced and want to move back in with you. On the other hand, that may be a reason to sell. Kind of depends upon your family.

I hate to appear crass, but I've found that a serious attack of house envy can trigger an attack of CHDD in me. I can't remember if the Bible says I'm not supposed to covet my neighbor's house or not, but when I launch into a case of Current House

Deficiency Disorder, that's usually the reason why.

And it usually has to do with a view, which is what my house is deficient in, and which I covet.

The last time this happened to me was about a year ago. I shot a video in the new home of a client that had a panoramic view.

The view and the home were both breathtaking. As were the prices in that neighborhood.

But that didn't stop me from spreading the fever by taking my wife over to show her their house.

Big mistake. Because when she catches the fever, pretty soon real estate agents and builders get involved.

The next thing I knew, I was tramping all over Spokane looking at lots and houses and floor plans and considering payments I couldn't afford and wondering if there wasn't a way to get my client transferred or fired so I could just buy his house cheap and be done with it, all the while thinking that I really wasn't that unhappy about where I was living in the first place.

Well, I thought that fever passed, but it didn't, and we're going through it all over again with another house.

Is there a cure for Current House Deficiency Disorder?

Not really. Like malaria, you just kind of have to ride it out. But there are some things you can do.

I've always found that taking a good hard look at what a new house payment would be is a good way to bring me back to reality.

And if that doesn't work, I think about the pain of selling my home, and paying a fat real estate commission.

And if a new house still seems like a good idea, then I think about actually moving, and how much I hate moving.

And if that doesn't work, I start thinking about how much I'm going to enjoy living in a new house.

And being over Current House Deficiency Disorder.

For a while.

Surviving Survivor Groups

It happened the other day. I was listening to a report on All Things Considered about the billion dollar settlement Dow Corning, maker of silicone breast implants, had agreed to.

What caught my ear was not the size of the settlement, or how much each woman who had a boob job may get. No, what caught my ear was the name of one of the groups representing the women involved: "Silicone Breast Implant Survivors."

Wow. What a great name. It made me glad to be an American where my freedom to abuse the meaning of words is protected by the First Amendment.

"Survivors."

The word has power. It's got depth. It evokes admiration and pity, all at once.

And right then and there, I realized I don't belong to any survivor groups.

Well, I've got a t-shirt somewhere that says I survived the road to Hana, and another one that says I survived a three-day marketing meeting at Washington Water Power, but those don't count.

The problem is by not being in a survivor group, I can't claim I'm a victim, and if I can't prove that I'm a victim of something, then I can't prove I'm not responsible for my actions. And I've been an adult long enough to know that being responsible for your actions, especially mine, just isn't any fun.

Now, some of you nit-picky types are probably thinking, "Wait a minute, let me get this straight. The Silicone Breast Implant Survivors are women who didn't like the chest they were born with, so they voluntarily went to a doctor, and voluntarily paid that doctor big bucks to take them — voluntarily — into surgery so he could, because they were paying him to, voluntarily put the baggies of silicone into their chests so they could have the body they wanted, right?"

Right.

"So what did they 'survive'?"

Hardening of the boobs, apparently.

Sort of like hardening of the arteries, but less lethal. Maybe other stuff that's tougher to prove. I mean, you never know.

But that misses the point, which is, if you're in a survivor group, you are by definition a victim; and if you're a victim, you can sue somebody.

And you're certainly not going to get anywhere suing a giant like Dow Corning if your group has a wimpy name like, "The Alliance of Women Annoyed at The Result of Their Plastic Surgery, 20 Years Later."

No. They've got it right. To get anywhere, you've got to be a "survivor." You've got to draw a parallel between surviving plastic surgery and getting off the Titanic.

So it seems to me that what we need are more survivor groups.

Bad management survivors.

Survivors of global warming.

Survivors of the stress of dealing with the IRS. That's timely.

And there are lots of drugs that we might be survivors of: Valium. Prozac. Henry Weinhards.

What about Tanning Booth Survivors of America!

"Your honor, look at me. I used to be young and wrinkle free, and now I'm old and ugly, and my face looks like a picture of the Grand Canyon from space."

"You're 70. You're supposed to be old and wrinkled."

"Did I mention I am a tanning booth survivor?"

"Why didn't you say so? That makes you blameless for your condition. Of course you're entitled to damages. Go help yourself to that pile of money."

EMF is another biggie. This is truly, the big bogeyman of the future. And the great thing is, everybody agrees it exists, but not what the long-term effects are. A situation made in Lawyer Heaven.

Oh sure, the engineers tell us Electro-Magnetic Force doesn't screw up our cell structure, but who pays their salaries? And how many of them own houses below high tension wires?

Besides, the world is full of information the experts "know" that proves not to be true. Just the other day, didn't we all read a report that said sugar doesn't make you hyper? See what I mean?

I'd guess our understanding of the long term-effects of EMF is about what it was for silicone breast implants 20 years ago.

We are all future EMF survivors, provided, of course, we don't die first. Everybody has something electric they can blame for whatever illnesses they may get.

I can see it now. We'll fan out, some of us suing the utility companies, some computer makers, others will go after giant electronics firms. First we'll bring Sony to court, then we'll bring it to its knees.

You'd think there would be a smokers survival group, but I think that the tobacco companies have pretty much already beaten that one in court, so what's the point?

That, and maybe not that many people survive smoking.

It will be wonderful. Whoever is left among us will be a survivor of something, almost by definition.

Survivor. Yes!

There is only one problem with attaching a powerful word like survivor to a product like silicone breast implants, and acting like you survived something besides your own lack of judgement, or vanity: What do you say to the old soldier who went through the Bataan Death March or the Jew who went to Auschwitz or Dachau and lived?

What do you say to the person who really is a survivor?

SPRING PROJECTS AND OTHER THINGS YOU'VE BIN GONNA DO

Bin Gonna Do

How's your bin gonna do list?

I've been thinking about this because October is almost here, and, I think this is correct, October is National Bin Gonna Do month.

Now, some of you guys in your 40s are probably thinking that bin gonna do was a mountaintop fire base in Vietnam.

"Sure, man, I spent some time in Bin Gonna Do in '68, I think," while the rest of you are thinking it's a menu item in a Thai restaurant. "Is the bin gonna do real hot today?"

No.

Bin gonna do is that thing you realize you have not done even though you've been thinking about doing it. Like when you notice that the light bulbs in the downstairs hallway are all out and you say to yourself, "Hmmm. Those light bulbs need changing. I bin gonna do that."

Those of you who have spent time in Alabama and Georgia may recognize its deep south cousin, "Done bin gonna do," as in, "I done bin gonna do that, but I done bin busy."

I've also been thinking about my bin gonna do list because last weekend, we took a family bicycle trip on a portion of the Centennial Trail, something that we've bin gonna do for a long time.

Now, you can get the bin gonna do's anytime, of course, but

there is something about October that really brings the household ones out. I think it has to do with our nesting instinct and getting ready to hunker down for the winter.

It makes you take a look around and see all the things you've been looking at all summer and never got around to doing. "Hmmm, the front door needs weatherstripping. I bin gonna do that."

In October, the bin gonna do list suddenly grows exponentially. Closets need cleaning out, junk piles out back need hauling away, windows need cleaning, the anti-freeze in the car needs changing, the list of things that you've bin gonna do seems endless.

This doesn't mean I actually do those things, you understand, it just means I'm more aware of them.

Bin gonna do's come in eight major categories. Household, automotive, recreation, family, financial, career, life's work and really stupid.

Household bin gonna do's are those never ending things that you see but just don't get around to, like changing that pesky light bulb in the hallway.

Now, I don't know about you, but for me to finally do those household bin gonna do's, they have to achieve a kind of critical mass where suddenly they become more important than whatever else I was doing at that moment.

Either that or my wife tells me to do them.

Automotive bin gonna do's are like the household variety, except that they are generally more expensive.

There's nothing quite like dropping your transmission all over Division to move the bin gonna do item, "Have somebody listen to the funny noise the transmission is making," right to the top of the list, is there?

I hate it when that happens.

Next comes recreation bin gonna do's. My Centennial Trail bike outing fits into this category. So does hiking, starting an exercise program, biking, rollerblading and dieting.

Some would argue that rollerblading belongs in the "really

stupid" category and dieting belongs in the "Life's work" category of bin gonna do's — but that's splitting semantic hairs.

In the family category, there are a wide variety of bin gonna do's, from remembering to call your brother on his birthday to all the school things with your kids, like making the teacher-parent conferences and volunteering to help make band uniforms.

At the risk of sounding like a totally derelict parent, I'll confess something right up front here. Helping make junior high band uniforms is not on my bin gonna do list. Parent-teacher conferences? Yes. Band uniforms? No.

Now, if you're rich, you probably don't have many financial bin gonna do's, because you've done them, which is why you're rich. I, on the other hand, have a long list of these. Like saving some money. And investing. I had a partner once who always had paying his taxes on his financial bin gonna do list.

That was a pretty good motivator for me to bail out and make a job move — something that had been on my career bin gonna do list for years.

Now the final category is the really stupid things you've bin gonna do. I think men have more of these than women. These can fit into any of the other categories. The really stupid bin gonna do's generally don't hurt anything until you, well, do them.

"Honey, I've made a decision: I'm giving up ENT surgery to be a stand up comedian."

"Why?"

"It's just something I've bin gonna do. Plus the nurses think I'm really funny."

As you can imagine, the convergence of a man's mid-life crisis period and a long list of really stupid bin gonna do's can wreak havoc on your family.

"Kids, say hello to your new mommy. Bambi, these are your new kids."

"Dad, Bambi and I have met. She and I were in home room in high school together, remember? So Bambi, I guess you're still out at the Deja Vu, huh?"

Now, you may be wondering how come some people have

very long bin gonna do lists, while others have pretty short ones.

Well some people will tell you that's because some of us are talkers while others are doers. I used to feel real guilty about this because my list of bin gonna do stuff is extremely long. But then, one day when I was sitting around watching football and drinking beer, I got to thinking that maybe I just think bigger than other people. Yeah, maybe it's not because I'm not a doer; maybe some people just aren't motivated to want to do as much stuff as me.

In fact, studying that very question is something that I bin gonna do.

Right after I change those light bulbs downstairs.

Spring Projects

What is it about Spring that makes a man feel like he's got to get a wheelbarrow in his hands?

What is it about the tilting back of the earth, the longer days, the sunnier weather that makes a man feel like he's got to build something?

What is it that drives us to those dreaded Spring Projects?

I thought of this a few days ago as I was driving home when I chanced upon a guy putting up a new retaining wall, or something. It was hard to tell exactly what his project was, but everything about his body language, his clothes, and the fact that it was 5:30 on a sunny afternoon in March fairly screamed to the world that he was working on his spring project - not because it had to be done by some artificial deadline, but because it was *time*.

Like a baby that suddenly needs to be born, our spring projects suddenly need to be worked on.

"Honey, I think I'll go outside and start that retaining wall project."

"Now? It's dinnertime. And Jason needs help with his homework."

"I know. Send him outside. I can help him while I work."

Right.

But it's not our fault. Because when it's time to work on that spring project, it's time.

Now, not every project one does in the spring is a spring project.

For instance, Yard and Garden Day absolutely does not qualify as a spring project. Neither does painting the house, which is a summer project — an altogether different animal.

No. To qualify as a spring project, something must be built — preferably something big enough that it puts us at risk of getting a hernia. Something that requires mixing up and pouring several bags of concrete is just about right.

I once had a neighbor who tore up and replaced all the concrete in his driveway.

"Why are you doing this?" I asked.

"Ah, you know," he said. "It was cracked."

It was cracked? Your flat, concrete driveway had cracks in it, so you tore it all out and replaced it? Your driveway's not the only thing around here that's cracked, I thought. Actually I thought the guy had too much time and money on his hands, but then I realized that what I was looking at was his spring project.

The thing that sets a spring project apart from all other projects is the personal nature of the thing. This is why any suggestions from our wives about "good spring projects" tend to get rejected out of hand.

"I have a spring project for you," our wives say. "Why don't you put that window box on the kitchen window that I've been wanting?"

"Ummm. I don't think so," we husbands reply.

It's not that we want to be jerks about it, it's just that, well, that's your project, not my spring project.

The genesis of a man's spring project begins late in the fall or early winter.

It begins as a casual observation. We look at something that has never bothered us before and we think, you know, I really ought to build a fence around my back yard. Or, I really ought to build a deck back here. Or, I really ought to knock out the wall between the garage and the kitchen so I have more room to work on the car.

Then winter comes, and snow covers everything. But inside our heads, the project germinates. At ten weeks, the project has a heartbeat of its own, and at 22 weeks, you can feel it kicking around in your head, wanting out.

I think men have a special look when they've got a spring project. Some people say we have a special glow about us.

"You've got a spring project in there, don't you, Roger?"

"Yeah. It's a big one, too."

And then one day, the snow is gone, the sun is out, and you know it's time.

There are few times when it feels better to be a man.

You put on your old jeans, strap on your carpenter's belt and, 25-foot Stanley Carpenter's Measuring Tape in hand, you go begin your project.

Now, don't misunderstand me; this doesn't mean you actually do any work. The first phase of the project is you measure. And you think.

Now, it could be argued that you had all winter to measure and think, but men know that you can't rush these things. There is a sequence that is right with nature and must not be broken.

With my projects, I measure everything. Then I measure everything again. Then I measure everything a third time to try to determine which of my first two measurements was the right one.

Then I try to figure out stuff like what my measurements really mean, since a two-by-four isn't really two-by-four, but something else, which I can never remember, exactly.

It's all academic, anyway, because by the time I get to Ziggy's or somewhere to buy my lumber, the guy asks me a question I can't answer because one of the measurements I absolutely need I have forgotten to get.

So I go home and start over.

The other crucial thing you have to remember about a spring project is just because it's a spring project doesn't mean it gets done in the spring. It's not unusual for a spring project to not get done until August. Or even the next year.

Some spring projects last for years.

I have always had a spring project. Unfortunately, for the past seven years it has always been the same spring project — remodeling the basement to add a bathroom. This past winter, my wife finally got the feeling that I was having trouble getting started on that project, so she hired a guy to do it.

I had been thinking about that job for seven years.

The guy she hired thought about it for twenty minutes and went to work. He started by ripping out what little work I had already done. What does that tell you?

Well, one thing it tells you is I need a new spring project.

Maybe this is the year I should fix those cracks in my driveway.

Driving With My Imagination on Cruise Control

Have you seen the new STA commercials?

"One person can make a difference."

What a great line.

It goes right to the part of the brain that controls being a good citizen. It speaks directly to our anxiety about being powerless in a democracy, about being individually helpless against the overwhelming problems caused by the output of an uncontrolled and uncontrollable mass of humanity.

"One person can make a difference."

It's almost Shakespearean. "…Or to take arms against a sea of troubles, and by opposing, end them."

"You can make a difference."

We, you and I, together, can clean up this mess we've made of everything. Yes! Sign me up! I am a good citizen. I do want safe streets, dead drug dealers, and clean air! What do you want me to do?

Park your car one day a week.

I beg your pardon?

Give up your car one day a week.

You want me to give up my car? How about lunch one day a week? How about I give up television? I could do that. Radio: You can have Morning Edition one day a week. You can have my firstborn male child one day a week, but you're not getting my car.

The problem is there are two different messages here. One is "ride the bus." The other is "Park your car one day a week."

While it's true that one message tends to beget the other, they are not at all the same thing.

Now, understand, I have nothing against riding the bus.

I don't do it, but I have nothing against it.

But riding the bus is transportation. Your car, on the other hand, is freedom. It's mobility. It's control of your own destiny.

Plus, if you're like me, it's the daily equivalent of a little therapeutic trip through Fantasyland.

Yes, I confess, in my car, alone, while I'm polluting the air, I am often also holding wonderful fantasy conversations that are solving all of my own, if not most of the world's, problems.

Now, I don't mean to imply that every time I buzz down to 7-11 for milk and bread I have a little psychotic episode where I hear voices or anything; not at all.

But when the hands, feet and eyes know the way, the car is the perfect cocoon for letting your mind conjure up a better world.

Sometimes these are rehearsals for the real thing, like talking to your boss. "Mr. White, sir, I need a raise. No? Okay."

Or solving a thorny family problem you know you have to face when you get home. "I know I said you could go to Melissa's slumber party, but that was before I knew boys were invited and her parents weren't going to be there. By the way, did I mention I'm sending you to a convent school next year?"

The isolation of a car is the perfect place to work out the

aggressions of the day as you drive home. "Maybe we should re-view the client-agency relationship, Bucko. You are the client and I am the agency. So don't tell me what your advertising should look like and I won't tell you how to run your business, okay?"

A recurring fantasy theme in our business is you walk into the client that is currently giving you the most grief, and you tell them to take a flying…um, take a hike.

Now, you might argue that one could still have those fanta-sies on the bus, but to be really therapeutic, I have found it helps to say that stuff out loud, to let the words resonate around in the air, filling real time and real space, even if they are just a fantasy.

In the privacy of your car, on say, Northwest Boulevard; that's no big deal.

The guy in the car next to you might wonder what you're doing, but who cares? Besides, he's probably immersed in his own fantasy conversation.

But sitting next to somebody on a city bus, telling your cli-ent where to put it, well, that's quite a different story.

They'll put you on Prozac for that.

Ventilating in the car, alone, is where nurses tell doctors off ("I've seen butchers do better work!"), where salespeople get to shoot obnoxious customers ("Thank you for returning that"), where bank tellers open trap doors that send would-be bank rob-bers and people who want their checkbooks balanced plummet-ing to their deaths, ("Next please?"), and everybody gets to fan-tasize about winning the lottery and explaining to the boss that you've just bought the company and she's fired.

Not all car fantasies are reality based, of course.

I, myself, annihilated Clarence Thomas's chance to get on the Supreme Court with my savage wit during his confirmation hearings.

And with my oldies tapes blasting, I have spent hours on stage with the Chad Mitchell Trio, The Kingston Trio and The Limeliters, not to mention having kayaked the Grand Canyon and helped John Roskelly get to the top of countless mountains.

In my fantasies, I'm a little taller, have bigger pecs, and I'm very articulate. Sort of a cross between Dick Cavett and Jean-Claude Van Damm.

And, of course, I'm infinitely sexier than in real life.

Talk about a fantasy.

The point is, it's all terribly therapeutic, and healthy for me, assuming that I don't zone out so bad I run a stop sign and get killed.

So, while STA has a great campaign and I'd like to give up my car and take the bus one day a week, I just can't afford it.

Now, if you'll excuse me, I have to explain to the President why his health care proposals aren't going to pass as long as I'm Speaker of the House.

Spring Pruning Madness

I think I know the inspiration behind the famous classic, <u>The Strange Case of Dr. Jekyll and Mr. Hyde</u>.

It isn't a story of transformation caused by the forces of society, or a cautionary tale about the evils of drugs. It's not even a parable about how sex and lust can change a man from an upright model citizen into a murderous monster.

I think it's about gardening.

Now I don't mean to imply that everyone who tends a garden goes through a sort of Jekyll/Hyde personality transformation. I'm sure that Phyllis Stevens who writes the gardening column for the paper never does.

But some of us do.

I know. I'm one of them.

There's something in the putting on of those heavy leather gardening gloves that turns me into a kind of cross between a barber, a heart surgeon and Freddy Krueger.

Some of you might argue that there is no difference between heart surgeons and Freddy Krueger, but that's splitting semantic hairs.

While some people shouldn't have children and some people shouldn't have pets, I think I shouldn't have a garden.

Actually, I never wanted a garden; but the people who lived in our house before us did. So they terraced the lot, making lots of space for shrubs and trees and bushes, most of which my wife and I planted.

We would go out to Ernst and buy about $200 worth of shrubs and plants, which if you've done it, you know isn't much.

"What will this look like in a few years?" I would ask the Ernst guy, who looked like he hadn't taken his medication that morning.

He'd think a while with his mouth open and then say, "Like that, only bigger."

My wife and I would nod like we were in the presence of Ed Hume and toss whatever it was into the cart.

Finally, the landscaping was done, the plants were planted, the trees were growing, and I did what I have always done to a garden. I ignored it. For years I ignored it.

It isn't that I don't like the look of well tended landscaping; I do. It's just that when it comes to the tending of the plants, A) I feel particularly ignorant, and B) I'm pretty lazy.

Once a year or so, my wife and I would go out and weed, and as we did, she would say, "We have to do something."

"Yes," I would reply. And do nothing.

Finally, of course, some of the shrubs got tall and disfigured by winter snows, and the trees we planted were sending up shoots everywhere.

Our neighbors would call over the fence, "Hey, Doug, do you mind if I pull out this little tree shoot that is growing over here? I think it's coming from your tree."

"Oh, no. By all means kill it."

Other shrubs were laying about like lizards, not growing up, but out.

So one day, I decided to "fix" my garden.

Now, you're probably thinking that I went out and bought a

few Sunset Books and read up on what makes a good garden grow and all that, right?

Wrong.

Instead, I applied Doug's First Law of the Garden. "When in doubt, prune."

So, I pruned and pruned, and when it looked scrawny and ugly, I pruned it back some more.

"Aren't you worried you're hurting it?" asked my wife.

"No," I replied, snipping off a branch that didn't look like it was putting out enough effort at growing.

And when I was done, the garden actually looked better. A little hacked up, to be sure, but better, nonetheless.

And so the tradition began.

One spring Sunday, I wake up, and the sun is shining, and I know, today is the day.

And like sweet Dr. Jekyll, I sip my morning coffee and look over my garden.

And then I go out to the garage where I keep my instruments. Hedge clippers, pruning shears, and, for big jobs, the chain saw.

My transformation begins when I put on my heavy leather gardening gloves.

These aren't just wimpy cloth gloves that keep you from getting a blister on your little finger. These are the direct descendants of the metal gloves that knights wore into battle and the leather gloves cavalry officers wore centuries later and that train engineers wore; and when I put them on, they say to me, "Let's go kick some plant."

I attack the first thing I come to.

"What have we here? A raspberry plant growing outside its designated area?" A deft snip of the shears, and it pays the price for its transgression— death.

I walk into a low hanging branch from a pine tree. There is not a moment's hesitation. Out comes the chain saw.

Yingyingyingyingying!

"That'll teach you to keep your branches out of my space."

I move to the former lizard shrubs, now growing vertically, sending new growth up everywhere.

"Hedge clippers!" I demand in my best surgeon voice.

"Hedge clippers." I answer back as my own horticultural surgical technologist.

Wap wap wap wap wap wap wap.

New growth flies everywhere as I trim the shrubs into green blobs that look like something a Rhino with a nasal infection might have snorted up and left behind. I try to make them round and symmetrical, but they don't want to trim that way.

As I hack away, I gain an appreciation for what a hairdresser must go through.

What do I do with this? Hmmm. Cut it! What the heck, it'll grow back.

Sometimes a shrub has a branch growing up out of the middle that offends me. Taking out my pruning shears, I follow it down inside the chest of the plant and I cut it out.

"Gee, I hope that wasn't your aorta." Oh, well.

I cut back everything. Nothing escapes untouched, unpruned.

Finally, the spring pruning frenzy over, I clean up the mess and put away my tools. And as I take off my gloves, I change from Freddy Krueger Falco to just plain me.

But even as I sit on my back porch, surveying my freshly hacked up plants, I can see where this one is lopsided and that one has a sprig I somehow missed.

My wife says, "I'll trim them."

To which I reply, "No, no, no. I'll just go put on my gloves again, and I'll do it."

Spring Cleaning

What is it about the first few nice days of spring that make you hear voices from the refrigerator?

Voices that say, "Look in here."

You're in the fridge, rummaging around for something to eat like you do every Saturday morning. Only this morning, with the sun shining for the first time in months, you hear that little voice, and you reach beyond last night's leftover pizza, beyond the containers of sour cream, way back to the dark and lonely recesses of your refrigerator, to that region Shakespeare's Hamlet was describing when, speaking of leftover food, he said, "…that undiscovered country, from whose bourne no traveller returns … " and you pull out a Tupperware container whose very existence says to you, "Look in here."

Big mistake.

You are about discover three things.

The first is the first natural anomaly of being married, which states that, against all justice and logic, the person who puts the food into the Tupperware is not the person who will take the food out of the Tupperware six months later.

The second is once you hear, "Look in here," no matter what else you had planned for the day, you are probably going to spend it cleaning, and the third discovery is a new and fuzzy life form.

When I discover something alien growing in Tupperware, I like to share it with my wife. "Did you want to keep these yams we had at Thanksgiving last year any longer? I think they were yams. Maybe they were sweet potatoes."

Back there with the sweet potatoes (or were they yams?) are several other Tupperware containers. They come out, too.

And a baggie with a chunk of greenish, calcified cheese.

And that sour cream? I check the date: Sell by December 91. Whoops! I don't need to look inside that one. Whatever is living in that container is going to die in there.

It's out of here.

With all the space freeing up inside your fridge, you notice that the shelves are covered with all sorts of crud and the walls look like your kids had a squirt gun fight in your fridge with grape juice.

So you start cleaning.

Now, what's weird about all this is your fridge has been like that since, well, since last spring. And it's never bothered you before.

But today, with a few sunny days behind us and winter officially gone, suddenly, cleaning the fridge seems like the right thing to do.

Unfortunately for your weekend plans, it is not the only thing to do.

My wife seems especially susceptible to hearing voices from cupboards and closets. "Look in here."

The next thing you know, every plate, every glass, every pot and pan is out on the kitchen counter tops while the shelves get scrubbed down. And more often than not, the very act of pulling out all that stuff we never see except when company is coming is enough to trigger a massive dishwashing binge because it is all <u>dusty</u>.

It was dusty yesterday, but did it bother anybody?

No. But yesterday, you weren't in the grip of the spring cleaning virus, either.

At this point, a sort of cleaning feeding frenzy begins. Looking for more 409, you take a look under your kitchen sink, and it says, "Look in here, sucker!"

"Honey, call the EPA. I have discovered a new Superfund site."

You have probably also discovered that an SOS pad, left to sit in its own caustic juices for nine months, will rust into almost nothing, but this little lesson in inorganic chemistry will most likely be lost on you as you rummage below your sink for refills of Windex and Simple Green.

What won't be lost is that the area under your sink is also demanding immediate cleaning attention.

If you have been through this enough times, you may learn that there are certain rules you have to follow to maintain any semblance of control over your life while this spring cleaning thing runs its course.

One is never, under any circumstances, to look behind the

washer and dryer, unless you're prepared to take time off from work for a hernia repair. You can look back there in August when it is somehow easy to say, yeah, well, one of these days I'll clean up that mess.

In fact, if you have one, it's a good idea not to go into the basement at all during spring cleaning.

I know, I know. There is a voice behind the door to the basement that seems to be calling, "Look in here!" but you must resist.

You must also resist the urge to look into your child's bedroom while your fever rages, because children, defined here as everybody under the age of about 27, seem to have a natural immunity to the spring cleaning virus. Perhaps it's God's way of protecting them from noxious chemicals.

Can you plan for this event? Yes.

Does planning make it go better? No.

While you know it is going to happen, this cleaning frenzy is, by nature, a spontaneous event. It is better to just go with the flow, and clean what calls to you than try to make someone else clean what calls to you.

They're hearing their own voices. Leave them alone.

How long can you expect to be in the grip of this thing? Unless you're totally neurotic, about one full weekend. Then it goes away as suddenly as it appears.

I think for most of us, our big cleaning weekend occurred last weekend, so we're probably immune now.

But does that mean we're out of the woods and now we can just enjoy this nice weather? Not exactly. Because after a week of nice weather, a lot of us hear a voice out among the shrubs and trees of our yards. It says, "Hey, come here; I want to show you something."

My advice?

Don't go.

Why Men Avoid Reading Directions

What is the true test of manhood?

Is it performing an athletic skill of great agility? No.

Is it bungee jumping from a 150-foot crane (and hoping you're not strapped up to a 210-foot bungee)? No.

Is it having the sexual prowess of a porno star? I don't think so. That's not to say that wouldn't be nice, but that's not it.

No, the true test of being a real man is putting together one of those big gas barbecues without looking at the directions.

Now, if you're a man you're probably saying, "Yes!" because you intuitively see the challenge. A bag of nuts and bolts, some washers, some bent metal that might be legs, a few wheels, a grate and a box that looks like a cast iron cradle, and you with a screwdriver, a pair of pliers and a six pack of Bud, and saying to yourself "No sweat," and not even looking at the directions.

The challenge is to get that hummer together before the Bud runs out and you start to have trouble seeing.

There was a time in America when it was easier to be a man because everything came assembled. Well, most everything.

We probably all have childhood memories of our fathers trying to build a backyard swing or a model train set or something, and not getting it right, but generally, when you bought something in the '50s and '60s, you didn't have to put it together.

But today, a lot of stuff comes unassembled.

This makes for a lot of manly challenges.

And being a man is made all the more confusing because whether or not you consult the directions is not an absolute thing. The rules are not hard and fast.

For instance, if you buy your child a bike at Toys 'R' Us, and it comes in a box and you have to put the handle bars and pedals and kickstand and wheels on, looking at the directions is not allowed.

"Dad, how come when I pedal forward, the brakes go on?"

"Hmmm. That doesn't seem right, does it?"

On the other hand, while you are not supposed to look at

the directions when hooking up your VCR ("Let's see. Line in. Now why doesn't that fit? Maybe if I jam it. Ooops."), it is okay to read the directions when you are trying to figure out how to use it.

I have discovered that by the time I am on step four of reading how to do "timed recording," or some other complex use, I can't remember what step one was, and I have to start all over again. But I don't do that because by that time, I am so frustrated that I am seriously doubting that I will ever want to record something at a time when I am not around the TV, and because my daughter, who is 12, seems to have it down, and if I need to I'll just ask her to do it for me.

Another rule of maintaining your manhood is you must never ask your wife to read the directions to you. The corollary rule is, wives should never ask their husbands if they have read the directions, because the husband will then have say, "What do you mean, 'Have I read the directions?' What kind of question is that?"

Which is not exactly a lie, but it doesn't exactly promote open and honest communications — which is not uppermost in a man's mind when he has just discovered he has put the picnic table legs on backwards.

After years of marriage, most wives either just stay away completely, or they pick up the directions and casually say, "Oh, what's this?" and then read a few of them, to see if hubby is doing it right.

However, it's perfectly okay for one man to read the directions to another.

We call this bonding.

What none of us like to admit, of course, is that some guys are just more adept at getting by without directions than others, just as some guys are better athletes than others.

This is clearly evident when a man ventures into the uncharted region known generally as "softwareland."

Here, it is nothing to be ashamed of to spend days reading instruction manuals on how to make, say, your word processor underline or do some other seemingly simple task.

However, even here some men have a natural advantage. We have an artist who considers it beneath his level of being to consult a software instruction manual. His karma is one with our Macintosh system, and he knows what the machines are thinking and what they need to perform at their personal best.

So like Nike suggests, he just does it. He just fixes whatever is wrong without so much as a glance at the installation and operations manuals. When he does this, we all know we are in the presence of a true man.

Still, if you're just a normal human, it's okay to buy a book on how to do things, which accounts for the immense popularity of the Sunset Books on how to do everything in life your father should have taught you, but didn't.

In fact, probably the best graduation gift you can get for a young man is the Sunset Book on basic carpentry.

"This is a hammer. This is a nail. Hit the hammer on the top of the nail. Try to miss your fingers."

The higher the level of education the young man is graduating from, the more important the book, because there seems to be an inverse relationship between the amount of education a guy has and his inclination to read directions.

I have all the books. Not that they help, as carpentry-disadvantaged as I am.

Over the years, I have found it's best to avoid putting my manhood to a test it might not pass. I do this by not buying products with the warning, "Some Assembly Required."

And my wife has learned it's best just to pay the extra $10 or $20 to have the retailer put together whatever it is she is buying. She figures she gets the product put together right, and I get to keep my manly self-esteem.

A bargain for both of us, any way you look at it.

THE FIRST SEVENTH GRADE DANCE AND OTHER PARENTING TRAUMAS

The First Junior High Dance

"Be cool," I told myself.

You don't want to blow it here.

This is the time when you want to keep the lines of communication open. Be casual; interested, but not too interested. Probe, but not too hard.

Don't be too direct. That might spook her into clamming up. Clamming up would be bad. Very bad. As a parent, you need to elicit certain information from your daughter without appearing to mistrust her.

She might be keyed up, so you have to play off that emotional high, I told myself.

But that can be tricky. Sometimes that means she won't talk about a subject — while other times she won't talk about anything else.

I was waiting outside the junior high school for my daughter. The street was full of cars with parents, like me, waiting for their children.

It was dark.

I felt like a detective on stake out. Would I see her before she saw me?

What if she was walking out with a boy, and they were talking, what would that mean?

In a flash, I had my answer. She was alone. I felt a sort of relief. Alone was good, I decided.

She approached the car.

Be cool, be casual, I told myself. Let her tell her side of the story, in her own time, her own way.

She saw me, and got in the car.

"So, how was…the dance?" I asked.

"It was fun," she said and fell ominously silent.

Fun? What did that mean? She goes to her first real junior high dance and all she has to say is, it was fun? Did that mean, my daughter, my little girl, this barely 13-year-old who has lately taken to wearing a little mascara and blush, actually danced with a boy?

"So, did you dance?" I asked, trying not to sound like the Grand Inquisitor.

"Yeah," she said.

Oh, God, it was worse than I had ever imagined!

Suddenly, I lost all self control. I had to know the worst. I didn't care if it wasn't cool, or if I cut off all future father-daughter communications.

I blurted out all my fears, all my anxieties in one fell swoop. "Did you slow dance? With a boy? Of the opposite sex?"

"Geez, Daddy," she said, neither confirming nor denying.

Finally she said, "I didn't."

"Yes!" every fiber of my soul screamed. Reprieve. My brain told my body to go off red alert status.

"Attention, attention all major muscle groups. We have no close clutch and grab contact, you may now relax —repeat — you may all relax. Will someone please go down to the stomach and tell it to turn off the acid machine? Memory banks, will you do a scan to see if we have any Rolaids in the car."

"Negative on the Rolaids, brain."

Dang. I've got to remember the next time my daughter goes to a school dance, to pick up some Rolaids before I pick her up. Maybe a Demerol or two as well. In fact, just being unconscious for the whole day of the dance was starting to look like a good idea.

"Did you go to dances, when you were in seventh grade?" she asked.

"Yes," I answered. But I explained that mostly I just stood against the wall, trying to get the nerve to ask Linda Sagstad to dance. Asking anybody, much less a prize like Linda, was the social equivalent of bungee jumping off a crane without knowing how long your bungee cord was. You could splatter yourself in front of your intended pretty easily.

"All the geeks stand against the wall at our dance," she said.

Ours too, I thought, but having been one of them, decided not to say.

I was going to try to explain to her that asking a pretty girl to dance had very little to do with dancing and everything to do with the length of your emotional bungee cord, but decided against it. Too complex.

Besides, it was her dance that was paramount in both our minds.

Instead I asked, "So, who did you dance with?"

"Everybody," she said. "You're just kind of out there. Head banging."

Like Beavis and Butt-Head. That's cool.

"You didn't dance?" she asked.

"It was different then," I said, remembering seventh grade dances pretty vividly. "When we danced to rock and roll, we did a dance called the bop, which required this heel-toe-heel-toe kind of step, and while your feet are going heel-toe-heel-toe on autopilot, you also had to swing your partner back and forth and twirl her and I could never get it right. So I didn't rock and roll.

Not to mention that in seventh grade, I was a full head shorter than almost everybody, including the girls I wanted to dance slow with, which also didn't help in the nerve department."

I spent most of my seventh grade dances standing against the wall with my buddies looking at the girls on the other wall, saying stuff like, "I dare you to ask Judy Cleghorn to dance."

"No, I dare you first."

"I double dare you."

"I triple dare you."

"You're chicken."

"You're the one who's chicken."

We were <u>all</u> chicken.

I could talk that way a whole dance.

In the meantime, of course, some kids would be out on the floor, dancing, doing what we were all there to do in the first place.

By the time we got home, I realized that we had successfully passed yet another little mile marker on the great freeway of life — her first junior high dance. We had each passed it successfully, each in our own way.

And I kind of laughed at myself, because, in hindsight, I realized that it wasn't at the dances in junior high school that everyone tried to play clutch and grab in the dark, and dance so slow that making out became a real possibility; all that took place at the private parties.

I was feeling kind of foolish at my earlier anxiety when my daughter turned to me and said, "Oh, by the way, Melissa is having a party this Saturday night. Can I go?"

Being the Dominant Male Lion When You Have A Teenage Daughter

I've got to figure something out. You'd think I'd know this by now, but I don't. I always thought you knew this stuff instinctively, but that isn't the case.

I've got to learn how to meet boys.

I realized this the other night when, after a high school volleyball game I refereed, my daughter came over to me and introduced me to Nate.

"Hi," I said to her, giving her a hug, and before I could think about it, a kiss on her forehead, which I'm sure she could have lived all night without and which immediately classified me as some sort of a major dork.

"Um, Dad, this is Nate. Nate, this is my dad."

Nate? Nate is a boy.

Now, I know how to meet girls. I've got that down.

If Nate had been a girl named Nadine, I'd have slipped right into the Superdad role, cranked up a few kilovolts of male charm and said, "Hi Nadine, it's nice to meet you."

I'd look her square in the eye with just the right mix of attention, confidence, male protectiveness and paternal acceptance, and ask her something inane like, "Did you get a chance to see the whole match?" To which she'd reply something like, "Um, well, um, like, well, like, most of it."

"Great," I'd say adding a few more volts of charm.

By this time, my daughter, who has seen all this before, and knows that everybody near me is at risk of passing out from high blood sugar, I'm oozing so much sweetness and charm, will usually ask my approval of whatever the plans are for the evening: "Can Nadine spend the night tonight?"

And the two of them would go off, and I would know that I had made a favorable impression on Nadine, but far more important that I hadn't embarrassed my daughter in front of her friend, which as any parent can tell you, is easy enough to do.

Like I said, I know how to meet girls. I've been doing it for almost 13 years. Piece of cake.

But lately, my daughter has been introducing me to boys. And it's not at all like meeting a girl.

"Um, Dad, this is Nate. Nate, this is my dad."

In a flash, I was struck by the fact that lately, and I mean just in the past month or so, I had been meeting a lot of boys.

"Um, Dad. This is Justin. He's a friend of Jason's. Justin, this is my dad."

"Dad, this is Bo and Cord. You met them in second grade, but you don't remember."

Bo? Cord? Justin? Jason? Nate? I think there's a pattern here.

Uh-oh.

We have boys in our life.

Now, I have known, as all father's do, that someday there would be boys in my little girl's life. I mean, she's always had friends who were boys, but in those days, the boys and the girls were all sort of the same. I mean, they all wore <u>undershirts</u> for Pete's sake, so from me, they all got pretty much the same treatment.

Well, those days are gone.

And in all this time while I was developing my Superdad with his high voltage charm machine, I never once thought about which father persona should meet these boys.

Should it be the authoritarian father, a sort of cross between a high school vice-principal, and Judge Lance Ito?

"Nate; how do you do? Next case."

Or should it be the squinty-eyed Clint Eastwood dad where a barely perceptible nod barely acknowledges Nate's barely human presence.

"Nate?"

All of a sudden, I'm in this who-is-the-dominant-male environment.

And I'm not very good at this. I don't know about you, but "dominant" is not the word that leaps to your mind when you meet *me*.

But this is an important moment. Suddenly, we're no different than the lions on the Savanna of Africa. And there's a young male lion hanging around a female member of my pride.

Should he be taught a lesson? Should I growl?

"How do you do?"

If I'm the father lion, shouldn't I let him know I'm not giving up my females without a fight?

I thought about doing my Godfather father. "Nate: Let's talk about sleeping with the fishes," but he didn't look old enough to get it.

On the other hand, if this is a male dominance thing, and

I'm supposed to be the father lion, maybe I could just crush his hand as I shake it.

If I shake it. Maybe I should let him just stick his hand out there into that void that exists between men and hang there a while, while I consider his maleness, and let him wonder if I accept him as a member of the male tribe or not.

"Um Dad, this is Nate. Nate, this is my dad."

Now, Nate, you understand, is just about the most normal kid a father could hope to see on the other end of an introduction from his daughter; good looking, pleasant, nicely dressed, no shaved hair that I could see, no cigarette behind the ear or ring through the nose. Just a really okay kid. Like Justin and Jason and Cord and Bo, for that matter.

He's just standing there, occupying his space, and looking at me with a look in his eyes that I suddenly recognize from a time some 35 years gone.

Eyes that say "You're the father of a girl I know, and I have to meet you. So I am." Not defiant. But not apologetic, either. Maybe a little uncomfortable, is all. But in any case, filling his space, and doing a pretty good job of it.

Oh, what the hell.

"Hi Nate, it's nice to meet you," I say, flooding Nate with about the same high voltage charm that has worked so well on so many little girls. It doesn't feel quite right, but it doesn't feel all that wrong, either.

Still, I give him a little Clint Eastwood squint just to let him know that we have a little man-to-man thing going here: You're the young lion. I'm the old lion. And I'm not leaving yet.

As we're walking out of the gym a few moments later, I'm thinking: I wonder if I did that right, and thinking that, if I'm going to be meeting more boys from now on, I'm going to have to get my dominant lion act down.

And then I think, wait a minute. I'm the one who kissed the pretty young lady he walked over to me with. And what male doesn't understand the dominance in that?

And as I strut outside, I wonder if anybody else can see my magnificent mane.

Starting Seventh Grade

This year, my daughter started seventh grade.

Do you remember your first day of seventh grade?

Me, too. In fact, of all the years I went back to school, including college, the only one first day I seem to have any clear memories of is seventh grade.

Well, that's not quite true. I have a vivid memory of being a first grader, and having to wait on the steps outside Crown Hill Elementary School, enduring the ultimate in humiliating insults hurled at us by second graders — the big kids.

They would chant, "First grade babies, born in the gravy." Boy, could they be cruel.

Today, of course, we would sue the school district for negligence and mental anguish, so it wouldn't be so bad, but in those days, we just had to take it. I couldn't wait to be a second grader so I could humiliate someone, but by the time my second year rolled around, no one seemed very interested in chanting insults anymore, and I wasn't brave enough or bully enough to do it alone, so I never got my chance.

But except for that, nothing about any first day of school is particularly distinctive in my memory, except seventh grade.

Junior high.

I think that's because when you're a kid, and you enter junior high school, your whole world changes.

Sixth grade is to life what the pre-season is to the NFL. It looks about the same, it acts about the same, it has most of the same players, but ultimately, it doesn't count. You thought it counted, they told you it counted, but it doesn't.

With the entry into junior high, you know instantly all that has changed. The real game has begun. It's now time for real life.

I had prepared for real life by buying a bright red, three ring binder, the kind that zips closed with two handles that pop up to make it sort of a brief case. I stocked it with about a dozen pencils and enough blank paper to write War and Peace.

Even today I have a hard time believing I had come to seventh grade, where image and social standing is everything, equipped with what amounted to an industrial sized nerd pack.

My older brother had tried to warn me that my choice of notebooks wasn't cool, but I brushed aside his protests. I liked it. And it was practical, my mom said.

That should have told me something, but I could be pretty oblivious in those days.

The first thing that struck me about junior high was, the entire scale of the world had changed: The size of the place is bigger, and all the kids comprised only three grades. Instead of the 90 kids in my grade, there were now hundreds.

And not one of them, except me, had a fully zippered red briefcase-type notebook, I quickly noticed.

In the halls before school, the first thing I knew I would have to learn was how to mill. After all, you can't mill around if you can't mill.

Knowing exactly how to carry yourself as you mill around is important, because you want to strike just the right pose between looking bored and looking lost.

But on the first day of seventh grade, when you're the youngest and most vulnerable, it's hard to mill properly. Especially when it seems like everybody else is greeting long lost friends.

This makes for some instant bonding. You bond to any familiar face.

I became instant old friends with kids from my old school I barely knew.

Pretty soon, all the seventh graders had formed groups of four and five — group protection against the unknown terrors the big kids might bring down on you. "Seventh grade babies born in the gravy."

In the halls, the groups moved like human clots moving down the carotid artery of the school. As one group met another, superclots formed, and the whole school was in danger of stroking out and coming to a standstill when a bell rang, dispersing us to Home Room.

Home room? What was home room? And what was first period? And second period? And when was recess? What do you mean there's no such thing as recess?

My brother had tried to tell me about all of those things, but I didn't listen then, either.

I found it all pretty bewildering.

But what made the first day of seventh grade so different, and perhaps memorable, was not just the structural changes in the school and the school day, but the fact that these were sort of layered on, if you will, over the changes that had taken place in me.

Being pretty typical, I think, somewhere between leaving sixth grade and starting seventh, I had become a member of the hormone patrol.

So the first thing I did when I got to home room was, I fell in love.

I remember being immediately smitten by Sandy, a lovely girl with an overbite and a stutter that made her all the more endearing. Unfortunately, while I gazed at her, imagining what it would be like to actually talk to her, the teacher handed out locker assignments and explained how the combination locks worked.

Didn't hear a word he said.

This was when I discovered that looking at a pretty girl could short circuit my auditory nerve. I think it's a phenomenon that happens to all men. It begins in the seventh grade and pretty much stays with us for the rest of our lives.

The net result was, I couldn't get my locker open, so I had to haul around my bright red notebook all day, which was a little like walking around school with the word "Geek" stenciled on my forehead.

It was, all in all, a day to remember.

I'm happy to report my daughter had a good time her first day at school.

She met some new friends, but complained that some of the guys were nerds.

That doesn't surprise me.

And who knows, maybe some day, somewhere off in the future, she'll say to some guy, "You know, the first day of junior high, I thought you were a real geek."

I'd like that if that happened.

Feeding My Daughter

It was as great a personal challenge as I had faced in twelve years of parenting.

"Your mission, Mr. Hurd, should you decide to accept it, is to keep your daughter fed while your wife is away at school for three weeks."

Hey, no sweat. I can do that.

"And to prove that you, a man, are every bit as capable of preparing the family meals as your wife, a woman, it will be considered cheating if you simply take your daughter to Zips twenty-one nights in a row."

Hmmm.

It seems that taking my daughter out for fast food every night and then considering myself a good cook and parent is sort of like taking my car to Jiffy-Lube and claiming to be a good mechanic.

Dang. This may be harder than I thought.

Now, if it sounds like my wife does all the cooking around our house, that's because she does, but not because I, the man, demand it.

It's more because A) she was raised in a farm family where life revolved in an orbit closely held to the gravity of the family dinner table, and B) perhaps because of that, she <u>likes</u> to cook and make salads and pastas, and roasts and au gratin potatoes and have it all simmer and smell and come together for an event where we sit down face to face and talk to each other for a few minutes while we gorge ourselves on all that delicious stuff, and

C) because, truth be told, she's not that crazy about the alterna-tive, which would be whatever I cook.

When my wife cooks, the aromatic and tasty journey is as important as the dinner table destination. When I cook, my primary goal is to make my tummy full, and the sooner the better, and I don't much care what it tastes or smells like.

Left alone, it's not unusual for me to have a dinner consisting completely of toasted English muffins. Or bagels. It's not that I'm particularly partial to toasted things, but because they're quick.

This is not to say that I can't cook, in a remedial sort of way. I mean, given enough time and forward planning, I can have meat loaf, potatoes and a frozen veggie all become edible at about the same time.

My wife, however, was worried that I would not be a real parent, and would simply buy burgers and pizza every night. And then she said those words that were both challenge and insult — "You have to plan your meals."

I hate to plan anything. And I avoid it whenever possible.

But I know a challenge when one comes along, and I took it.

If planning was what it would take to keep us fed and alive, then planning is what I would do. I would show the world we men can keep our children alive.

First I conducted a quick review of the basic food groups around which I would build twenty-one well balanced dinners. The Chinese group, the Italian group, the hamburger group, the fish and chips group, and the Oreo cookie group. Oh, yeah; and the chicken group.

Hey, this was going to be easy.

I called my daughter together for a family meeting.

"Look. Mommy's going to be gone for three weeks, and we can eat whatever we want, which means we don't have to eat our vegetables or anything if we don't want to, so what do we want?"

Her complete list consisted of Parmesean Noodles.

"Great," I said. "What else?" She couldn't think of anything, so I added beer and Dove Bars to the list for me, and with my meal planning complete, went shopping.

Now normally when I help my wife with the grocery shopping, I go right to the magazine section and read the latest Cosmo or Swimwear USA magazine. I'm not as much help as I might be.

It's been a long time since I actually had to wander up and down the aisles and make purchasing decisions.

I started in the meat department. Holy moly! No wonder some people become vegetarians. Who can afford this stuff? And what's the difference between a rib eye and a New York steak? Besides the price?

Clearly, I was out of my league.

Next came the vegetables.

I was beginning to wish I had done a better job of planning. Does my daughter like corn on the cob? I couldn't remember. Not only that, but I couldn't remember how to fix it.

Fruit! Here I knew my stuff. I loaded up on apples and oranges and bananas. At least my daughter wouldn't get scurvy while my wife was away.

Then I hit the frozen foods section.

It was all there: every conceivable meal from every corner of the earth. Ready to pop in the microwave and eat. And there aren't even any dishes to do.

Father Cooking Heaven.

A voice from within said, "You're cheating."

"What do you mean I'm cheating?" I said, loading up on precooked, frozen and breaded fish filets, french fries and pizza.

"It's not what your wife would do," came the voice. "Popping a frozen dinner in the microwave is not the same as laboring in the kitchen over a hot stove creating a delicious meal for your family."

The voice was right. And in a flash, I knew that I had been taking all my wife's planning and cooking somewhat for granted.

I felt awful.

But still, I didn't want to fail in this test of parenting. I knew I should forego the frozen foods and get real food that I prepared from scratch.

Or at least, room temperature.

It was a true crisis of conscience.

Finally, I resolved the issue the way any man would. "Look", I said to the voice, "I won't tell about the frozen food if you don't."

To which the voice replied, "Hey! Don't forget the frozen burritos."

Fear, Loathing and Bellbottoms

You don't need to be a social scientist to know that something is terribly amiss in the Clinton administration. There is a social evil that is out there, growing each day, gathering strength, making subtle inroads into the lives of citizens everywhere. This nation has at least a generation at risk, and the Clinton administration has not done a single thing about it.

You wouldn't expect the Bush administration to see it coming, but you would think that Bill and Hillary, of all people, would be hypersensitive to the immense consequences and potential damage of this threat, and they would be marshalling the efforts and resources of the federal government to fight this thing, to nip the problem in the bud before it grows into another boondoggle that the government cannot control.

Too late the government launched the war on poverty. Too late the government launched the war on drugs. While there is still time, I am writing to the President to protect our children and ourselves by launching an all out war on bellbottoms.

You're probably thinking: "I thought bellbottoms were dead." Well, you're right, they were. But like some sort of fashion Frankenstein, they are rising from the dead and threaten to return.

We need no less than a cabinet level Bellbottom Czar to fight this thing. I suggest Sonny Bono.

We need a program in the school, like D.A.R.E. We need an Officer Huddle from the Fashion Police. We could call the program B.A.R.E. for Bellbottoms Are Really Ugly. (I realize that the acronym doesn't work exactly, but anybody who would wear bellbottoms probably wouldn't notice.)

Now, I know that some of you in your forties are probably becoming a little apoplectic at that news that you may have to wear bellbottoms again, and you're probably fighting back the urge to yell at your paper, "Oh yeah? Oh yeah?" and if you don't have the urge to yell, you're at least thinking to yourself, "Yeah, well, not me; not in bellbottoms, not ever."

Right.

A classic case of bellbottom denial.

Bellbottom denial is a documented response to the severe fashion abuse of the late '60s and '70s. Victims of bellbottom denial block out entire decades of their lives, and really and truly can't remember that they spent years wearing Aztec print, hip hugging, rhinestone lined bellbottoms, or mutton chop sideburns or shirts with Elvis collars, or platform shoes, either.

Well, whether you are in bellbottom denial or not, the signs are all in place: Bellbottoms are coming back. I know this because in the latest issue of Mirabella Magazine, one of my favorites, many of the skinny fashion models are wearing them. Not the huge flared numbers like Goldie Hawn wore on Laugh-In, but bellbottoms just the same.

This should not come as any big surprise. Fashions, after all, are cyclical, and, sooner or later, those who invent the clothes that tell us who we are simply re-invent something from an earlier era.

Like suspenders. Suspenders? (Okay, braces for those you who shop at Nordstrom.)

If ten years ago, someone had told you that in 1993 your closet would have three sets of floral print suspenders, suits with pleated trousers and fat ties that look like they were designed by a computer drafting program that has a few lines of code missing, would you have called that person a fashion visionary or an idiot?

I know, I know; what's the difference? But that's not the point. The point is, if suspenders and pleated pants can come back from the fashion dead, why not bellbottoms?

And it's probably not an acceptable answer to say that bellbottoms are a lot uglier. After all, when it comes to fashion, ugly is in the eye of the beholder.

But there is something about the notion — make that the vision — of bellbottoms that puts them in a whole different category from, say, the rise and fall of hemlines, or of the comings and goings of shoulder pads or skinny or fat ties.

Maybe it's because there is something about bellbottoms that recalls not so much a fashion look as the whole era. And while other cyclical fashions tend to move us forward in time (suspenders look like the '90s even though I know the last time they were cool was the '50s), bellbottoms have the distinct look of the '60s and '70s.

And to paraphrase Lilly Tomlin, "The '60s were nice, but I wouldn't want to live there all the time."

And I especially wouldn't want my daughter to go through all that.

So we must protect our children from creeping bellbottomism. We must teach our children to just say no to the bellbottom pushers; we must help them learn from our own experience, learn that if they give in to bellbottoms, then next will come wide white belts, and love beads and platform shoes and peace signs, and the re-release of Sergeant Pepper's Lonely Hearts Club Band, and granny glasses and women in Oshkosh overalls and maxiskirts.

We must teach them that if the country gives in to bellbottoms, there is only one place it can all end: In the return of the polyester leisure suit, of course.

And who wants *that*?

Learning to Tip in Davis, California

I coach a volleyball team, and I recently got the chance of lifetime.

The chance to teach one of those lessons that I know will stay with my players for life. A lesson that ranks right up there with the meaning of sportsmanship, of giving your best effort, and of the real meaning of winning and losing. A lesson about how you say to the world what kind of person you are, what your values are and what you stand for.

How to spike a volleyball? Nah.

How to make a difficult honesty call a the net? (An honesty call in volleyball? Get real.)

No, this is one of life's fundamental lessons, and I was called upon to teach it.

How to tip a waitress.

I know you're thinking, hey, that's not your job, that's the job of the parents, or of the school system.

I know. But by chance, it fell to me.

It happened because I took a team to the Sacramento area for the annual Davis Volleyball Festival.

The Davis Festival is a seven day event that draws some 400 teams and 7,000 athletes from all over the country. There are 5,200 matches. It is like Hoopfest gone berserk. In volleyball, it is a big deal. And it's fun.

It was to be a great learning and growth experience. My girls, all just 12 and 13, had exceeded all previous expectations of them, so I was pumped. "Yeah! Let's go down there and kick some butt," I thought.

This is where I would become super-coach and motivate them from good to great.

"This is the big one," I said to my team. "This is where we show the world what we've really got. I need each of you to dig down inside yourself and always give me your personal best. Nothing less than 110% every time. We need to you to play the smartest ball you've ever played, moving to the ball, reading the sets and getting a wall up to shut down the hitters. When you're tired, you need to push through it; to find that reserve of energy and give a little more effort than the other teams. We need great serving, great passing and great hitting all day, every day!" I was practically John Wayne.

"Any questions?" I asked, as we huddled together, ready to give a rousing team cheer.

A hand went up. "Are we going to have time to shop?"

This caused a brief out of body experience where I wondered, briefly, if boys traveling from, say, Yakima to Spokane for Hoopfest ever asked their coach if they could be sure to hit NorthTown for some shopping before heading home. I didn't think so.

So much for being super-coach, I thought.

Oh, well. If this was going to be a learning experience, it appeared I was going to be learning a few things right along with the players.

The tipping lesson occurred because we had decided that each girl would receive a daily food allowance and when we weren't actually playing, they would order and pay for their meals on their own.

We were teaching responsibility here. And financial management. Not to mention nutrition.

What we didn't realize was, with the prospect of a California shopping mall in their futures, the girls would quickly realize that any money that wasn't spent on food or left in a tip could be spent shopping.

I'm surprised they didn't all develop eating disorders.

I got the feeling that with some of them, if it cost a nickel to go to the bathroom, they'd have found a way to throw up instead.

In this climate, you can imagine how much they wanted to leave a tip.

"Why do we have to tip?" they asked at the first restaurant we stopped into.

"It's how restaurant workers make their money," I said.

"Don't they get paid?"

"They do," I said, "But not much. Usually minimum wage, which is only about $4.50 an hour or something." This might have been a mistake, since $4.50 is about three times scale for babysitting on the South Hill.

"$4.50! And I'm supposed to leave them more?" was the reply. "How much more?"

We all agreed that 15% was the accepted minimum, but it was to slide upward or downward based on the quality of the service rendered.

I have never seen a faster transformation. One moment they were sweet, generous 13-year-olds; the next, hard bitten business managers evaluating employee performance for incentive purposes, in a deep business recession.

"She didn't smile when she asked for our order," said one, mentally docking a point off the tip.

"Yeah, and hasn't brought the ketchup. I'm knocking five percent off her tip," said another.

"My toasted cheese sandwich is squishy and she wears too much makeup," offered a third.

"Hey, don't blame your waitress for the food," I said. "That's not her department. And remember, a lot of waitresses are raising families on tips, so don't be too quick to cut them off."

"What's 12 percent of 79 cents?" one of them asked, slashing and burning through the deadwood of California's restaurant trade.

"Look you guys," I said, "this an opportunity to be gracious, to help another human being. Don't look at the specifics, look at the whole. Did she do her job well? Was she pleasant? If so, be generous, round up your tip to 20 percent or more. You can afford it. If she isn't pleasant, well, still be generous. Being a waitress is hard work."

I felt like a union negotiator explaining to management why a worker who makes three times what they make should make 20% more. With shopping in their future, I could see they weren't buying it. Nothing personal, you understand, said their steely looks, but it's my shopping bonus you're talking about.

"Does anybody have change for a nickel?" asked one, putting a fine point on it.

This picking nits over tips continued throughout the week, and I was afraid we were leaving a trail of bad feelings wherever we went to eat.

Worse, I didn't think the girls had gotten the concept of tipping as being a way of saying thank you to a server. They saw it as a tax — and an involuntary one, at that.

Then on the last day, when we were pressed for time, a middle aged Denny's waitress with five kids and enough mothering instinct to smother everyone in the place served the girls, and they transformed back into themselves.

"She was neat," they told me at the end of the meal, "and she could use the money." And they all left tips that, on a percentage basis anyway, were quite generous, especially for my little group of tightwads.

And I knew they understood why we tip, even if it doesn't always work out that one is deserved.

And I figured that maybe learning about tipping was like learning to spike a volleyball. If they could do it right once, it was only a matter of time before they would always do it right.

So I turned to them and told them I was proud of them. And I was.

And then, since I hadn't left a tip yet, I asked if any of them had change for a nickel.

Signing Yearbooks

My daughter gets her yearbook today.

Just finishing up seventh grade, she is getting her first real yearbook, the flimsy books they give the kids in elementary school being the yearbook equivalent of the training bra.

When she brought that book home last year, I asked if anyone had written anything in it, and I got one of those "What are you talking about?" looks that communicates to everyone within eyeshot that at the ripe old age of 12, she is bone-weary of having to contend with a mentally deficient parent, and she summed up how incredibly out of touch with reality I was with a single word: "Written?"

This year, however, she is in seventh grade, and things are decidedly different.

In fact, we had planned to take a vacation right now that would have pulled her out of school for the last few days — the all important yearbook signing days.

I won't make that mistake again.

My wife and I were informed in no uncertain terms that to miss a couple of days of yearbook signing is to gut the year of all meaning and significance.

What about everything you learned, I asked, forgetting entirely that the whole point of school is social instead of academic.

Who cares, was the reply. "I <u>have</u> to be there for yearbook signing."

I had forgotten that the yearbook is a lot of things, not the least of which is validation that you exist.

Or existed.

And the proof of this is not so much in the photographic proof of the rows of pictures, but in the yin and yang of the yearbook signing ritual; how many books did you sign, and of equal importance, how many signed your book.

To have a blank book is to be worse than merely unpopular; it is to be non-existent.

This was why, every year during the last days of school we frantically searched out everyone of any significance whatsoever in our lives, and asked them (in some cases fairly pleaded with them) to sign our books.

"Cindy! Will you sign my yearbook? Please?"

"I don't know you, you little cretin."

"Don't you remember, we were in band together, and I sat next to you, until they found out I didn't play an instrument and I transferred out on the second day of school. You remember me, don't you? Don't you?"

"Oh, okay."

Yes! Validation. Cindy the Beautiful signs your book, and gives meaning to your life, and a reason for you to stay in school.

By high school, a clear and universal measure of your popularity is how much of your yearbook's white space is filled up with long dissertations from your friends about how wonderful you are.

In fact, a kind of reverse snobbery can take place; actually having to decline people's request to sign your book because of space limitations.

Now, you may be wondering if, as a writer, I cheated and explained the rules of yearbook signing to my daughter.

No way. I know that there are some rules of life that are sacrosanct, and that just as the mother robin must let its chick learn to fly on its own, so every child must learn what to write in yearbooks with no parental influence.

Besides, the rules are so confusing, trying to explain them would only make things worse.

I mean, how do you explain that how much you write can be, but isn't always just as important as what you write, and all of its value is weighted by your relationship at that moment, with the book's owner?

When Cindy the Beautiful signed her name to her picture, and did not add a comment, was she not saying who was who in the popularity pecking order and that, yeah, you existed as far as she was concerned, but just barely?

And when your best friends wrote that you were the most popular person that there ever was and how scary the future was and good luck and we'll see you lots this summer, weren't they saying that, contrary to the laws of physics, you were the center of the universe? And if your best friends had written less, wouldn't you have just *died*?

Of course. But you can't explain that. That would irretrievably taint the honesty of the whole process, which is, by and large, pretty honest.

There are five generally accepted levels of yearbook signing.

The Signature Only, (The Cindy signature) which indicates you didn't hardly know the person but were willing to recognize their existence; the Signature with a Greeting like "Good luck!" (sometimes known as the "Teacher Entry") which indicates a speaking acquaintance, but nothing you could call a friendship;

The Short Entry (often a historical note — "Mr. Willis sure was mad when you left that can of Ultra-Slimfast on his desk!"); The Long Entry which can be both historical or personal in nature, and the prized Very Long Entry, which is reserved for the index pages with all of their white space and which document both what you did together and why you are so perfect.

There is also the bogus entry. That's where you autograph the picture of the kid who, by year's end, is already in reform school, and you say something like, "Going out with you was the highlight of my year, and I hope you're not pregnant. Love and kisses, Bernard."

When you're a kid, you think that's soooo funny.

Like teacher and janitor signatures, though, bogus entries don't really count in the personal validation sweepstakes, unless you're really desperate.

Of course, when all the entries are in, the yearbook is probably the most accurate picture of your child, and your child's friends, and what they have done, are doing, and will do, you could ask for.

So, while I hate to look like a parent whose teenager has taught him to roll over and play dead on command, I realized that in this case, my daughter was right and should not miss the last days of school.

So we rescheduled our vacation.

But it's not a total loss.

After all, now I'll have a yearbook to read, won't I?

It's in the Genes

At first I thought it was my fault. I thought I was lacking as a parent in some way — that I had failed my daughter.

The guilt was crippling me — keeping me awake at night, distracted at work, the whole bit.

And then I read where scientists had isolated the gene for our biological 24-hour clock, and the gene that controls addiction, and I realized, it's not me, that's the problem, it's her.

But it's not really her fault, either.

It was suddenly so clear: My daughter just doesn't have the gene responsible for cleaning up her room.

You have no idea what a relief it was.

Of course, we didn't actually have genetic counselling or anything, but you can tell just from looking at her room that she is lacking in the neatness gene.

Either that, or she has the very rare aviary gene for nesting, and her nesting materials are previously worn clothes. A 300-pound barn swallow would feel right at home in her room.

Now I understand what she means when I look into her room and she looks at me and says, "Don't say anything; it's my room and I like it this way."

It's not parental. It's genetic.

Once I had this revelation, I realized how much this genetic thing was affecting my life. For that matter, all our lives.

For instance, it also became quite evident that I am lacking the gene that enables one to figure out which shirt goes with which pants. It's like being color blind, except for fashion. I'm fashion-blind.

I can stand for fifteen precious morning minutes looking into my closet trying to figure out what combination of pants and shirt will look okay, and when I finally make my choice, about three times out of four my wife says to me, "You're not going to wear that, are you?" To which I mutter, "Ah, no. This was just a test to see if you were awake yet. "

Now when she asks if I can't see that my clothes don't go, I can say, "No, <u>I can't</u> see it: I don't have that gene." I can say the magic words, "But, it's not my fault. I'm fashion blind. It's genetic."

I really know that I don't have the gene for choosing ties. The medical test for this gene is known as the COBCTTN test, which stands for Casual Observer Blowing Coffee Through The Nose, which is what your receptionist does when she looks at your tie when you first walk in the morning.

"Nice tie," she says, blotting the telephone. "Pick that out yourself?"

You can now go to the store, and buy a tomato that is genetically altered to taste better. That's kind of subjective isn't it? It makes me wonder what their advertising slogan will be. I think a good one would be: Is it real or is it Genentech?"

They are finding that there is a gene for everything. (Or is it a lack of a gene? I forget.) And not just stuff like breast cancer, multiple sclerosis, alcohol addiction, and heart disease, but important stuff like where your 24- hour biological clock is located. Some people even seem to have a gene for a seven stroke handicap.

This will be great. In the same way that you will be able to know that you are genetically programmed for some dreaded disease and take corrective action, you'll be able to use genetic identification to help you make the major decisions in your life:

"I'd like to marry you Hal, but you don't have the money making gene or the dish washing gene, not to mention the diaper changing gene. Plus you have the genes for a hairy back and a bald head. Sorry."

Of course, we already know that most of what we are is in our genes; my parents were short, and I'm short. Mario Andretti drives race cars and so do his sons. Frank Sinatra is a singer and his kids ... Hmmm. Well, it doesn't work in all cases, but you know what I mean. We see the effects of our genes all the time.

But now it's getting so specific. And it's going to get more specific as they find more things that are controlled by our genes.

"The bad news is, your baby does not have the gene for common sense. She'll grow up without a lick of it. The good news is, with no common sense at all, she'll be qualified to be a federal judge or head up the Army Corps of Engineers, or maybe the whole Interior Department."

Imagine how it will impact, say, the law.

"Ladies and gentlemen of the jury, while it's true my client doesn't have the rare bank robber gene, I think our experts have shown conclusively that he lacks the personal restraint gene, which may account for why he is currently mooning the judge."

Hear the message? It's not his fault. It's genetic.

There are some questions still to be answered, of course.

For instance, the question we all want to know is, is there a gene for being fat? Or one for being skinny that only a few of us have?

And is there one for growing old? And more to the point, if there is, can we turn it off?

I mean, if they can identify the gene that causes addiction, you'd think they could find the one that triggers the mid-life crisis.

The big question, of course is, if all this stuff is programmed right into our genes, and our kid's genes, then what are we doing as parents?

I don't know about you, but I'm shutting the door to my daughter's room until she gets the neatness gene.

Or she gets attacked by a 300-pound barn swallow.

Whichever comes first.

The Party

As a parent of a 14-year-old, I knew that someday, it would happen.

And last week, it did.

I got the question every parent dreads.

I was just sitting there, minding my own business, alone in the living room when my daughter walked in and stood in front of me.

She was poised and calm. Serious but not somber; young, but not to be trifled with; for a moment, just a split second really, she didn't say anything, letting her presence set the tone for what she had come to talk about.

And in that split second, she reminded me of no one so much as Marcia Clarke. Which made me feel like Judge Ito. I half expected her to begin by saying, "Your honor ... " but, of course, she didn't.

Instead, choosing her words carefully, she got right to the point.

"Friday night, could I have some friends over for a ... get together?"

"Objection! Your honor," screamed the part of my brain that wants to keep her a little girl forever. "Clearly out of order! She is way too young."

"Shut up!" replied the rational Judge Ito side of my brain.

"You want to have a ... party?" I said, introducing into this family court the dreaded "P" word.

"Not a party, not really; more of a get together," she answered quickly. And, I might add, confidently. She was prepared.

We live in a house where the meanings of words are important; and it was clear that a "get together" was different than a "party." I think we both tacitly agreed that a party was a big, open-ended event about which word could spread and non-inviteds might show up at, as in, "Hey I hear Allyson's having a party! Let's go!" A party was a license to get crazy. A party was where there was no adult supervision. No looming adult presence.

I had been to parties all my life, and I was darned if I was going to let my daughter throw one.

But a get together, now that was something else. A get together was a go-cart with a governor on the carburetor; it was Drivers Ed. to having your license. It was a party with training wheels.

With a looming adult presence, it was controllable.

"And who would attend this get together?" I asked.

"13," she said, and ticked off the names of the girls. I knew them all; the A list. No sweat.

She paused. This was it. Time to get to the real heart of the matter. Time to get to what we were here for.

"And...?" I said, from the bench, as it were.

Picking up my prompt, she listed the boys she wanted to invite. Some I knew; some I didn't.

She immediately ran down their rap sheets. All good guys. All clean records. All to be released in my house, on their own recognizance, in the presence of girls they are "going out with," to use the current vernacular, which, curiously, doesn't mean they actually go out anywhere, together.

The part of my brain that was defending my daughter's little girlhood asked to approach the bench.

"Your honor," it said, "have you lost your mind? Do you remember being an eighth grade boy? Do you recall the single, all encompassing, overriding ambition you had at that age? It was to get yourself and your girlfriend to any place at any time so you could make out! So you could do the old tongue-tango! And do you remember the perfect environment for that? A party? And when asked, do you remember how you innocently faced your parents and, using that wide-eyed 'who, me' look to hide your dirty little mind, you told them that at your parties you just played records and danced when what you really did was play <u>16 Candles</u> over and over and went into the darkest corner you could find and under the physical pretense of dancing, stood there and made out? Remember that? And do you really think the ambitions, not to mention the hormonal levels of eighth grade boys has changed all that much in 35 years? Ask her what they are going to do, your honor!"

"What are you going to do?" I asked my daughter.

"Maybe play music and watch videos and stuff," she said a little too wide-eyed and innocently to make me feel completely comfortable.

Well, at least she didn't say, "Play <u>16 candles</u> and make out," I thought, although I must admit I wasn't completely sure that she <u>didn't</u> say exactly that, except she used the words "Play music and watch videos" and I'm just too dense to understand the code.

I asked all the logistical questions: times, food, house rules, clean up. She had it all worked out.

"What about party crashers?" I asked.

"They don't get in," she answered, "but I don't think there will be any."

I had no doubt she was right.

"What does your mother say?" I asked rhetorically, knowing that I was the last hurdle in my daughter's divide and conquer strategy.

"She says it's okay with her as long as it's okay with you," was the Marcia Clarke wannabe reply.

Defense counsel stood up. "They'll be playing kissy-face, your honor, right under your nose, looming adult presence or not, if you let this plan proceed. They'll find a way; you know they will. Do you want that? Do you want your daughter and her friends to grow up and prefer the company of sex-crazed boys to you and all your paternal protectiveness, or do you want to deny this first step, and keep them and her, little girls forever?"

But we both knew the answer to that one.

What I wanted didn't matter. The answer was standing before me. She and all of her friends weren't little girls anymore.

Well, if I couldn't control the fact that they would engage in some 14- year-old smash mouth action, I could control where. And with my looming adult presence, perhaps how much.

At least this time.

Her body language was saying, "I'm not rushing you, but we need a decision, your honor."

"Okay," I said, with perhaps a bit more resignation for a time suddenly past than I had intended.

And then I got something from my daughter that I doubt Lance Ito ever got from Marcia Clarke. A thank you with a hug.

A hug that had just a touch of goodbye in it.

The Stress of Eighth Grade Volleyball

You wake up in the morning and before you're even fully awake, it hits you. Today's the day.

You try to put it out of your mind, but you can't — not really.

Today is the day of the big game. The day the season starts.

You go to work, but your mind is somewhere else.

When you should be concentrating on work, you can't.

"I'm sorry, I lost my train of thought. What are we doing, here?"

"A rhinoplasty, doctor."

"Oh."

And when you should be concentrating on work, you find yourself thinking about the other team.

What if they are bigger than we are?

What if they're animals?

What if we go out on the court and they maul us like a bunch of hockey players?

And then you think, get a hold of yourself. This is what all the practices have been for.

In the middle of the afternoon, in an important meeting, when you are about to explain why your plan will bring a greater return on investment than anything comparable on the market and all these big lawyer types in suits are just hanging on your every word, you think about the game and you blurt out, "What if they're all on anabolic steroids? It could happen!"

Some of the suits look at you like you've gone over the top, but others look at you and recognize the symptoms, and they know it's game day.

Been there. Done that. He'll be himself tomorrow.

Finally, it's time.

On your way there, you start to get pumped up for the game. Hey, what's the big deal? We're ready. What have they got, anyway? A bunch of wimps.

You're like a prize fighter getting psyched up, dancing around the ring, waiting for the first bell.

Except you're in a '92 Ford Explorer and all that bouncing and talking to yourself is making quite a spectacle, and everybody on Division is either speeding past you or staying way behind you, and nobody is making eye contact.

Finally, the moment comes. The moment you've been both dreading and looking forward to. You enter the gym. The coach has put in her starting line up. You draw a deep breath. You read the numbers. Did we make it?

Yes! The coach is going to start your daughter.

So you go up into the stands, and you assume the concerned parent posture: elbows on knees, hands cupped over your mouth. Teeth clenched so tightly, if the game doesn't begin pretty soon, you're going to need some orthodontia work before the end of the day.

And so the eighth grade volleyball season begins.

Now, to be fair, I can't imagine that eighth grade volleyball is all that much different from junior high soccer, basketball, wrestling or any other junior high sport.

In the stands, we parents observe certain unwritten rules of behavior.

The primary rule is, never lay blame on anyone. There will be plenty of opportunity to spread blame around later, in high school athletics, and later still in adult recreation programs.

So it is considered bad form to watch a child do a real dumb thing on the court and say out loud something that would be perfectly acceptable while watching, say, the Seahawks play, like, "Who is that idiot?" Because, in all likelihood, the parents of that child may be sitting right in front of you.

Or worse, it could be your daughter somebody else is talking about.

So nobody says anything.

Hence, the elbows on the knees, hands over the mouth position, from which, if some sound does escape, it's just a muffled grunt.

At the junior high level of competition, all comments are to be encouraging and positive.

Consequently, everything is "okay."

Your child serves into the net: "That's okay!"

Your child shanks the ball into the wall and through the window: "That's okay!"

Your child passes the ball in a perfect arc to the steroidally malformed six-foot-four monster-child on the other side of the net who crushes the ball to floor for game and match point: "That's okay!"

It is acceptable to shout general encouragements like, "Get the next one," and "Side out," and, "Hustle," as long as they are directed at the team in general and not at anyone in particular. As fans, we parents feel compelled to yell something to get into the spirit of the event.

However, it is considered politically incorrect to be too specific. Like for instance, "Hey, number 12, move your butt," just won't do.

That's the coach's job.

This is a bit of an aside, but I should mention here for the sake of journalistic integrity if nothing else, that the two coaches I watched, the Chase and Northwoods coaches, did nothing of the sort. They were both very benign. Nice Job. A little serene for the heat of athletic battle for my taste, but still, nice job.

The final rule of parental behavior which is, everyone must assume uptight body language; arms folded tightly across the midsection, and everybody is hunched over like they all have debilitating acid indigestion.

Which is probably not too far from the truth. Except, of course, when a point is scored, and everybody stands and cheers, to the great relief of all the internal organs.

Eighth grade is the last time that the non-jocks, non-dedicated athletes really get a chance to play and wear their school colors. By the next year, between the pressure to choose between such things as volleyball and band, and the limitation of school teams to just 12 or 15 players, insures that all but the best athletes will be cut from the team.

So this is their moment to play, and a last moment that some of them will remember for the rest of their lives.

And win or lose, it wouldn't do to stain that moment with ugly parental behavior.

So that's why we parents have our code of conduct in the stands. Why we try to recognize every kid's great efforts and forgive anything less.

And why, after the game, when our kids say to us, "You're funny. When you're watching the game, you always cover your mouth with your hands," we can look at them innocently and say, "Really? I wonder why I do that?"

Steering the Car

My daughter soloed last weekend.

Right on schedule. Actually, she soloed twice.

But I'm getting ahead of myself.

Every once in a while, as your child travels down the great freeway of life, you get to watch them pass a mile marker that you recognize from your own journey toward adulthood.

This happened to me this weekend.

This is great when it happens because it gives you, the parent, a kind of navigational fix on your child's position — at least relative to your own experience.

It gives you a chance to go back and look at the maps of your childhood and plot the way points and compare them to your child's way points.

And for at least a brief moment, as a parent, you know, absolutely, where they are in their own expanding universe.

Now, the reason this is such a revelation is because as an adult, you don't know when they pass these mile markers. You only know that they have.

The first kiss mile marker, for instance. Remember that?

Sure you do. Everybody does.

Since it took all the nerve I had to cross that major threshold, I also remember the intervening six weeks until my second kiss, and what I was thinking about most of that time, and why my grades went south, and spending a lot of time checking my palms for hair growth and worrying about going blind.

The point is, did you go home and announce to your parents that you had received, or delivered your first real kiss?

"What, and be grounded until I was 22?"

Of course not.

So your parents probably never knew exactly when you passed that mile marker. They only figured out later that you had.

Like when one day your father comes in and says, "I think it's time we had a talk about kissing and stuff," and you answered, "Sure, Dad. I'd have thought you'd have had all that worked out by now, but hey, what is it you want to know?"

"Hmm. Never mind."

But once in a while, you pass a mile marker that's right out in clear sight.

We passed the first one on this particular journey about a year ago when she was 13.

I was taking my daughter to school, and while I was trying to get my seat belt fastened, she matter-of-factly reached over and began steering the car.

Now, while I was grateful for the help, and not having to steer the car with my knee and risk plowing into the parked cars I was heading for, I was struck by the fact that never before during seat belt fastening roulette had she reached into my adult domain and taken control of steering the car.

She had been quite content to let me drive off the road.

And at that moment, I knew exactly where she was on her map.

She was at the mile marker called "Steering the car."

It is the first step toward driving the car.

During steering the car, every time you pass some invisible geographical boundary, where all the streets are familiar and the potential dangers minimal, your 13-year-old has a compelling urge to feel what it is like to be in control of a ton of moving steel.

It is during this time that they suddenly get an awareness of the general relationships between moving cars and the rules of the road, and when you have enough time to make a left turn without getting nailed and when you don't.

This is great, except it creates a 13-year-old back seat driver, and who needs that?

"Nice signal Dad. Ever thought about using your blinker to tell people you're going to turn, or would that be too much work?"

Sound familiar?

Steering the car generally gives way fairly quickly to the other steps that lead to driving such as starting the car, washing the car — a step I have yet to see any evidence of in my daughter, and finally to turning the car around.

This was the mile marker we passed this weekend.

I was out spreading Roundup on the weeds in the driveway, and had to move the car.

"Can I do it?" she asked.

Bingo! Mile marker time!

Now, my first impulse is to scream, "No! You're too young. Who let you out of diapers? And when did you start to walk? And what do you mean you'll probably take Driver's Ed. this year? You? My baby?"

But my baby is almost 15.

I checked my map and looked at my "backing out of the driveway and turning the car around" mile marker. Fourteen, almost 15.

Right on schedule.

There was nothing she could run into (without total mental and physical shutdown) there was no traffic and there was no reason not to let her cross this threshold.

"Sure," I said. "Get the keys."

Now, when you were cleared to start the car and turn it around, how long was it before you backed the car a little farther than you needed to, and pulled forward a little farther than you had to?

Right. Not very long.

In my case, it wasn't but about a month before turning the car around began to include a trip to the end of the block and then to the end of the next block and pretty soon to a trip to the beach and to my friend Greg Deer's home about a mile away.

"What are you doing?" he asked incredulously the first time I drove up.

"Turning the car around," I answered.

"Cool," he said.

Technically, of course, I was underage and driving without a license.

This was scary because when you're fifteen and driving for the first time, you feel as if there is a giant spotlight on you and loudspeakers that are blaring, "Attention Attention! This driver is obviously underage and should be arrested immediately. Will somebody please call the police?"

Actually, if you want to get technical, I was also driving a stolen car, although I figured if I got caught the chances of my parents pressing charges would have been minimal.

What I remember was how exciting driving was.

The car! The freedom! Where was Willy Nelson singing <u>On the Road Again</u> when I needed him?

I was still weighing the wisdom of what I had allowed to happen, and thinking that maybe this should be one of those little father-daughter moments, you know, not bring my wife into this event just yet, kind of keep it our little secret, when my daughter strutted into the house, tossed the keys on the counter and said to everyone present, "Guess who just moved the car all by herself?"

Well, I thought, I didn't really want to keep it a secret, anyway.

I also decided that now was probably not a good time to tell her that I not only knew exactly where she was in this moment in time, but that I also knew where she would be in the next few months, pushing the boundaries, and driving first around the block and then around the neighborhood, and that I wasn't going to tolerate it. No sir, it would be against the rules, so don't even think about it.

But then I remembered that the first time you solo in a car, it's a pretty amazing feeling, and I decided not to spoil the moment. There was time enough to rain on that parade later, I decided.

Later that afternoon, as we were preparing to leave, with barely so much as look for permission, she started the car and backed it out of the driveway.

As she put the car in park and moved to the other seat, I thought, I'd better not let that conversation wait too long.

Caller ID

There isn't much in the form of high technology I hunger for.

I don't care if my computer has Intel inside. All I really care about is that it runs my word processor program.

I'm not sure I want on the information super highway. I figure I'm on the information hiking trail, and I'm going where I want to go just about fast enough, thank you very much.

But there is one high tech gizmo that I want.

Caller ID.

This is the little box that tells you the name and number of the person calling you. Technically, I guess, and this sets all those ACLU hearts all aflutter, it tells you the name and number assigned to the phone being used to call you, but as far as I'm concerned, that's close enough.

The little box called caller ID is a big step up from what we use in our family, which is intuitive caller ID.

This is where we guess who the caller is and decide whether we want to answer the call or not.

You probably have something like it in your family.

"That's your mother," I say to my wife when the phone rings. "Do you want to answer it?"

"How do you know it's my mother?" she says.

"We've been skiing all weekend, it's six-thirty on Sunday night, she wants to know if we got home safely from skiing and if Allyson's braces still hurt and if she is taking solid food yet, and she probably wants to give us a medical update on all of her friends, both of whom are failing rapidly, and there was no call left on the answering machine, which means this is her. You want to answer it or not?"

Call it my male intuition.

Usually we answer it. And usually, I'm right.

"Yeah, she's right here. Want to talk to her?"

(Don't you love it when you're right, and your wife's only comeback is to call you "Smarty pants" under her breath as she takes the phone from you?)

I have to admit that Intuitive Caller ID has been made more difficult, though, by having a teenager in the family. This is because my daughter has friends who have had their telephone receivers surgically grafted to their ears and who will call at all hours of the day or night.

I can't imagine what it would be like with more than one teenager in the house.

Actually, it was because of my daughter that I realized I wanted caller ID about six months ago.

Prior to that time, we'd get these calls for my daughter, "Is Allyson there?" they would ask, and Allyson would ask, "Is it a boy or a girl," and I'd say, "I don't know," because I didn't.

Mario sounded just like Natalie.

Then one day, a voice deeper than mine said, "Is Allyson there?" And suddenly knowing who was calling seemed like a good idea.

Caller ID, of course, presents about as many social problems as it creates, it seems to me. For instance, if you've got it and your friends know you've got it, and if you don't answer the phone now, will you have to lie about it later?

Right now, I don't feel especially compelled to answer the phone, especially when I'm alone. I figure whoever it is will call back. This is easy and democratic of me, because, not knowing who it is, I just reject everybody.

But if I know who it is, will I feel the same?

I don't know.

I mean, how many of us want to have to face anybody and say, "You called, but I didn't want to talk to you, because, well, you bore me silly."

Not very many, I should think.

So instead, we'll probably all become more proficient, social liars. "I know you called last night, but I didn't answer because, um, I had the flu, and I thought I might be sick. Especially if I talked to you."

I can't imagine dating with Caller ID in place. Most young men count on the element of surprise to help them get dates. They figure that if they can just get their intended target on the line and ask her out, she may not be able to come up with an excuse quick enough, and he might just get a date.

But if those same young ladies get to see who is calling before they answer the phone, there's no telling what might happen. I mean, I don't think it's unreasonable for a bunch of Pi Phi's to look at their Caller ID box and say, "Hey, anybody here want to talk to anybody at the Beta house?"

"Are those the guys who eat from a trough? I don't think so."

You see the problem.

Because in many cases, it's not simply who is calling, but why they are calling that makes us want to avoid the call.

So what we need to go along with Caller ID is Caller Subject ID.

What a great idea! It could be like Voice Mail.

"Hello, welcome to Caller Subject ID. If you are a close friend or family member, and you are calling to invite someone to dinner, press one. If you are calling to announce you are getting divorced, need money or getting into Amway, press two. If you are an acquaintance, and you are just calling to chat, press three. If you are a pervert, and this is an obscene call you would like to make, press four. If you are an attorney, and this is anything other than a social call, press five and then go drink cyanide. If you are a telephone solicitor, and you want to tell someone that your carpet cleaning crews are going to be in the neighborhood, and we have been selected for a free carpet shampoo, press six. If you are calling about money we owe you ... " well, you get the idea.

But that's down the road.

For right now, I just want to know who's on the other end of the line when my phone rings. And when I already know, intuitively, it's not my mother-in-law.

And when someone asks for my daughter and they have a voice deeper than mine.

Day-Timer Upmanship and Other Things They Don't Teach in Business School

Day-Timer Upmanship

When the catalog comes, I always glance through it.

I know I shouldn't because I know that I'm not supposed to buy anything out of it, but I look through it anyway.

To sneak a look at the sexy things in the catalog, I tell myself, "Maybe I'll find something in here for my wife," but I know I'm lying to myself.

I just like looking at that stuff.

And then, before I know it, that insidious catalog thing takes over. The photos are so good, and the models so perfect looking, and their merchandise so alluring, that I project myself right into the fantasy world they inhabit, and the next thing I know, in my mind's eye, I see myself as younger, taller, more successful, better dressed, well-respected, absolutely in control, and the one thing I am not now and I probably never will be: Organized.

Such is the power of the Day-Timer Catalog.

The Day-Timer catalog. 60 pages of calendars that promise to make sense out of the chaos that is your life even while they make you <u>look</u> like you know what you're doing.

The Day-Timer catalog is to your business life what Victoria's Secret is to your private life; something that says if you just buy <u>this</u>, you'll look like <u>that</u>.

But, as anyone can tell you, life just isn't that simple.

I should say here, for the record, that "Day-Timer" is a brand name and should not be used as a generic term meaning all calendar-organizers, which is exactly what I mean when I use the term.

And just like there ought to be a disclaimer somewhere in the Victoria's Secret catalog that says just because you're buying their stuff doesn't necessarily mean that you are going to look just like their models (there being the slight problem that maybe your body isn't nearly so perfect as theirs and all that), there ought to be a disclaimer in the Day-Timer catalog that says just because you spend a ton of money on the most elaborate daytime organizer known to man, you may not necessarily get organized.

What they don't tell you is that for those things to work, for you to get organized, you have to change.

Well, that's a drag.

Actually, it's a good thing they don't have little warning signs on them, or my Day-Timer would have to say, "Caution: The person carrying this Day-Timer is not nearly as organized as he might appear."

And there are several other things they could tell you in the catalog, but don't. Like once you have one, you will have to live with the Day-Timer Paradox, which says, "When you don't need your Day-Timer, you will always have it with you; and when you do need it, you won't." And the more important the need, the less likely you will be to have it.

"Then we're all agreed that we'll meet at 10 o'clock next Friday with the presidents of both companies to discuss our role in the merger, right?"

"I'll have to get back to you; I forgot my Day-Timer this morning. I think that's the day I'm having open heart surgery. "

You may wonder — where does this all begin?

At the lowest level of the Day-Timer food chain are the month-at-a- glance calendars. These are the sorts of things that some businesses give out for free at the end of the year.

We always get a pile of them from the Spokesman-Review. I think it's what they make with the paper they have left over at the end of the year.

"As our way of saying thank you for placing a million dollars worth of advertising in our paper last year, we'd like you to have these genuine vinyl-covered, somewhat embarrassing calendars that none of our reps would be caught dead with."

"Thanks."

"Think nothing of it."

"I don't."

You learn pretty quickly in business that you just can't open one of those free things up in a meeting with someone who has a Day-Timer they actually paid for. You just can't.

So you buy your first Day-Timer. Inevitably, it is a one-month pocket version. When I did it, I splurged and bought the nice leather holder.

I thought I was so cool, so business: "Am I available next Wednesday? Well, I'll just check my Day-Timer and see."

Unfortunately, you quickly learn there is a hitch.

"Uh, next Wednesday is next month, and I don't have that little booklet with me. I'll have to call you back." I carried the pocket version around with me for two years and almost never had the right month with me.

This was made all the more embarrassing by the fact that I had a client who was into serious Day-Timer-upmanship.

Day-Timer-upmanship occurs when you see someone else's Day-Timer and it's neater than yours, and you think, "I should have one of those."

When that person is your client, this is not a good thing.

When I had a monthly pocket version, he had the junior one-page-per-day edition.

"Two can play this game," I thought. So I bought the full-size one-page-per-day edition.

He countered with a full-size, two-pages-per-day, genuine pigskin edition; and before I could retaliate, he had abandoned that for a full size, two-pages-per-day, plus auxiliary writing pad, with built-in calculator, Rolodex, complimentary pens and pencils and Webster's New American Heritage Dictionary edition.

Check and Mate. Apparently, two can't play this game when one of them is me.

He had to carry all this to work in a small suitcase, you understand, but that only added to his aura of authority.

Some people play reverse Day-Timer-upmanship where they get their Day-Timers smaller. And then there is reverse-reverse Day-Timer-upmanship where you get your Day-Timer smaller; but you stuff it with three years of lunch receipts, business cards, old parking tickets and notes from your wife to pick up milk at Rosauers on the way home.

It makes you look very important.

In the breast pocket of your suit coat, if you're a woman, it also makes you look like you've had a breast removed. If you're a man, it makes you look like you've had a breast added. But I guess that's neither here nor there.

Now, it takes a while, but sooner or later, you realize that you are what you are; and your Day-Timer isn't going to change that. And you settle on a size and format that seems to work for you.

And you learn that your success is not based on the size of your Day-Timer.

Probably.

Messy Desk Syndrome

What is it about being men that makes us so prone to that scourge of business life, that insipid, debilitating illness that sucks life from the heart and soul of our work while it robs the entire nation of productivity and, in the process, wastes billions of dollars in lost time and needless paper shuffling?

What is it in the male condition that makes us so apt to come down with the dreaded Messy Desk Syndrome?

Now, I know that some of you women out there who must work with men who have Messy Desk Syndrome are saying, "Are you kidding? Men don't come down with MDS like it's some sort of external case of the flu. They're born with it!"

It starts when they're in diapers. I mean, little girl diapers look like they're from a human being, while little boy diapers look like something from a mutant form of life that is all large intestine. Little girl diapers look like something that needs to go into the wash, while little boy diapers look like they need to go to a toxic waste dump.

And messy diapers lead to messy rooms and messy bathrooms and messy dresser drawers and messy garages and messy relationships and messy marriages — so why should the place where they spend eight hours a day be anything, anything but a complete and total MESS?"

To which I reply, "I don't know."

Male bashers.

Now, it should be said that not all men suffer from Messy Desk Syndrome.

For instance, my boss, Jack White, has an immaculate desk. And that's when he's there, at it. When he leaves, it's worse: when he leaves work, his desk has nothing on it.

Frankly, I think it's a little weird.

And there's a difference between having a messy desk and being busy, which can result in piles of work that need to be done. The primary difference is people who are busy and have lots of piles of work on their desks generally know where everything is, while people who have Messy Desk Syndrome don't necessarily have to be busy to not know where anything is.

Did you follow that?

How do you know you've got Messy Desk Syndrome? How do you know you're not just busy, and that's why your desk looks like it does?

One telltale sign is when you have Messy Desk Syndrome, things disappear.

Like phone call reminder slips. And the card you wrote your next haircut appointment on. And the 15-page video script, shooting schedule and cost estimate you've been working on.

"How much is it going to cost? You mean, money? Let's see, I just had the estimate in front of me a minute ago ... now where did that go? It was right here, Oh, here it is. No, that's a note to myself to buy my wife an anniversary gift. Anniversary? Dang, I knew there was something I was forgetting last month. Oh well. Wait a minute! Here it is. No, that's not it. That's my driver's license renewal notice. Listen, can I get back to you on that estimate?"

Now, those of you who don't suffer from this condition are saying, "Why can't you just buy an in-basket and a Day-Timer and get organized?" It's not that easy. I keep losing my Day-Timer and I've got an in-basket.

Somewhere.

We men have a code when we're in messy desk paralysis.

If we are secure in our self-esteem, we say, "Can I get back to you on that? I don't have those numbers right in front of me at the moment," which is messy desk paralysis-ese for, "I had it here, I was working on it, and now it is gone, disappeared, for which I have no explanation, and why I am rummaging through the wastepaper basket while we're on the phone, thinking I may have tossed it away and you need to respect my malehood and get me off this hook!"

To which the appropriate reply is, "Sure, no big deal; go ahead and fax it to me when you find it," which is code for, "I understand completely that papers can vaporize and that I am not rendering a judgement of incompetence on you, even though you can't find a 15-page document that should be right under your nose."

If we are insecure and lacking in self-esteem, we blame someone else. "Listen, my idiot assistant must have done something with it. I'll get back to you."

The key phrase is, "I'll get back to you." In any case, the reply is the same.

When someone is in messy desk paralysis, it is considered bad form to hold his feet to the fire by asking something direct and potentially embarrassing, like, "Well if it's not on your desk, where is it?" (To which the lame answer is, "It is on my desk: I just can't find it, even though my desk is only two feet by four feet.)

It is extremely bad form to ask the worst question of all: "Did you look in your files?"

Files? Are you kidding?

When you have Messy Desk Syndrome, filing something is to paper what cryogenics is to dead people. It's like putting it in a deep freeze where no one will see it for a hundred years or so.

That's because of the Universal Rule of Filing, which says, "There is no thing on earth which can't be filed under various headings, most of which can't be thought of later when you want to retrieve that thing from a file."

Plus, people with Messy Desk Syndrome almost always also have Messy Filing System Syndrome.

Now, you're probably wondering about the scope of the problem, and wondering if all men have it (as some people claim) or just some men…and I have done some research on that, and I have those numbers right here … somewhere…let me see …

Can I get back to you on that?

Planning the Company Picnic

If you stay at a job long enough, sooner or later it <u>will</u> happen to you.

You're trying to be a good employee, to show up for work on time, add value to the corporation, not tell any jokes that the females will find sexist or the PC police will find inappropriate, do everything that your boss and your boss's spouse wants and still one day, your boss shows up in your cubicle with that concerned paternal look on his face that says, "I've got some bad news," and you know, you know your time has come.

You're about to face the worst thing that can happen to you. The true corporate no-win situation: "I want you to serve on the company picnic committee," your boss says.

Now, if you are fresh out of college, new in your job, and still think that people are basically good and that picnics are fun, you may think, "Wow, cool."

If you're a little older and you've been in the working world a while, it is likely your whole career will flash before your eyes. Then you smile and say to your boss, "Wow, cool."

"I knew I could count on you," your boss says. "I'll just leave this big sword here in your cubicle so if the picnic turns out to be a drag, you can fall on it and save us all a lot of trouble."

The problem with a company picnic is it is one of those things that everybody can agree exists and everybody has a kind of mental image of, but no two people share quite the same image.

The first thing the committee has to decide is when the picnic will be.

You can do this by guessing at the weather, "July is always sunny!" "Are you an idiot, it's got to be in August!" Or by trying to find the date when the fewest — or fewest most important employees — will be on vacation.

Or you can do it the easy way and call the bosses wife to ask her when she wants it.

There is also the question, is this little shindig going to happen on a work day, in which I'll be glad to come; or on a Saturday, in which case it's on my time, and I'm not sure I want to spend my Saturday socializing with people I work all week with and don't care for all that much.

After you decide when to have the picnic, you must then decide where.

"I know. Let's have it at Medical Lake!"

"Why? Are you running low on Prozac? I say Hill's Resort at Priest Lake."

"And drive two hours back and forth?"

"Well, not all of us drink so much that driving is a problem."

The "where" question can get real testy real fast.

The "where" question really boils down to "on the water somewhere" or not; and for most people, a picnic without a lake is unthinkable.

This adds a whole new level of stress to the event for women because once they know it is going to be on the water, they begin visualizing everything bad that can happen, from drowning children to being seen in a swimsuit.

And seeing some of their male colleagues in a swimsuit.

"Somebody tell Harold to put a shirt on."

You'd think that once the committee has decided when and where the company picnic would be, the big fights would be over.

Wrong.

You still have to decide what food needs to be planned.

Here the choices are: You can have the event catered, and eat like there is no tomorrow (not a pretty sight), and blow your budget on food; or you can go cheap — buy a ton of food at Costco, haul it to the site, set up a field mess hall, and try to serve it before it grows toxic levels of ptomaine or E. coli.

This looks like an okay idea until you ask the question, "Who serves it?"

The picnic committee? Uh huh. Good guess.

Suddenly, hanging around in the sun for two hours over a hot barbecue, standing next to picnic committee members you hate, serving food to people you don't like, starts to look like a real possibility.

"How long has this potato salad been in the sun?"

"Look, lady, I don't want to sound irritable standing over these hot coals or anything, but that little kid over there just ate two pounds of potato salad with his hands, and he seems to be doing okay. So just eat it, okay? What department do you work in anyway?"

"Payroll."

"How would you like your burger?"

Finally, of course, there is the toughest question of all the committee has to solve, which is, besides eating, what are you going to do?

Do?

This is where the softball players take up arms against the

volleyball players, and both of them beat up the horseshoe lovers; where non-athletes gravitate away from athletes, and those with children move away from those without. Where the left-brainers go into planning high gear while the right-brainers get feeling emotionally claustrophobic, and everybody on the committee starts feeling like John Paul Jones, who, as we all recall, was the one who said, "I have not yet begun to fight."

Company picnics are a lot like any other big party, of course. They can succeed or fail due to all types of phenomena you have no control over — inclement weather, weird social interaction, a plague of locusts.

You just never know. So you do the best you can, and then you get out of the way and let the event sort of run itself and hope for the best.

Well actually, not the best.

You don't want the picnic to be too great a success. You don't want everybody raving about what a great job you did.

Not because it's bad for your career or anything, but because starting next month, the boss will be looking for someone to start planning the office Christmas party.

Laser Combat

The voice of our Creative Director, Subcommander Zero, came over the office intercom. "Will everyone who is going into combat please assemble in the briefing room?"

So there it was. It was time. In an hour, we would be going into combat against another advertising agency. Not figurative combat, fighting for an account, but literal combat.

Laser combat.

I wondered: Will I be afraid? Will I panic? Will I be man enough? Will I have nightmares later? Will I suffer Post Laser Quest Stress Syndrome?

Fifteen of us citizen-creative-soldiers gathered around the table.

Subcommander Zero diagrammed the killing ground of Laser Quest. He explained how our strategy was to take the high ground during the first thirty seconds that everyone had before their laser guns were activated, and then shoot down on the other guys from above.

North Idaho Deer Hunting Rules apply: If it moves, shoot it.

It sounded simple enough. We moved out.

We had reserved Laser Quest for three back-to-back sessions, each fifteen minutes long. At Laser Quest, computers track your success; who you shot, who shot you. (Actually, they say "tagged," which is far more politically correct than "shot." Personally, I'd sort of hoped they'd say "wasted." I mean, after all, this was combat wasn't it?)

The first thing we had to do was sign in so the computer knew who you were.

As I got in line to give my name, I suddenly realized that nobody was using their real name.

This wasn't a place for Daniel or Michelle or Doug. It was a place for Bulldog, Speedqueen, T3, El Quervo and Jackal. It was like a cross between being in Top Gun and at a citizen's band radio convention.

I had an immediate identity crisis.

Who was I? Goose? Maverick? No, they were jet jockeys. I tried to think: what was the sergeant's name in the '60s TV show "Combat?" And then I thought, who wants to be Vic Morrow, anyway?

What was the name of the goofy guy in the jungle in Apocalypse Now? I am blank. What was the name of anybody in any war movie?

In all combat, the name means everything. It has to be threatening, but cool. It should imply a slightly crazy, psychotic, or unstable quality. The name "Steve Hasson" came to mind. Then I thought, no, people would just wave at me.

"Grenade," I blurted to the attendant.

So there it was. I was Grenade. I liked it. It said, "Go ahead, pull my pin." Having a macho combat name like Grenade caused me to swagger just a little.

In fact, as everybody signed in, suddenly there was a lot of swaggering going on.

First you go in for a briefing about how the game is played. Each player wears a vest with colored lights on the front, back and shoulders. To score a hit, your laser must hit the lights.

Our team would have all red lights, the other guys, green. Actually, theirs were sort of a pukey, yellowish green. Very wimpy.

I was Grenade. A bomb ready to explode. Yeah. Stay clear, man.

As we suited up, I noticed that the other team had more women than we did.

Fine. If they wanted to play with the big boys, let'em. This was war. There would be no prisoners. No mercy.

The killing ground at Laser Quest is a large wooden maze with ramps on either side leading to a high ground. The maze walls have holes in them that you can shoot through (or be shot through), and there are mirrors above that expose your lights and that the lasers can bounce off of.

If you are killed, uh, wasted, your vest vibrates and your laser goes dead for about five seconds.

Finally, the door opens and we bolt into the maze. It is smokey inside so you can see the track of your laser.

It is also dark. Really dark.

Moving through the maze I immediately get lost.

Could it be my whole team has played Ditch Doug, and I don't know about it? Nah. They wouldn't do that to me. Would they?

My adrenalin is pumping. Finally I find the ramp to the upper level. Like police snipers, we take our positions on the wall.

Suddenly, our vests and guns light up. We are live. This is it.

I take aim at a green light below. Suddenly laser beams from everywhere are shooting at me, and I learn a hard lesson. When you aim, you expose the target lights on your laser gun, so whomever you're shooting at can see you.

My vest shakes.

Dang! I've been in combat exactly 12 seconds, and I'm already dead once. But like the game of cops and robbers we played as kids, I count to five and come back to life again.

Then I get shot again.

I'm beginning to think that I have misnamed myself. A more appropriate name might have been Dead Meat.

At the end of the first game, I am 11th out of 30. Respectable, I think, for a first-timer.

The next game I fall to 15th. My learning curve is either falling behind the others or going the wrong way altogether.

In the third session, I make a critical tactical error. I leave the high ground and enter the lower maze on a search and destroy mission.

"Let's go get'em," I say to a comrade. "Follow me."

He doesn't.

I'm beginning to think my code name is wrong. Maybe it should be Stupid.

As I'm wondering about that in the maze, I suddenly encounter the beautiful and deadly Jezebel.

In the smoke and dark, she looks sort of like Cindy Crawford, but with the psychotic killer mentality of a Dennis Hopper character.

She shoots me like there is no tomorrow. Like I'm every man who has ever done her wrong.

I spend more time dead than alive. Every time I turn around she is there, blowing me away. I try to escape, but the maze keeps feeding back into her sights.

Just about the time being dead starts getting very tiresome, the game ends.

When the scores are shown, Grenade is dead last. 30th out of 30.

Still, it was a lot of fun. As we all left to tell war stories at Birkenbiners, the words of Arnold Schwartzenegger came to me: "I'll be back."

But next time, I'll have a more appropriate name: Target.

The New Power Dressing: Corporate Grunge

We recently made a major agency presentation to one of our clients. They are going through an agency review, where they called in major ad agencies from all over the west coast, and the review committee included people we don't normally deal with on a day-to-day basis.

So we really had to impress them.

We knew it wouldn't be enough just to show them that we had a depth of knowledge about their business. It wouldn't be enough to show them that we could think strategically and globally while employing great creative tactics.

It wouldn't be enough to show them that we were grounded in technobranding expertise and relationship marketing and that we knew what a home page was.

We had to go above and beyond all that. We had to convince them we deserved their three million dollars in billing.

So we pulled out all the stops. We wore <u>suits</u>.

Now, I know what you're thinking, "Wow, man, I hope you didn't have to present on Friday, because Friday is casual day; and nobody, outside of the retentive types who work in the Seafirst Building, wear suits on Friday."

Well, we were in luck: we presented on Thursday, so we got to keep our integrity, such as it is in advertising, intact.

Actually, we used to wear suits around here a lot.

I discovered early on in this business that when you are asking people to trust you with a couple of hundred thousand dollars of their advertising money, it helps if you wear at least a tie.

There is something about handing your ad budget to someone who looks like a hippy fresh from the '60s that makes marketing managers nervous.

"Smedly, there's a homeless person sitting our lobby; get rid of him."

"Oh, that's not a homeless person, sir; that's the creative director from our advertising agency."

"It is? Oh. Well, get rid of him."

So, we wore suits.

But then, several years ago, we decided to make a mini-trend that seemed to be floating around the region our official dress code; that of dressing in jeans on Fridays.

Yeah! Dress down Friday! How cool, how very hip!

It seemed to fit the creative spirit that has to be nurtured in an advertising agency if it is to survive. After all, we don't want people to think we're wound too tight, or they won't think we can be "creative."

Of course, what we didn't think about was that as we were freeing the account executive types from wearing a suit on Friday, we also were liberating the artists and writers from the minimal constraints they were already exercising in their dress code, with the general result being that, as an agency, we free fell from something like "no-tie" day directly to a grunge rock and roll look.

Somehow, when we envisioned a casual dress day, having artists looking like the drummer for Pearl Jam wasn't exactly what we had in mind.

And around here, it wasn't long before everybody conveniently forgot the part about Friday being dress down day, and every day became dress down day.

At first, not wearing a suit and tie was liberating; but having a casual dress day isn't without its problems, as well. Not the least of which is trying to figure out just what does casual look like?

What you learn real quick is wearing a suit is the easiest way to dress for work. After all, even the most style-challenged of us can match up a suit and shirt and tie combination without causing too much visual damage. But when you venture into casual land, the rules get very murky.

For instance, I wore a shirt and tie with my blue jeans the other day to a client meeting. "What is this? The new corporate grunge look?" I was asked. I chose to take it as a compliment.

I mean, does "casual" mean jeans? And does that mean designer jeans or your basic Levi 501s? (As if anybody over forty can fit into 501s anymore).

Or does casual mean stuff from Lamonts? Or Nordstrom? Or The Gap?

It's important, because while I can deal with Lamonts, Nordstrom makes me nervous. And I am not allowed in The Gap without a fashion guide — usually my wife or daughter.

I don't know how it is with the rest of you guys, but for me, a trip to The Gap is a study in patience and humility. My daughter and wife give me a bunch of clothes that look great on The Gap's six-foot, two-inch Italian-looking stud-bucket models.

But when I come out of the dressing room wearing those same clothes, even strangers stand there with their mouths hanging open in something between catatonia and shock, until my daughter renders her studied eighth-grade fashion judgement: "I don't think so, Dad."

For me, visiting The Gap is not the cool experience it seems to be for, say, David Geffen.

There are some advantages to getting more causal at work, however.

Last year, taking a cue from Horizon and Southwest Airlines' summer uniforms, the agency style setters moved boldly into Bermuda shorts. A move that looks and feels, curiously enough, just right for a Spokane advertising agency.

In fact, I was about to adopt the shorts and polo shirt look, when my wife pointed out that all my shorts are athletic shorts, not the cool Horizon Air uniform type shorts, which are pleated and look really good on those six-foot, two-inch, stud bucket airline-type guys.

But she said I should have some of those.

It just takes a trip to The Gap.

I think I'd rather wear a suit.

Manners for Today's Technology

I'm a big fan of Miss Manners.

This is because, like most men, I don't have any. Or, at least, not a full set, if you know what I mean.

I used to blame my parents for this deplorable situation.

"You failed me. I'm not fit to eat in polite society."

"You're not fit to do anything in polite society. We tried to show you how to eat with a fork, but you wouldn't listen."

"What's a fork?"

You see the problem.

Eventually, I stopped blaming my parents for my lack of manners. Instead, I blamed my sex.

"Hey! I'm a man. Real men like eating from a trough more than a plate. It's in my genes."

But now I think that's just a cop out. It's just, well, bad manners.

I can live with that.

But I don't read Miss Manners to figure out how to eat without smearing honey mustard salad dressing from the corners of my mouth to my ears; I'm getting that down.

(My wife thinks the answer is smaller bites; I think it's refining the hand-eye targeting mechanism.)

No. I like Miss Manners because she applies rules of etiquette to the awkward new situations in which we may find ourselves in the 90s, like how to deal with co-workers who wear too much aftershave or perfume.

Her answer? Delicately have a close friend point out that the scent may be stronger than they think. Boy, was I glad to read that, because I used to work with a guy you could smell coming at fifty feet, and my first inclination was always to say, "Holy Moly, you smell like a beta site for the Old Spice company. Go back to smoking; you smelled better."

But the problem is, modern living is moving faster than Miss Manners can keep up with, and there are new situations we encounter that there are no clear manners developed for.

For instance, here's a situation I'm sure we all find ourselves in at some time or another, and often feel we don't know exactly what the appropriate behavior is: I was at Ernst the other day, where the check out lady had a ring through her eyebrow. Now, even though seeing such a thing puts me right into sensory over-load which puts my anal sphincter muscle into spasm and causes my eyes to bulge out, I am sophisticated enough to know that, A) a ring through the eyebrow is not nearly the worst body part you can stick a ring through, and B) a ring through the eyebrow doesn't necessarily mean the person is weird, or anything, or C) she has other rings through other body parts I'm not likely to see, and D) I should plan on doing more shopping at Home Base.

But the question remains: what are good manners in this situation? Are you supposed to look at it? And if you are, are you supposed to pretend it's - well - normal, you know, like an every-day thing, like a ring on the finger? "Wow, nice eyebrow ring. Get that at Mandells?"

Or are you just supposed to ignore it like it isn't there? But if you do that, aren't you defeating the purpose of what that sort of body ornamentation is done for?

I'd sure hate to offend anyone brave enough to puncture their body. Obviously, I need a little help here.

And I don't think I'm the only one.

I mean, technology alone has outpaced our ability to develop appropriate manners for it, and not in just such exalted places as cyberspace or the Internet.

For instance, what do you do when you find out that a co-worker is playing a pornographic CD on their computer, and doing it on company time?

Well, first of all, if it is your company, you fire them. Or pro-mote them, depending upon whether you think they have showed initiative or not.

But if you're just a co-worker what do you do?

"I know I'm not your supervisor, but I'm going to give you two days to get that smut off your computer. But first, download it to mine."

And it doesn't have to be so clearly offensive. How many of us must deal with co-workers playing computer games during work hours? What are appropriate manners there?

This problem is made more complex when they are playing a really cool game, and they play it better than you. Do you politely tell them to get back to work? Or do you get a game lesson and then tell them to get back to work?

Or do you just shut up and mind your own business?

Unfortunately, Miss Manners is silent on the point.

Cellular phones also offer their own little etiquette voids, because some people don't always tell the truth about where they are.

"I can't talk now, honey, I'm in a budget meeting. No, I don't know why it sounds like I'm at the Deja Vu."

Now, even those of us who are manners-challenged know that lying except to save your job, your marriage, make a lot of money or being under oath in a criminal proceeding is never acceptable. But what about being a passive observer to such reprehensible activity?

Do you correct the caller, or ignore the lie?

Hey, it's a problem. Probably depends upon who paid the cover charge at whatever dive you're in at the time.

Well, clearly, there is a need for an updated manners manual to guide us through these confusing times.

In the meantime, does anybody know for sure, if you don't have a salad, do you still start with the little fork on the outside?

Bad Hair Days

One of the ladies I work with is having a bad hair day.

It's her 17th in a row.

Now, I should tell you that she looks great. The only reason you would know she's having a bad hair day is because she keeps announcing it to everyone. It seems that she went to get her hair cut and came back with one side hacked off about three inches shorter than the other.

She says. I can't tell for looking.

But then, I take your basic male approach to haircuts which says the difference between a good haircut and a bad haircut is about three days.

Unless you're the President of the United States, in which case it's three days and about 185 dollars.

Here's a question for you: If you had an unlimited disposable income, would you pay 200 dollars for a haircut? I don't think so. Especially if I had Bill Clinton's hair which looks A) pretty good to begin with, and B) like hair that won't look much different no matter how you cut it.

Is there an ironic twist of fate going on here, with Clinton, of modest means, spending $200 bucks on a haircut, and his political arch rival, Ross Perot, a billionaire, looking like his mother still cuts his hair with hand clippers for free out on the back porch. "There you go, Rossy; now go play in that big pile of money."

Now, if the First Lady spent two hundred dollars on a haircut, I'd be inclined to think it was money well spent.

For all that, if our own city council approved spending 200 dollars on new haircuts for themselves, I'd consider it money well spent.

But why is it we seem to be hung up on bad hair? Why do we only pick on hair when there are so many other things that can go bad on you?

Ties, for instance.

When you go to work today, take a critical look around; and what you'll find is a lot of people having a bad tie day. If you work for the city engineering department, it could be most everybody.

What is it about engineers that make them gravitate to baby blue ties with dark blue and yellow diagonal stripes? And to ties that stop about two buttons up from their belts?

Something in the symmetry of it all, no doubt. It makes you wonder if when they hand out engineering degrees, they also hand out ties from Goodwill.

"Congratulations: Here's your degree. Here's your tie. Go and design great sewers."

But your choices aside, some days your tie just doesn't want to stay tucked up underneath your collar where it belongs, or lie flat on your chest. Clearly, the hallmarks of a bad tie day.

I've noticed that the older I get, the more I'm apt to wake up to find my face is so deeply furrowed that it looks like I've slept on a relief map of the tectonic plates of the Pacific Rim. This could be a bad face day.

I don't know about you, but when I look in the mirror and see a bad face day, I am grateful that I am already married, because I don't think that anybody in a dating situation, seeing my face in the morning, would voluntarily agree to spend the rest of their life with me. It. My face.

For men facing a bad face day, there is only one cure. A shower. If that doesn't return the face to normal, too bad. We just have to go around looking like Merle Haggard all day.

Women, of course, get to put on makeup, which is something of a double edged sword. Done right, makeup can enhance and beautify. Done wrong, and you get a bad makeup day, which can make one look like anything from Raggedy Ann to the child of Morticia and Gomez Addams. "Wow! Nice chin line! And what a lovely color purple your cheekbones are this morning. That color isn't found in nature, is it?"

There are other bad days, some less obvious than bad hair or bad makeup.

Like bad stomach days. These often follow heavy drinking and are sometimes associated with bad head days. When these combine, you almost always get a bad hair, makeup, tie, shirt and socks day going. That's when you show up for work and someone pulls you aside and says, "You look awful," and they mean it as a compliment.

As a writer, I'm here to tell you that we, as a class, often suffer from bad finger days. On those days, we are grateful that we live in a time of word processing and we know the backspace delete key and spell checkers are the true saviors of us all.

And if writers have bad finger days at the word processor, does that mean that Chet Atkins and Itzak Perlman also have bad finger days on their instruments? Probably.

And if they do, do surgeons? "The good news is, I repaired your hernia. The bad news is, I was having a bad finger day, and I slipped and sliced your femoral nerve, which is why you can't feel anything in your right leg. And never will again."

Radio and television announcers have bad mouth days where the lips and tongue just don't seem to want to cooperate with one another. When that happens, we all sound like Elmer Fudd.

All of these, of course, originate from bad brain days. "This is your brain. This is your brain on a bad brain day. Notice how it looks a lot like scrambled eggs." I figure the president was having a bad brain day when he paid $200 for his haircut.

Let's just hope he doesn't have too many of those.

How to Be the Perfect Employee

Have you ever wondered if maybe Shakespeare didn't get it right, and that when Julius Caesar said to Brutus, "Et tu, Brutus," that maybe, just maybe, before he stabbed him, Brutus said, "Hey, I'm sorry Caesar, but we're downsizing here. We're eliminating one whole supervisory level of government. Yours."

Just wondering.

Of course, stabbing your boss to death is kind of a severe way to force early retirement on someone; but you have to assume that the early Romans were just finding their way through all this new management stuff.

Fortunately for us, we live in a kinder, gentler time, where, except for in the U.S. Post Office, killing everybody you work with as a labor relations tool is frowned upon.

What's great about working during this time are the wonderful words we are inventing to help us understand it.

Words like "downsizing."

Doesn't that have a nice ring to it? So much more pleasant

and easy to say than its older verbal cousin, "layoffs," or its crotchety old grandfather, "you're fired."

You know how today you're trying to explain to your children what a hippie was? Well, someday, if we live long enough, our great, great grandchildren will ask us, "Grandpa, you were around in the '90s; what was 'downsizing'?" And we can say, "It meant you got laid off. Permanently. About the same as being fired. Except in those days, before the Great Lawyer Purge, you couldn't be fired; because if you got fired, you got to sue, because the lawyers had us all convinced we weren't responsible for anything."

And the word I heard the other day: deselection.

You know how you can be selected? The opposite of that used to be rejected, but that's so harsh.

Plus, it's not quite right.

Rejected comes with a whole truckload of negative emotional baggage that really has no place in business.

So they've invented a new word. Now you can be "deselected." You're not being rejected, you're being un-chosen. There now, doesn't that make you feel better?

One can only hope that this new business language makes it into the dating lexicon: "Gee, I heard Suzie broke up with you."

"No, she was downsizing her relationships and I was deselected."

"Yeah, that happens to me a lot, too."

All of this, of course, is tied to re-engineering, which is to the '90s what searching for excellence was to the '80's. If you look it up in the dictionary, it says, "The rebuilding of a corporate structure from the vantage point of new paradigms that generally does not include you. See SEP and RIF."

Now the question is, if you're a man, how do you survive this frenzy of re-engineered downsizing deselection?

Assuming, of course, that you want to, which is a whole other commentary.

How do you become the perfect employee — the one who, when push comes to shove, nobody wants to deselect?

Well, assuming you don't work for the county where one employee told me their motto is, "We don't care because we don't have to," or for STA where their new motto is, "Budget? What budget?" (It used to be, "Ride with us," as in, "You're 12 million dollars over budget and that's before the bamboo trees arrived!" "Yeah, well, ride with us on this, will you? Ride with us." Or in academia where they have this thing called tenure, and all this re-engineering stuff is amusingly academic — you do the dishes.

Say what?

You do the dishes.

You know, in the office kitchen that everybody uses but nobody likes to clean, and where there is that sign that says your mother doesn't work here and a duty roster of whose job it is this week to load the dishwasher and clean the place that everybody ignores, and where the office refrigerator that hasn't been cleaned or defrosted in a decade lives, and giardia and other water-borne diseases thrive?

Do the dishes. Make it your domain. Make it sparkle.

I know; some of you are saying, what about working long hours and doing a good job? To which I say, get real. When has doing a good job ever equated with job security?

And I know that some of you recalcitrant macho types are saying "Real men don't do the dishes."

Bad attitude. Worse, wrong attitude.

In the first place, just where do you think most of the deselection is going to come from? The bottom of the corporate food chain where bodies are cheap, or the middle where they're not?

And in the second place, don't you think that there are likely to be some women on the deselection committee? Women who might look at a man who does the dishes and cleans the kitchen as a corporate asset? A keeper? Let me put it another way: In the re-engineered world, real men get deselected.

"We have to choose between Bill and George. Both are supervisors who have outlived their corporate usefulness. Which one goes?"

"Well, I would hate to lose George because he cleans the kitchen and does the dishes everyday."

"He does?"

"Yes."

"The dishes? Hmmm. Well, certainly we don't want to lose a man who does the dishes ... "

"The problem with George is, he hasn't done a lick of work in three years, he dresses awful, and he has a hairy back that's gross to look at at the company picnic, he's overpaid and he costs the company a fortune in accrued benefits."

"Still, if he does the dishes…"

You see what I mean. We're talking product differentiation here, and you're the product. I mean, who would you chose?

Now you're probably wondering, is doing the dishes and being a perfect employee a guarantee of job security in this time of re-engineering and downsizing?

Well, no.

But it can't hurt, and the training you get might come in handy for your next job.

MOONING IN MOSCOW AND OTHER POLITICALLY INCORRECT MEANDERINGS

Third Floor Mooning at the University of Idaho

Once in a great while, once in a millennium, events take place that make us all witnesses to history.

We watch, awestruck, as events unfold.

You can tick these momentous events off on one hand. The explosion of a supernova; The Emancipation Proclamation; Crick and Watson's discovery of the DNA double Helix; the lawsuit of Jason Wilkins.

Jason is suing the University of Idaho for negligence because he hurt himself when he fell through a third story window while mooning the people below.

Well, okay; maybe a mooning lawsuit isn't in the category of a supernova blowing itself into interstellar bits, but you know what I mean, this is big stuff.

Now, for those of you who attended college before the 1960s and may not know, I suppose I should explain that mooning is the act of dropping your pants and showing someone your bare butt.

Anatomically speaking, the amount of rump exposed is about the same as what you would see on a beach with someone wearing a thong bikini, sometimes referred to as butt floss.

The difference is mooning is not done on a beach, where it might just masquerade as a fashion statement; it is done somewhere else.

Anywhere else.

Like out a car window at a stop light, or while passing a bus load of senior citizens on their way to Winnemucca to do a little gambling. Or my favorite, at a party, when the right combination of beer and illicit drugs makes everybody spontaneously burst into a refrain of Blue Moon, and down go the pants.

Prior to Mr. Wilkins ill-fated mooning, the risks of mooning were two: one was that if you were still of dating age and you exposed your butt, the women present might decide that your butt, in the flesh as it were, wasn't suitably cute enough to justify a dating relationship; and two, if in the act of dropping or raising trou (as the phrase goes) you inadvertently exposed the opposite side of your body, you could be arrested for indecent exposure, and be forced to post a sign outside your home for the rest of your life, stating you were a sexual pervert and warning little children to stay away.

What Mr. Wilkins did, according to the report in the paper, is to climb up on a heater at a third floor window and attempt to moon the people below, when he fell through the window.

Right now, if you are somewhere where you can see a third story window, I want you to imagine falling out of it, backwards, with your pants around your knees!

It staggers the imagination!

What goes through your mind?

Do you think, "Gee, I sure hope there's a Tri-Delt watching."

Or are you more pragmatic. "Well, I've got a few seconds before I hit terminal velocity, so maybe I'll just pull my pants up."

Or are you furiously swatting away the shards of glass that are falling with you, and praying that none of them land <u>under</u> you and puncture your aorta when you hit?

I myself would be thinking, "This is not at all what I had in mind."

Now, I know that some of you older mooners out there are sniffing that mooning in its purest form is never done against glass, and therefore, the whole event is bogus.

And to you I say: You miss the point!

Because, up to now, this event would merely be material for the Guinness Book of World Records (highest fall from a broken window while mooning: Jason Wilkins, Moscow, Idaho, 1994) except that he is suing the University for negligence and not properly supervising the residents.

Meaning himself!

Yes! It's almost like suing your parents because your IQ isn't high enough!

And he didn't even have to leave Moscow, Idaho to get an attorney!

I'll bet his attorney is thumbing his nose at all the big guys at Winston & Cashatt right now. "We'll see who makes new law. Let's see: A third of $940,000 dollars is ... well, my secretary can figure it out later."

This is landmark stuff. If you're sober and not responsible, (as opposed to drunk and tumbling out windows, another U of I student proclivity) then what isn't possible? The fundamental nature of college changes. You don't go to college to party and get a degree — you go to party until you hurt yourself so you can sue the school!

This is an aside, but if I were an attorney in Moscow, I'd be making sure that a tour of my offices was part of every student's orientation to the University.

"Hi, welcome to the University of Idaho. If you do anything really, really stupid in the next four years and fall out of a window because of it, give me a call. It could be very, very profitable for both of us."

Given the sorts of students who seem to migrate to the University of Idaho, I might even give third floor tours.

"Can we stay in a group please? You'll notice that below all these third floor windows, there are nicely tended shrubs that can help break just about any fall, so a fall out of these is worth about $900,000. Up ahead we have a fire escape that you could get drunk and fall off of, and of course, the roof is always an option. Survive this and it's good for at least three million, of which, naturally, I get to keep one million."

Now, I know that some of you are writing letters to the editor of the paper and whining about the fact that Mr. Wilkins should take responsibility for his actions and not blame the University, but lets face it, where is the money in that?

I mean, you can't take personal responsibility to Safeway and buy any groceries with it, can you? I find the whole thing inspiring.

As a parent with a child who, in a few years, will be heading off to college, it has certainly been a lesson for me.

The lesson is I'm sending my daughter to Whitworth.

Clichemongering, and Wavemongering Your Way Into Political Office

I don't know about you, but I am always sorry to see the primary election come and go.

This is because, the primary is full of candidates who, I think, probably woke up one day and said, "Hey, Honey, I think I'll run for the city council," or "Gee, I'm not doing anything this week; maybe I'll spend 20 grand or so and see if I can get elected to, um, City Treasurer. Yeah! Treasurer." To which the spouse probably replied, "That's nice dear, just be sure you call if you're going to be late for dinner."

Now, tell the truth: Haven't you sat and watched the city council meetings on channel five and watched the city council members sit in those nice cushy chairs while concerned citizens stand at the microphone and talk about who knows what, and thought to yourself, "I could do that. I could sit in those chairs and stay awake as well as those guys."

Sure you have. We all have. So we all know, at least a little, that tug to sit in the cushy chair.

Personally, I'm not sure that being on the city council would be worth giving up "Monday Night Football" and "Blossom," but then, I've never been accused of being overly civic minded, either.

But generally, it's not too hard to understand when some ordinary citizen decides he wants to be the new Jack Hebner or Orville Barnes. Or Mike Brewer.

The truly struck want to be the new Shari Barnard. What the heck, if you're jumping in, why not jump in all the way. Be Mayor!

The reason the primary is so fun is that all these people need to gain name recognition, and the only way to do this is to make your name stand out from the rest, which is why primary candidates are so inclined to employ the ancient political art of "clichemongering."

Now, a lot of you think that clichemongering is a bad thing because it sounds very much like rumormongering and fishmongering, both of which leave a bad smell behind. But in fact, clichemongering is the great grandfather of the sound bite, and we all know how highly regarded that is in American politics.

The first thing a new candidate must learn about chichemongering is constitutional guarantees notwithstanding, all cliches are not created equal. There is a sort of hierarchy at work that you will have to master.

The first rule is, you generally don't want a cliche that invites a question. For instance, this year, one of the candidates said, "I'm the one who will put more cops on the beat." Now, on the surface, that looks like everything you would want in a cliche: a strong take-no-prisoners kind of statement.

Wrong. It invites the question, yeah how you going to do that? Walk into the police station with a riding crop and beat on desks? "You! Outside. You there at the typewriter, stop what you're doing and go arrest a drug pusher! You with the donut, go find a burglar or something. Oh, excuse me, Chief Mangan."

Plus, that kind of clichemongering doesn't tie the cliche to the candidates name (witness the fact that I can't remember who said it), so it's really a wasted effort.

Another great cliche that I always eagerly await is "Give the government back to the people."

Again, this has a nice appeal. A sort of salt-of-the-earth approach. None of this professional politician stuff. This is often used by candidates who seem to feel that they shouldn't be seen in a tie. Either that, or they just don't own one.

The problem with this cliche is A) This is an election, not the French revolution, and B) I think I can speak for The People when we say, we don't want the government back. If we did, we'd attend more city council meetings.

After all, our local elections have less to do with taking the government back from some sort of mythical political aristocracy than with what poor shmuck we're going to give it to next.

There are some tried and true cliches: "Experienced, Dedicated." And one of my favorites: "I will work for you," and, "Vote for me for a more responsive city government."

I've heard that before.

A good clichemonger will always thank their family and supporters, even though the former probably has no choice and the latter, it usually turns out in the primary, are non-existent.

Well, thanks anyway.

So what is a new candidate to do if not resort to cliche campaign themes?

Well, wavemongering is one possibility, although I wouldn't recommend it. Wavemongering is where the political candidate stands on a busy corner and waves to all the passing motorists, showing at once that he is both normal and will stoop to any level to get a vote. This campaign tactic was made popular by Steve Hasson, and then promptly improved upon by the savvy beggar class who sport signs that say "will work for food."

Instead of waving, which, at the very least, implies that the best we can hope from a candidate is a lame imitation of Steve Hasson, I'd at least advise candidates to stand there stoically with a sign that says, "Will work for your vote."

What I'd really like to see someone say is "I want to be elected because I need the job," but I suppose that's too much to ask.

When all is said and done, I doubt that most clichemongering really works anyway. After all, we are an upscale and informed electorate. We know the issues, and we do not elect those who simply mouth the most cliches.

Not at all.

We vote for the candidate with the most yard signs.

The Strangeness of Being Older Than The President

So. We finally have our rock-and-roll President.

And I am now one of the many millions of Americans who is suddenly older than the President of the United States. Not a lot older, but older, just the same.

And personally, I think it's kind of weird.

Because for the first time in my life, I can relate to the man in the job.

For the first time in my life, it's not a job held by someone clearly older and wiser in the ways of the world like some benevolent grandpa type. Now it's held by someone who might just hold cabinet meetings with Marvin Gaye singing "What's Goin' On?" in the background. Someone whose influences in life can't be all that much different from my own.

Even though he says he didn't inhale.

What's weird is until January 20th, I never knew how much I liked my President filling a parental role. How comforting it is. Now my president fills what might be called a little brother role. This does not make me feel better. (Does the image of giving the President a "noogie" come to mind?)

Of course, if I live long enough, maybe the President will fill a child role. I can already guess how I'll feel about that.

Your discomfort is all part of aging, you say. Maybe, but I don't think so.

You see, it doesn't bother me anymore when I go into McDonald's and everybody working there is younger than I am, and they all call me "sir," not because they have to because it's company policy, but because their mothers taught them to call everybody old "sir" out of respect; and it doesn't bother me when

I go to the doctor and find out that the person who is going to open me up and repair one of my malfunctioning internal parts is only a little older than Doogie Houser, because I figure if Doogie The Surgeon sees something in there he hasn't encountered before, he will ask for advice from somebody older and more experienced. ("Uh, call old Doc Jenkins and see if he's ever seen an organ that looks like a bullfrog where the spleen should be, and ask him if I'm supposed to take it out or what.")

But whom does a President ask?

Hmmm.

When the President is as old as George Bush or Ronald Reagan, I automatically figure they're supposed to know all that President stuff. By virtue of their age, they're supposed to know what to do to fix the country. Never mind that there may be all kinds of evidence to the contrary.

But having a President that is younger than me is kind of strange, because, all of a sudden, the President of the United States is no longer older and wiser; now the President is just the same, even if he is smarter. And if there is one thing that I know about people my age, I know that sometimes, not always, but sometimes, we're still faking it.

Ah. It finally comes out.

Now, I'm not looking for a show of hands or anything, but don't you fake it sometimes?

Yeah, sure you do.

We all do. Somebody asks you a question that you think you should know the answer to but you don't, and the next thing you know, you're out there winging it — making it up as you go along.

You'd think that by our forties, we'd know what we're supposed to know, but we don't always, so we fake it. And if you and I are faking it at our age, why should we think he's not faking it — when he's younger?

The dilemma is I know that inventing it as he goes along is what we pay him to do. For that matter, it's what we pay all our chief executives to do.

I'm just not sure I like <u>knowing</u> it; I think I liked it better

thinking the President was old enough to have all the answers —
sort of like Walter Cronkite.

What I'm experiencing is nothing that millions upon millions of Americans have not experienced before me, of course.
Everybody, if they live long enough, someday gets to be older
than the President of the United States and must experience the
same sort of feelings.

(It is odd how one's perspective changes: now I know what
they were talking about when Kennedy became President — being
so young and all. Although with me being 14 at the time, Kennedy
certainly seemed old enough to me.)

But this is the baby boomer President. This guy is not quite
my age. This guy is from the "Bummer, man" generation.

"Mr. President, the economy is in the toilet."

"Wow, bummer, man. Let's get Michael Jackson to hold a
concert and we'll call it, like, Economy Aid. Maybe Willy Nelson
will show up."

Of course, the President always has lots of advisors around
him, but except for Lloyd Bentson, most of Clinton's advisors
look like their first reaction to bad news would be "Wow, bummer, man," as well.

I wonder why I didn't think of all this before the election?

Not that it would have made any difference.

It was time for a change.

There's a saying that goes, "Be careful what you ask for because you just might get it." Well, I'm in the generation that,
through demonstrations and political activism, has long told the
world that it should be running things.

Well, now we'll see, won't we?

So I hope the President does a good job.

Or at the very least, fakes it as well as his predecessors.

Being a Workin' Man

I don't know about you, but I am really glad to see the NAFTA debate come to a vote.

I was glad to see it end partly because I am a firm believer that there are certain things that we, the public, are probably better off not seeing.

And how the political system actually works is one of them.

We all know that in Congress, to get anything you want you may have to give something: "Okay, lemme get this straight. You gonna vote for my 250 miles of 49-foot high Mississippi levee at seven billion, and I'm gonna vote to extend the Interstate highway system from Spokane to a place called Pullman so folks can get to something called the Apple Cup sooner. I got that right?"

Politics is a little like embalming. We all know it works, and we all know what it does, but that doesn't mean we all want to see it actually happen.

But the real reason I am glad to see the NAFTA debate end is I was getting real tired of hearing about "the working man." Especially when I discovered, about halfway through the debate, that, in spite of holding a job most of my adult life, when they were talking about "the working people of America," they weren't talking about me!

You get paid, Doug, but you don't 'work', was how it was inelegantly explained.

"Hmmm. Exactly wrong on both points," I thought to myself.

I wanted to say, "You face a blank sheet of paper in a typewriter, knowing that whatever you write on it will eventually be on television, radio, or newspaper and be read over and over by hundreds of thousands of people who will all share an opinion of it (and you), based on what you've written, and see how many pounds you sweat off in an hour."

But I didn't.

And as for being paid, have you ever seen how the reporters at the Spokesman-Review dress? You can't just chalk that up to an accident of fate. Writers, as a class, suffer a serious case of disposable income deprivation.

But, I realize I'm splitting semantic hairs.

You're a working man or you're not. And I'm not.

But at least I'm not alone.

Who else doesn't qualify? Most everybody, when you get right down to it.

I would say that teachers, don't qualify, for instance.

Now, I know that you teachers are saying, "What! I come home every day with something that resembles Stouffer's Mashed Potatoes where my brain should be after facing six classes a day of 30 kids each, any one of whom just might be packing a gun, and not one of whom has the slightest interest in learning what a dangling participle is, and you say I'm not a working person? Besides, what about all my NEA dues?"

Sorry. To be a working person, I think you have to get dirty. And you have to have tools.

That means we can eliminate everybody in the health care field, beginning with administrators, doctors, nurses, and ending with everybody in the insurance industry.

There's probably a surgeon somewhere high-fiving an anesthesiologist saying, "Yeah! We work with tools, we're working men!"

Wrong.

We are not talking about little itty-bitty tools like scalpels and suture needles and cauterizing guns here. We're talking about big tools. Like jack hammers and torque wrenches. So unless you repair a hernia with chain saw, you don't qualify.

And anesthesiologists? "Is the IV in? OK, I'm going to turn this valve, and the patient will go nighty-night. That'll be 800 bucks please."

Definitely not. You're just not who they're talking about when they invoke the noble image of "The American working man."

This is not to imply that you have to have a high income to be bumped out of the category. (The teachers are over in the corner grumbling, "You're telling me.") People like waiters don't make it either. ("Hi, I'm, Jeremy. I'll be your waiter tonight." "Hi Jeremy, I'm Doug. I'll be doing the eating.") This, in spite of the fact that most people in the food service industry work for minimum wage, lousy tips and go home dead tired.

Who else? Well, I think we can eliminate artists, photographers, bankers, accountants, stockbrokers, all sales people, everybody in marketing, engineering, and all lawyers right off the bat.

So who are the working people?

I think we can all agree that truckers are working people. Anybody immortalized by Dave Dudley in "Six Days On The Road and I'm A-Gonna Make It Home Tonight" certainly qualifies. Although, I'm not sure why truckers are when airline pilots aren't.

Maybe it's an altitude thing.

Naturally, anybody who works with a shovel qualifies as a bona fide workin' man.

(Those of you who are asking, "Hey, I put in my own sprinkler system last year; does that mean I qualify?" Forget it.)

To be a working man, you've got to build something or weld something or work on a machine. And I'm not talking about some pantywaist machine like a computer, I mean a real machine, like a bulldozer or a lathe. Something that you get real dirty working with.

Carpenters are working people, although I think the new class of air-driven tools where they don't pound — so much as shoot — houses together puts them at risk of losing that title.

I think the main definition of a working man is you're a working man if Congress feels compelled to protect you.

It's been a couple of weeks now, and I'm getting over the disappointment of finding out I'm not really a working man. But I have to admit, it's not all bad.

After all, if I'm not a working man, I may not know precisely what I am, but, at least I'm in pretty good company.

Except, of course, for another group of nonworkin' men: Congress

PhotoRoboCop

I believe it was Robert Frost who first observed, "Something there is in nature that doesn't like a camera giving speeding tickets."

Or was it Ansel Adams?

Well, it doesn't matter.

The point is, the city didn't get a huge grant, and now we are not going to enjoy the obvious benefits of Photo-radar.

Photo radar is that perfect marriage of technology wherein a camera is wired up to a radar gun, set up on a street, and it takes pictures of speeding motorists.

Sort of a cross between RoboCop and Candid Camera: PhotoRoboCop.

I think there are some obvious benefits to photo-radar. The main one being if you're speeding, it may be because you need to get somewhere in a hurry; and with photo radar, you get to get there, instead of wasting more time as one of our local policepersons stops you and goes through the whole ticket drill.

"Can I see your license, automobile registration, proof of insurance, tire-tread caliper test results, most recent blood test, birth certificate or photo facsimile thereof, and proof of citizenship? Would you take it out of your wallet, please? Thank you. Mr. Hurd, were you aware you were doing 57 in a 20?"

"Gosh, no, officer; I wondered why I went up on two wheels around that last corner. I thought I just needed new shocks. Guess I'd better get this speedometer checked. I'll do that right away."

"Uh, huh. These are new boots I'm wearing, Mr. Hurd, so if you don't mind, before they get completely covered, I'll just write the ticket."

With photo radar, this little social transaction, which can be very damaging to your self-esteem, is gone.

Instead, you get a letter.

"Dear Mr. Hurd:

"How, you doing? We have a little problem down here at the city. Wonder if you could come down and talk to us about it. Seems our little radar-robo-cam picked you up doing 57 in a 20. Didn't seem possible, so we checked our gear. But there you are, looking like an F16 flying low on Northwest Boulevard at 0800 hours. If coming down is a drag, why don't you just send us your $138 fine and we'll call the whole thing square. We take cash, checks and all major credit cards. Sincerely, Your Police Department. P.S. Don't make us come after you."

Now, I ask you? Isn't that a lot more civilized than having a personal confrontation thing with a live officer?

Oh, sure, civil libertarians have their noses out of joint about it because somebody, someday will get a ticket in the mail and in it will be a picture of somebody in the car who shouldn't be. "Dear, you got a ticket in the mail today. It seems you were speeding down Division while some woman was kissing you on the neck. Who was she? Anybody I know?"

But hey! Those things are going to happen.

And the police PR department says they would only be placed in areas where there is a high incidence of traffic accidents. Right.

If I had this little unmanned money-maker, I wouldn't put it where accidents happen, I'd put it where people speed the most. In what the police call their cabbage patches. The places they go hang out when they need to write a bunch of tickets.

And as soon as I had one paid for, I'd get another and another until I had PhotoRoboCops monitoring the whole city.

And pretty soon, I'd have enough money to solve the real traffic problem in Spokane, which isn't people speeding, its the way everybody feels compelled to run red lights.

PhotoRoboCop would develop into VideoRoboCops, and we could mount them on every traffic light in town. They would come with basic military-industrial complex target acquisition hardware that would home in on cars entering the intersection after three seconds of yellow.

There you'd be: dashing through a red light, cars coming the other way screeching to a halt, pedestrians diving for the sidewalk, and your face would be captured in that little targeting square we came to know and love so well during Desert Storm, saying "Out of my way, I'm coming through!"

Now, in as much as everybody seems to ignore red lights in this town, I'd have a three-for-one sale on running red lights tickets at first, where you get to run three lights before you get one ticket.

If you didn't, there would be a rash of rear-end accidents, with people getting out of their cars yelling stuff like, "What are you doing stopping for a red light like that, you moron?"

But eventually, VideoRoboCop would capture every red light offense and beam it by microwave to traffic ticket central where a steady stream of letters with fines would go out, and bad drivers and the colorblind would send back huge fines supporting the whole endeavor.

As computers kept track of the worst offenders — the people who are congenital speeders and red light runners — new targeting information about them could be fed to the cameras, and little message boards could be mounted on the stop lights, and drivers could be ordered to get out of their cars and lie spread-eagled on the ground until an available officer could be dispatched to come by to arrest them.

And if they resisted, the system could fire little heat seeking missiles up their tailpipes…Adios, red light runner!

I get a little excited about the possibilities.

But, it is not to be.

The grant the city needs to start PhotoRoboCop didn't come through. I'm sure that, like me, you're very disappointed.

Oh, well. Maybe Robert Frost was right, after all. Maybe there is something in nature that doesn't like a camera giving speeding tickets.

Or was it Ansel Adams?

Finding New Tax Revenues

The city council is looking for new things to tax. They need more money.

Well, who doesn't?

They have proposed licensing cats, which I find odd, because no one ever really owns a cat. The best you can hope for is a shared residence and a mutually agreed upon living arrangement.

The problem is, the city council is just not being creative about this taxation thing.

They seem to be looking only at the revenue-raising side of the tax equation. They need to look at the behavioral side. This is the real heart and soul of taxation. It's what all of our loopholes are based on — modifying people's behavior by modifying the tax code.

You want businesses to invest in new equipment? Give them an investment tax credit. Want people to buy homes and spur the economy? Give a tax break for home mortgage interest.

Smoking is bad. Put a hefty tax on those things. Make those smokers pay through the nose for hurting themselves.

Same thing with Gin. Drinking is a marginal moral activity, so tax it. Make it expensive enough so people don't do a lot of it.

That's the theory, at least. It doesn't seem to work too well in practice.

So, how can we make the city a better place to live? Let's look around and see what behaviors we'd like to modify through taxation. What can we tax that will raise a lot of money and simultaneously make Spokane a better place to live?

I think we can all agree that one of the first places we could raise a lot of money is by taxing bad haircuts.

You don't have to be Vidal Sassoon to know that Spokane has more than its share of bad haircuts running around. And taxing bad haircuts would have the social benefit of making everyone look more like young Republicans than someone who got in a fight with a berserk Marine Corps barber with cordless clippers.

And wouldn't that be nice?

We would have hair cops. Hair cut tax collectors. They could be stationed right at places like Supercuts and collect the tax right on the spot, like sales tax. "Let's see, tax on three scalp grooves cut above the ear is eight dollars a groove. Only doing it on one side? Bad symmetry: $10 surtax. Oh, You want to carve a dirty word into the back of your hair? That's an additional $52."

When Michael Bolton comes to town, we could tax him for his hair before he sings. I think we can all agree that anybody who wears their hair like a balding Amy Irving deserves the maximum tax.

You're probably thinking, isn't a bad haircut kind of a subjective thing?

Not really, I think we all know ugly hair when we see it. But even so, that's no big deal. The property assessors routinely go out and place a value on your home for taxation, and that's pretty arbitrary. The assessors are running seven years behind schedule, but that's another commentary.

What about wigs and toupees? A bad wig counts as a bad haircut. Unless you wear it on TV. Then it gets taxed as the Mother Of All Bad Haircuts. Bald people pay nothing. They suffer enough.

What I like about taxing bad haircuts is we don't know which members of the city council have cats. But we do know which ones have bad haircuts.

We'll see how they vote when it's obvious they're going see their taxes going up.

See how easy this is?

What other behavior do we want to modify?

It is so obvious.

What is the most universal New Year's resolution? Yep. Lose weight.

Everybody wants to lose weight. Jenny Craig is getting rich off people who want to lose weight. Let's help those people! Let's tax them!

I just have to believe that if the city taxed that portion of your weight that went off the top of the chart, we'd modify lots of behavior.

If you knew that once a year you were going to have to go down to City Hall for a weigh-in, think you'd stick to your diet? We could weigh in at the same time as we get our license tabs.

"Would you step on the scales, please? Whoa, you're a little porko, aren't you, Mr. Hurd? Well, all those Domini's sandwiches are going to cost you, let's see, $346 in the city fat tax."

We're out of shape. Out of shape people have more heart attacks.

Health care costs skyrocket for heart patients with bypasses and replacements. ("Shopping for a new heart, are we? Here's a nice one that right up until yesterday belonged to a non-smoking, non-drinking marathon runner who liked to ride his motorcycle without a helmet. It can be yours, installed, for just $300,000 dollars. Pain medication not included.") Cutting health care costs is a big deal. When we weigh in and get our hair checked for the uglies, we could do a quick treadmill test and be taxed on our degree of failure.

At first, the city would be swimming in money. (After all, how many people do you know who are slim, in shape and have a good haircut?)

But in a year or two, we'd figure out that getting in shape and losing weight would cut our tax bill, and pretty soon, we'd all be svelte and healthy and have beautiful hair (or be bald) and run marathons every other Sunday. And we wouldn't care about the taxes on that stuff because we wouldn't have to pay it.

And as we got healthy and the tax base dwindled, the city council could get really creative and decide to tax stupid ideas, because there's a lot of those and they don't do anybody a lot of good.

And if the city council taxed stupid ideas, eventually, we would eliminate stupid ideas. And I think we would all agree that would be wonderful.

The only question is who on the city council would pay the tax on the idea to license cats?

The Problem with Licenses

One of the really great things about being in advertising is you don't have to have a license to do it.

You have to have a business license, but not a professional license.

This is both good and bad.

On the one hand, it is good because one day you can be unemployed, have terrible self-esteem problems, bad credit and a failing marriage, and the next day you can declare yourself an advertising professional (or, if you wish, an actual advertising agency) and like magic, you are no longer unemployed.

And now that you are an employed professional, you will no longer have self-esteem problems. You will still have bad credit and a failing marriage, but that's normal for advertising people.

It's bad because anybody can do it. In fact, most advertising agencies are formed by media sales people who get tired of hawking commercials and decide to declare themselves ad agencies.

And because there is no license, you don't have to take a test or anything.

It's a curious little void in the vast licensing authority of our government.

Now, not all professions are so lucky.

Some professions that you wouldn't think would need licenses do.

I was watching television last night and saw a commercial for (I think) the North Idaho Denture Clinic.

This is the commercial that shows, in vivid close up photography, actual dentures being made — something I, personally, can live without, especially during the dinner hour when it seems to run a lot. The commercial shows what appears to be a perfectly healthy set of teeth and gums (minus the skull) being ground into shape on the kind of grinding wheel my father used to sharpen his favorite chisels on. While gum-colored plastic is flying everywhere, the soothing announcer tells us that not only is the price right, but every set is made by a licensed denturist.

Well, that makes me feel better.

Of course, I supposed that it is possible that "licensed denturist" is another way of saying "Not a dentist" in the same way that saying "nurse anesthetist" is a way of saying, "not a doctor."

Advertising isn't the only profession that doesn't require a license.

Many of you are probably wondering why Randy Shaw, the Q6 News Anchorman didn't have his News Anchorman License suspended when he recently went public with the news that he might run against Tom Foley for Congress, which also doesn't require a license.

Well, he might have, except there is no such thing as a news anchorman license.

Now, I know what you're thinking. "What! You mean that any nitwit can get on TV and feed me the news?"

Sure: Look at Q6.

For that matter, look at the newspaper. Like marketing consultants, journalists are not licensed.

The thing is, the government can't quite figure out what licenses are all about.

In some instances, like a driver's license or a pilot's license, it's a quality control issue. A license is supposed to indicate some sort of quantifiable skill level. If someone has a pilot's license, it says they are trained to fly an airplane and you are safe riding with them.

Unfortunately, the license doesn't work that way. I know. I've got one, and I sure wouldn't go fly with me. But I've got that license.

Today, drivers often go through Driver's Ed., get a learner's permit, and then get their driver's license.

That makes a certain amount of sense.

But does that happen when you get your fishing license? No.

I think our government is really failing us here.

You just can't look at the pictures of all those couples getting married in the paper each day and not help but think that if our government required a learner's permit before the marriage license was issued, some of those people wouldn't be getting married.

"Susan, you passed your marriage license test, but Harold, I'm afraid you failed Employability, Responsibility, Basic Communication and the Household Tasks section. Frankly Harold, I don't think you're qualified for a marriage license, and you really ought to graduate from high school first. You'll have to take the test again in six weeks. In the meantime, Susan, you have your marriage license, and if you find someone else with one, you're free to marry."

And while we're on the subject, have you ever wondered why if you have to get a license to be married, you don't have it revoked when you get divorced? I mean, why is somebody twice divorced? Why aren't they twice revoked?

With a license the implication is you must know something about what you're licensed for. And that's not always true.

Ask anyone who has ever had a home built or a remodelling job done, and they will tell you that you should never confuse "licensed and bonded," with, "competent and timely."

Not the same thing. Not the same thing at all.

And witness the ubiquitous business license.

Anyone can get one. Of course, a business license doesn't really mean you know anything about business; it just means the city knows who you are and expects to see some quarterly tax money.

I probably should have mentioned that when you decide one morning that instead of being unemployed, you're going to be an advertising agency (or its uptown snooty cousin — a "marketing consultant"), the lady at city hall who actually gives you the license gives you that sweet, neutral smile reserved for the mentally incompetent and soon to be bankrupt. Because she knows that as a class, people in advertising tend to know less about running a business than any other group.

Perhaps a learner's permit for a business license would be a good thing.

So, what's to be done?

Should we license TV anchormen?

Absolutely.

Should we license politicians?

Yes. Instead of term limits we could just indefinitely suspend their licenses.

Should we license advertising and marketing professionals?

Gee, I wouldn't go that far.

Finding Politically Correct School Mascots

We live in a truly amazing and enlightened time.

Just think about it. At a time when Bosnians are slaughtering Serbs and Serbs are shelling Croate villages and Floridians have declared open season on any European in a rented car, and everybody else is talking about universal health care, the Washington Board of Education wants to ban school mascots that might offend somebody.

In fact, according to an article in last weekend's Spokesman-Review, Bob Eaglestaff, the Principal of the American Indian Heritage School in Seattle, wants a law against Indian logos and mascots.

Well.

I think that we, the KPBX audience, are certainly well read and educated enough to know which way the politically correct wind is blowing, and being politically correct, we would all agree that any school mascot or name that gives offense to any person's heritage or race should be struck down like some sort of rabid cur.

This, even though, according to the article, there are many

schools with actual Native American populations who think their Indian-type mascots conjure up nobility and honor and something to be admired.

Wellpinit, for example.

But no matter. Some people are offended, and we wouldn't want that, would we?

There is one thing that bothers me, though.

Why are the Native Americans in this matter not extending their influence to the other downtrodden races and peoples who, by their definition, must also be mightily offended by being school mascots?

How can we even think about being politically correct to one group, without supporting the struggles of all groups?

Well, the short answer is, you can't.

So the proposal to ban or outlaw Indian mascots clearly does not go far enough.

For instance, I don't think we can any longer tolerate the Ferris High School Saxons. The people of Saxony, not to mention all people of Anglo-Saxon descent, will not be reduced to school mascots.

Shadle Park Highlanders? Gotta change. Wouldn't want to offend any people with Scottish blood. It's bad enough that the Scottish people had to endure the whole Mary Queen of Scots thing not to mention winding up as a high school mascot.

Rogers Pirates? Glorifies violence, not to mention it's blatantly sexist, in as much as there are no women pirates. The descendants of Bluebeard file a formal protest.

University High School Titans?

Well, let's see. A titan is a really big person, huge, titanic, or one of a family of greek gods, so I think that's pretty offensive to those of us below the national average in height, not to mention a violation of our constitutional right to church and state separation.

And what about the Wa-Hi Blue Devils?

I don't know what a blue devil is, exactly, but I'm pretty sure that the devil is supposed to be red, so the satanists among us, who already have enough to put up with without being subjected to having their deity be scorned as a miscolored high school mascot, are almost certainly offended.

And it's not just high schools.

The fighting Irish? Get with the program, people.

What about the Minnesota Vikings? Scandinavians unite! You don't have to put up with that crap!

And just where is the DAR when we need them?

How can the Daughters of the American Revolution stand by while the New England Patriots take our entire revolution from the British and trivialize it to the point where the likes of Paul Revere and Ben Franklin are reduced to team mascots.

And why isn't the Pope doing something about the New Orleans Saints? Don't the Catholics have some sort of theological monopoly when it comes to naming saints? Isn't trivializing saints about as offensive, not to mention risky to your immortal soul, as you can get?

Now, you're probably saying to yourself, all right, I get your point. Fine, we'll give all teams animal names.

I don't think so.

There are, after all, animal rights groups out there and we wouldn't want to offend any of them, would we?

Wouldn't be politically correct. So you schools with panthers, tigers and bears, not to mention bluejays, cardinals, bulldogs, dolphins and eagles be thinking about a new name.

So what's left?

Well, body parts are pretty neutral in all respects, although being the Shadle Park Patella's or the Mead Mudulla Oblongata's kind of leaves something to be desired.

Well, nobody said this politically correct/don't offend anybody stuff was going to be easy.

I just hope the Board of Education uses their common sense when considering this issue today.

Of course, in a politically correct world, that's probably too much to ask.

New and Improved...Labels

Do you feel it? A new national mania is coming on.

Labeling.

Across the nation, people are holding up Pepsi six-packs and looking at their bottoms like they are trying to figure out the sex of the can or something.

"Hmm. Looks like a boy Pepsi to me."

Actually, they are checking the freshness date.

As if it matters. I mean, have you ever wondered how fresh your Pepsi was? Me neither.

I've wondered if some of the wine I've drunk was bottled a month ago, but that's different.

Actually, the date I would like the Pepsi people to tell me is the last date I should even consider drinking it. Have you noticed that they aren't telling you when it's no longer fresh?

We don't need to know when it was made so much as when we can use it to strip the paint from our cars.

Even the government is getting into the labeling business.

Or, again, more accurately, deeper into labeling.

We are about to see the implementation of the Nutrition Labeling and Education act of 1990.

That's right — 1990.

I don't know about you, but I always feel better when the government decides I need more protecting, and does something about it, and in typical government fashion, waits four years to make it happen.

Aren't you glad your doctor doesn't work that way? "Doug, the reason your lips are always blue and you're out of breath is because your coronary arteries are clogged because you're 250 pounds overweight. I am putting you on a strict diet I want you to start in June of 1998. And in case that doesn't work, I'm going to schedule an emergency angioplasty for September 2, 2003."

With all the information already on food labels you might be thinking that we are suffering not from an information deficit but information overload, what with food labels already telling us not just the fat and vitamin count but also what is actually in the food, which might include piridoxine hydrochloride, magnesium and zinc, which presumably you could also get by sucking a galvanized nail.

But that's why you don't work for the government.

All government officials, including the ones we elect, know that they can never be done protecting us from ourselves, because when they are done doing that, most of them are out of a job.

In their zeal to protect us, the government has noted, with some alarm, that we, as a population, are overweight, and they figure this is because we are being duped into buying food labeled as low-fat, when, in fact, it may not be. This is the same observation that has made Jenny Craig, who could lose a little weight herself, a multi-millionaire.

Hence the new labeling rules.

This is the government's way of saying to us we're all weight challenged, and shopping-impaired. Or put in the vernacular, the government is saying to us one part, "Fatty fatty two-by four, can't get through the kitchen door," and one part, "You're really stupid."

The sad part is, of course, they're right.

"Gee, honey! Fresh Twinkies Light! Can I have two dozen?"

"Sure, And let's get a couple of cases of Natural Lite Beer to wash it all down with."

"Sounds like breakfast to me. What'll we get for lunch?"

Actually, some labeling is good. I'm sure I speak for all of us who don't smoke, that we consider the warning labels on cigarettes as good. They don't stop anyone from smoking, of course, but they do make us non-smokers feel morally superior to those who do.

If they wanted to stop smokers, a more effective warning might be "Caution: cigarette smoking can make you look really stupid and smell very bad." In the abstract, I think as a population, we are far more afraid of looking dumb than we are of lung cancer.

But I'm sure fashion labeling is still a ways off.

And who among us doesn't buy milk based on the date stamped on the top of the carton.

I'm always a little embarrassed to reach way to the back of the cooler where the milk cartons with the longest dates are, knocking over everything in between, but I do it.

The new labeling is supposed to help us make better, more healthy buying decisions.

In the future, if something is labeled as "natural," it will have to fit the government's definition of natural. And the new labels will also educate us to what "fresh" and "natural" means, and what saturated fats are and what evils they hold for us.

(I don't know about you, but the very words "saturated fat" conjures up an image of something with the consistency of axle grease and the color of Crisco.)

Personally, I think if buying healthy food is the goal, a check-out weigh-in system would be more effective. "I'm sorry, the government protecto-meter indicates that you're forty pounds over weight, so you can't buy these Ding Dongs. Would care to buy a carrot instead?"

Will all this new, truthful, educational and standardized labeling make us wiser, thinner, healthier shoppers?

Maybe. But I wouldn't be selling my stock in Weight Watchers or Jenny Craig just yet.

SHOPPING AT COSTCO AND OTHER THREATS TO MARITAL BLISS

The Costco Shopping Experience

It's getting to be that time of the month again at our house. You can tell because everyone is a little bit cranky, a little bit on edge. You'd think by now we'd know this thing rolls around once every 28 days or so and know how to deal with it.

You'd think that we would be able to take what amounts to an unavoidable physical thing and intellectualize it into no big deal, and we could help each other through it.

Unfortunately, it doesn't work that way, does it?

I mean, when your wife announces it's that time of the month, how many of you men have ever said something like, "Look, I know when this time of the month comes, it makes you tense and irritable and it's unpleasant for you; but it's unpleasant for me, as well. But we just have to endure it and try not to bite each other's head off. We both know that the worst of it only lasts a few hours, and then it's pretty much over. So can we try to make the best of it?"

Right. Not many. Because you know that your wife will look you right in the eye and say, "Look, it's that time of the month when we have to go to Costco, and you're going with me."

To which you probably reply, "Why do I have to go?"

It wasn't always that way, of course. At first, going to Costco was fun. Costco is, after all, sort of like a giant garage sale but with all new merchandise.

"Wow! Boomboxes for $189!"

"Is that a good deal?"

"I don't know. But when they're stacked up like this, it sure looks like it."

In those days, we tended to come home with 25 pounds of M&M Peanut Candies, 25 pair of white athletic sox, three boxes of wine and the occasional radial tire.

It had to do with the novelty of it all.

Somewhere along the way, the novelty wore off.

I think it was in the parking lot. Too many people going too many directions looking for not enough parking spaces. And all of that complicated by unmanned shopping carts rolling around.

Makes me nervous.

When my wife and I go for our monthly trip, we go into our Top Gun mode. One of us pilots, while the other navigates and looks for parking spots and bad guys.

"Maverick, we have a Bogey on your right, and a possible parking target dead ahead at 12 o'clock high. Enemy movement toward parking target coming in at 3 o'clock."

"Roger, Iceman, we have target acquisition. Hang on. We're going in."

Next you have to through the check-in routine.

"Excuse me, sir, but your card has expired."

"It has? Expired? Are you sure? There must be some mistake."

"There's no mistake. Step over to the counter, please. You have the right to another card. You have the right to another photo on your card. If you need a card and you cannot afford one, you do not have a right to shop here. Do you understand these card rules as I have explained them?"

There is something about paying for being able to shop in a place that I haven't quite figured out. But I do it. Not having a Costco card is like not quite being a fully accepted member of society.

Once we have cleared Costco's border guards, I routinely go into sensory overload. So many things, so little money! I go directly to the palm-sized video cameras.

Want!

I check the prices, but the fact is, I wouldn't know a good price from a rip-off in those things.

Meanwhile, my wife, who knows what she wants and where she is going to find it, starts heading for the frozen food section. We tend to eat a lot of their frozen chicken breasts.

After I move out of the stereo section, I skip the clothing and move right into tools. Again, I want one of everything. Whoa! A Makita palm sander! Only 46 bucks. Never mind that I hate sanding to the point where if I have a project that requires sanding, I won't do it, period. Even <u>with</u> a palm sander.

I generally reconnect with my wife in the books section. By this time, she has loaded up the cart with a month's worth of frozen food and other stuff I didn't even know we were out of. Unlike me, she knows her prices, so she has a pretty good idea of what we are saving.

It is, after all, the reason we are there, enduring crowds and parking and people pushing oversized shopping carts loaded up with 75 rolls of toilet paper in the first place.

It is usually at about this point in our trip that we have the true Costco Experience; we encounter something we didn't know we needed but instantly decide we can't live without.

This time of year it's apt to be something like lawn furniture.

"We need new lawn chairs."

"We do?"

"Yes. And these are a good deal."

"They are? Well, then, we'd better get some."

So we load up a half a dozen or so. One year it was garden hose. I think I bought 300 feet. The Costco Experience will do that to you.

By this time, my shopping endorphins are really starting to flow. "I think I should check out the tires, floor jacks and pneumatic tools," I say.

"I'm getting in line," my wife replies. This is wife Costco-ese for, "You can go where you want and see what you want, but when I get to the checker, you be there, Bucko."

I usually meander into line with a final turn through the candy section.

"What's this?" my wife asks as I add my last impulse treasure to the pile that's going to cost somewhere between $400 and $600.

"M&M Peanuts. They're for work."

"25 pounds? How long will they last?" she asks.

"About a month," I reply. "Just about a month.

Is it Clutter or Dirt?

Each morning, I look at the newspaper, and I look at the pictures of the newly married couples, and I can't help wondering if these couples, starting their life off together, have found common ground on the most basic and fundamental issue facing any marriage.

I fear, most of them have not.

Oh, yeah, most of them have settled the minor points of living a life together. Whether there's a God or not, whether to have a Visa or a MasterCard, where to live, whether to have a TV in the bedroom or not, how many children to have, whether they're both going to work or not ("If we're both going to eat, we're both going to work."), and all the sexual stuff ("I'm telling you, it's not normal for a woman to spend a third of her life in flannel jammies." "Yes, it is: My mother did it." "Well, there you go."), and who's going to get the next new car and whether or not it will be a four-wheel drive pickup with a chrome roll bar with eight sets of headlights on top and an air filter sticking up through the hood.

But I doubt most of them have come to grips with the real menace to most marriages. The one that absolutely requires a balance, or the marriage is doomed to failure. The definition of what constitutes dirt and what is merely clutter, and how much of each is too much.

Those of you who have been married a long time are nodding sagely and muttering to yourself, "Yeah, ain't that the truth."

We know that what happens is if a couple has a dissimilar definition of clutter and dirt, one of them will always be yelling that they live in a pigsty while the other will be wondering what all the noise is about.

"How was your day, honey?"

"We live in a pigsty. Look at this place."

"That good, huh?"

The not very subtle message here is if one of you thinks you live in a pigsty, then one of you must be a pig. Almost by definition, you have moved into divorce territory.

The problem is one of agreement: dirt is a beauty-in-the-eye-of-the-beholder thing. If you both want to live in a home that is so clean and clutter free company could drop in at any time and you wouldn't have to apologize for how your house looks, great.

Or if you both like living with empty pizza boxes on the coffee table, great. You've got no problem.

The problem comes when one wants to live in a home that resembles a surgical theater, and one wants a home to have a more "lived in" feel.

Around our house, we generally define dirt as anything that you pick up with a vacuum cleaner or wash off with a cloth. Everything else falls under the heading of clutter.

Clutter is by far the bigger problem. Certain things are made to create clutter.

Like twelve year olds, for instance.

For a while I thought that boys generated more clutter than girls, but now I'm not so sure. I think pound for pound, my daughter can generate as much clutter as any boy her age.

There are many modern devices to fight clutter, devices architects insist on building into homes.

One of these is a closet. It's an area where clutter can be stored out of sight, where, by some quirk of physics, it no longer exists.

Architects know all about the clutter battle, and the dumb ones build lots of closets into their homes. The smart ones know that won't work because there is a law of nature that says, "Your junk expands to fill the closet space allowed for it," so instead of building in more closets, they make the living room bigger, which makes you feel better when you are buying the place, which is all that's really important.

Actually, it's a little known fact that the best clutter fighter is a laundry chute into which all manner of clutter can be stuffed and made to magically and instantly disappear.

Personally, I've never quite gotten the hang of a closet. There is something about a living room chair that attracts my coats, ties, sweatshirts all kinds of things that should go into a closet.

My daughter may never know what a closet is for. We have allocated a conveniently placed bin for her stuff in an effort to try to keep her clutter at least in one place. Sounds like a good idea, right?

Well, it's not.

Her bin goes from empty to overflowing in no more than 12 hours. And the overflow goes right where her clutter always went — everywhere.

Some clutter is specialized. Make-up for instance. And the bottles and holders and solutions that go with wearing contact lenses.

But like I said, the problem is not that there is clutter, but rather on agreeing how much is acceptable and how much is too much. And in agreeing what is clutter and what is dirt. And how much is acceptable. And where.

For instance, a work bench is supposed to be cluttered. It works better when there's spare lawn mower parts, assorted wood screws and socket wrench sockets strewn about. So you don't want to be messing with that. You may also discover that you can tolerate far more clutter in your child's bedroom simply by closing the door. But for this trick to work, it has to work for both parents or it doesn't work at all.

Now, after all this, you're probably wondering if, having been married for twenty years, my wife and I found our own balance in the dirt versus clutter question.

We're working on it. We're working on it.

Buying The Big Things

A friend of ours recently went out one Saturday to buy peat moss and a few plants for the garden.

When she got back, her husband asked her what she got, and she answered, "I got four Begonias, three bags of peat moss, a hedge trimmer that was on sale and a Dodge Grand Caravan LE. And a bag of weed and feed."

To which he answered, "I wish you wouldn't impulse buy like that; I've got weed and feed."

What happened was the Dodge dealer was having this parking lot sale where she was buying the peat moss and there was this Grand Caravan LE that had her name on it, if you know what I mean, and she was feeling real good about herself and them and all the cosmic signs were right, so she bought it.

She went out for peat moss and came back with a new car. Seemed pretty logical at the time.

And the point of all this is making a major purchase like that was okay with her husband. (He probably figured, correctly, that he was never going to outlive all his debt anyway, so what difference did it make?)

A perfect example of Major Purchase Compatibility.

Now, the reason I told you that story is because one of the young ladies I work with is getting serious about her boyfriend.

You can tell because the word "marriage" is beginning to slip into her casual conversations about him. She seems quite happy with him, and from what I can see, he's a pretty okay guy.

But those of us who are older and wiser, well okay, maybe just older, we know that there are certain building blocks in a successful marriage that you can't know if you have or don't have until you are actually married. We know that there are certain basic compatibilities that you cannot test outside of the pressures of marriage.

And there is no compatibility more important or fundamental to marital happiness than Major Purchase Compatibility. Or to put it in the vernacular, how you buy the big stuff.

In the olden days, buying big stuff wasn't a big deal. The man did it.

"Well, I sold the crops and both the cows and bought us a new buckboard. Four horses, anti-lock brakes, driver's side airbag (whatever that is) …"

"I was sort of hoping we'd have money left to buy shoes for the kids."

"What's your point?"

But with the advent of the modern two-income family, not to mention all the stuff we all want that's so darned expensive, I think we can all agree that those days are gone forever.

This has been especially hard on we men who generally have a genetic propensity to feel that any spending on ourselves doesn't really count as spending — it's more like an investment — while any spending on anything else is … well, profligate.

You can see this at work any day of the week at Sears. All the salesman in the power tool department has to say is, "This table saw is so powerful, that when you turn this baby on, not only do the lights in your house dim a little, but the lights in your neighbor's house dim a little, too." And the husband is saying, "Hmmm, That's the one I'd better have." Never mind that the only thing he's ever made is a wobbly sawhorse that has never had all four legs touching the ground at the same time.

But ten minutes later, when his wife is looking at new drapes, he says, "Drapes? What's wrong with the sheet that covers the front window?"

The scary thing is, he probably really doesn't know.

Now the definition of what constitutes big stuff is relative to your disposable income. Or when you're young and married, your lack of disposable income.

When you're first married, a fifty dollar expenditure may be a big purchase. (I'm here to tell you that if you have a career in advertising, $50 will always be a big purchase, but that's another commentary.)

What becomes important is not the amount that constitutes a big purchase, but how you each go about making the purchase with the other's approval.

If not blessing.

What's important is how you achieve Big Purchase Compatibility.

There is no one right answer. Like so many things in life, couples have to find out what works for them and stick with that.

For some couples, there is the territorial imperative method. "I'm the man, so I buy all the stuff for the cars, the garage, the camping gear, the snow blowers, and lawn mowers; and you're the woman, so you buy the furniture, the kitchen appliances, stuff for the kids and the washer and dryer."

Now, in this politically correct world, few couples are so boorish as to actually verbally make such a declaration, but we all know couples where that's the reality, don't we?

Others, frustrated by each other's spending habits, make out a list in order to impose some discipline. The problem with the list idea is, while everything on your spouse's list may be valid, none of it is important. At least, not as important as the stuff on your list. So that system breaks down right away.

If you stay married long enough, you develop more subtle approaches. One person I know takes a guerilla warfare approach. She goes out on shopping patrol, little search and destroy recon missions, scouting probable locations for what she wants, and when she finds it at a price she thinks is right, she ambushes her husband by saying, "Come with me," and she shows him what she's found, and why they should make this major purchase.

The thing is, "Come with me" is also what she says when she wants sex; so when she says that, he automatically gets a little agitated and doesn't think altogether clearly. But that's neither here nor there: The point is, they achieve Major Purchase Compatibility, and that's the important thing.

Now, it should be said that not all couples achieve this exalted state. I think we all know of couples who go out to buy new furniture for <u>them</u> and come back with a new stereo piece for <u>him</u>.

They have great sound systems, but hey, there's no where to sit to listen to it.

In our family, we have adopted a two-tiered formula. On tier one, we discuss major purchases, and we actually shop together for them.

Sometimes this is purely a cosmetic exercise in domestic tranquility, you understand.

"So what do you think? The Macintosh Performa 636 with CD ROM or the Compaq with Windows and the communication software?"

"Whichever you think is better, Dear."

"I want the one that has enough power to dim the house lights when I turn it on."

On tier two, the prevailing philosophy is, "It's better to ask for forgiveness than permission, especially since you can almost always take anything back."

"How do you like the new couch?"

"Did we need a new couch?"

"That wasn't the question."

"Oh. Well. In that case, I like it fine."

So do I have any advice for my co-worker to see if she has Major Purchase Compatibility with her boyfriend? Not really. Like I said, I think you've got to live with it to see if you've got it.

Except maybe, I would advise her not to go out for peat moss until you can afford a Dodge Caravan.

Entertainment Books

Some say that life begins at forty.

Not true.

For those of you who are 38, and have yet to get a life, I realize what a disappointment this news must be. And I'm not sure who you blame. It could be a fraud perpetrated by 60-year-olds who are still mad about growing old and take perverse pleasure in watching 40-year-olds get their hopes up only to be dashed by the effects of menopause and self-destructing prostate glands.

Or it might simply be an advertising gimmick to keep people in their forties spending money on products designed to make them think they're still in their twenties.

In any case, scientists now know that life doesn't begin in your forties. It begins, at least for most people in Spokane, when they get their Entertainment Book.

I mean, don't we all know people whose approach to life is, "Hey, I've got my Entertainment Book; let's get together somewhere."

Ah, the Entertainment Book, that ubiquitous two-inch stack of perfect bound two-for-one coupons. That fund raising marvel. That book that every group on the planet that needs to raise money sells, and that lives under the front seat of about half the cars in Spokane.

"My kids hockey team needs uniforms; wanna buy an Entertainment Book?"

"Uh, I bought one from KPBX, and that was before my kid wanted me to buy one to support their band trip to Washington, D.C. So now I have two. Have you tried Elizabeth?"

"All three of her kids are selling them for school things, and so is that group she is the president of, "Mothers For Assault Rifles.""

"I wonder if she's tried George Nethercutt?"

Now, personally, I'm not offended by someone offering to spend time with me because — or as long as they can do it for half price — although I can imagine some people who would.

And so far, when my wife and I have suggested getting together with another couple and we pull out our Entertainment Book, no one has made us feel cheap and tawdry and poverty-stricken by saying, "Oh, come on; let's just go where we want and pay full price for it, shall we?"

"Full price? Are you kidding?"

In fact, something quite the opposite usually happens. Something that can only be described as Entertainment Book roulette takes place. Everybody pulls out their Entertainment Books and tries to find a place for which everybody still has a coupon.

"How about Eagles Nest?"

"Oops. Nope. We used that one. Chic-A-Ria? Everybody have a coupon for that one?"

"What's it like?"

"Who cares?"

Which is the point, of course. The Entertainment Book is sold to restaurants, hotels and other businesses on the premise that, given a two-for-one coupon, most of us will try a restaurant we normally wouldn't be expected to.

Of course, the reason that works is we're all such whores, we'll go anywhere for half off one menu item.

To which I say: Right on.

Now, that doesn't mean that I like using it.

In our family, we buy the book strictly for the guaranteed payback; I can look through the book and see a guaranteed return on my forty-dollar investment without getting past McDonald's and Zips.

But I must admit, when it comes to actually using it, actually shoving it across the counter at the server, I have a little buyer's remorse, and I wonder if it's worth it.

This probably stems from an earlier experience with similar books where, when you showed your coupon, the servers treated you like you developed a case of spontaneous leprosy, ("Not another one of those…") and there was about a fifty-fifty chance they would announce in a voice everyone in the restaurant could hear something like, "I'm sorry, but those discount coupons are only good on Mondays and Tuesdays, and never for the prime rib, so if you don't have enough money to pay for two dinners, perhaps you'd just like something to drink, besides, you tight-wads are supposed to tell me before you order."

"Believe me, it won't happen again."

To be fair, that kind of thing hasn't happened with the Entertainment Book, but you can see why I'm still a little gun shy, and why, when I push the coupon toward the McDonald's kid, I look like a man expecting to be slapped.

Curiously, it is only Entertainment Book coupons that seem to affect me in this way.

When I rent a snowboard for my daughter and use a half off coupon, I put it down like a triumphant chess player: "Twenty bucks? Take this! Check and Mate. Ha! Half off! I win."

Actually, I lose. At half off, I figure I can pay for it for her. If was full price, I'd make her pay for the whole thing.

And it certainly doesn't bother me to pay for my ski lift ticket with one of those discount tickets, or to load up the cashier at Rosauers with them. "Wait a minute, I've got a coupon for a nickel off that Preparation H here somewhere… "

But restaurants…

I have come to grips with my Entertainment Book problem by facing up to my fears and feelings of inadequacy by doing what any real man would do: I make my wife present the coupon.

But that's okay, because she is strong in the knowledge that she is doing the right thing. That she is protecting and growing her financial investment; wisely using the family funds, and feeding her family all at the same time.

And more often than not, it's all happening in a place where we normally wouldn't be caught dead if we weren't getting two-for-one.

Choosing Your Long Distance Company

Today the topic is an identity issue that each of us must face

— and answer for ourselves. A modern dilemma brought on by the convergence of affluence, technology and an aberrant Supreme Court decision.

At issue is a decision we all must make, and decide for ourselves, as individuals and as families, and then have that decision scrutinized and challenged under the hot glare of the lights of free enterprize.

It's a decision that gets to the core of who each of us, individually, is. Are we flighty or serious? Are we profligate or frugal? Are we Bud or Miller Lite? Levi's or Men's Warehouse? Are we button-downed, stay-at-home-and-quote-the- Wall-Street-Journal, or are we party animals?

The question we all must answer is: Are we AT&T or MCI?

Some of you are probably thinking, "Who cares?"

Well, I'm here to tell you: AT&T cares.

The reason you gotta decide is they are going to ask, and you can't be both, not at the same time.

Now, there are a few things you should know about switching your long distance service. First of all, you know all those happy people in the MCI commercial who sit in that big room in front of computer terminals and wear head sets and smile like they've all taken a big hit of nitrous oxide and say stuff like, "Friends and family from MCI lets you save up to 40% calling the friends and family you call most!"?

You know those people?

Those are not the people who are going to call you.

Those people are having way too much fun to be real telephone sales people who get routinely hung up on and sworn at by people like you and me, who don't want to be called during dinner and asked about our long distance service.

People who've had obscenities yelled at them for eight hours aren't nearly that chipper.

Plus, the people who have called me haven't sounded nearly as normal as the people on TV. In fact, the first guy who called me sounded like he wasn't on a job so much as on … parole.

"Yeah. Is dis Douglas Hurd? Yeah, Mr. Hurd, dis is Vinnie

Testosterone from MCI, know what I mean? How are you to-night, Mr. Hurd? Yeah, well, I'm hungry too. Well, getting to da point, Mr. Hurd, a Mr. Morris Smith of Walla Walla ... "

"Smyth"

"Whatever. Mr. Smith indicated ... hey, Walla Walla. I think I gotta cousin doing twenty to life in Walla Walla. Ever get down there?

"To the big house? No."

The other thing that you need to know is, the moment you say, yeah, okay, fine, switch me over, AT&T will know.

And they will not be happy.

So you can expect a call from them the next night.

Now, if you're lonely, all this attention might be great. If you're not lonely, it's not so great.

"Mr. Hurd? This is Mr. Cummings from AT&T. Can we talk for a moment? It seems you are dissatisfied with our service."

"Ah, well, no, not really."

"Then, I tell you what I'm going to do. I'm going to switch you back, and to show you how much we at AT&T appreciate your business, I am going to send you a certificate for 10 minutes of free long distance. Good night."

"Good night."

Guess who called back the next night? Right: those party animals at MCI, saying, Doug, Doug, I thought we had a deal.

Now, I guess that every person has to deal with these situa-tions their own way, but it was here that I made my smart money play. I said, "They gave me a better deal. Offered me ten minutes of free long distance to switch back."

(Which means I can be bought for about three bucks.)

"But what about the 40% savings we offer?"

I hate it when they do that and I have to do all that math in my head. Let's see: 40 percent of three dollars is ... three times four, move the decimal point ... a dollar twenty? Can that be right?

So, I switched again.

Now, you should know that when you switch you don't just say, "Okay" and that's that.

No. Somebody calls you back and confirms it. That night. And they try to sell you whatever it was you didn't sign up for the first time. And then, somebody calls you back again to confirm the confirmation, by which time, you want to call the whole thing off.

After about a month of this, battle fatigue sets in, and you have to decide to be one or the other, and you realize that the whole issue isn't about money or long distance quality any more than a Rolex is about time.

It's about image. Yours and the company you're going to deal with.

So you make a final, final decision.

In my best adult imitation, I said, "Hey, that's it. I've had it with you people. I like MCI, I'm staying with MCI. I may not have any friends, and I don't call my family, and I certainly don't have a best friend I would wish you people on, I just want you to leave me alone. I'm staying with MCI. Got it?"

You've just go to be firm with these people, you know what I mean?

There was a silence and then the person on the other end of the line said, "Actually, sir, I'm with MCI. You're with AT&T. So, would you like me to switch you again?"

Selling Your Home

A friend is selling his house. He's got boys growing up, his house has appreciated, interest rates are down. In short, the time is right.

I didn't want to tell him that when it comes to selling a house, the time is never right, any more than there is a right time for, say, taking yourself out and having yourself publicly flogged.

"Gee, interest rates are down. I think today I'll sell my house. Either that or go down to Riverfront park, strip to the waist and ask a stranger to flog me with a cat o'nine tails, because either way, I'm going to feel the same when I'm done."

The first thing is, if you do have to sell your house, you want to do it either before your kids are old enough to know what it means — which is before the age of about six — or after they are grown and gone. Because the moment you casually mention over dinner that you might spend Sunday driving around looking at houses, your kids will respond like you are going to ship them off to the Gulag.

"Look at houses? What do you mean look at houses?" your 12-year old will wail. "Are we going to move? What about my friends? What about my making first tuba in the band? What about hanging out at Hastings with my friends? I hate my life! I hate it! Can I have more macaroni, please?"

No, it's better to conduct the negotiations in secret. Then, when they finally do become public family knowledge, you can soothe the children in the time honored way parents have always soothed their children.

You lie.

"Don't worry, honey. You'll still keep all your old friends. You'll just have lots of new ones, that's all."

Right. You're moving from Mead to Post Falls? You'll see your old friends again — when you hit college. What you don't tell your child is that half the reason for moving might just be his choice of friends.

Even though hysterical, your kids are still apt to recognize a strong bargaining position in all of this: "If we move, would I get my own bedroom? And could I have my own phone and a private entrance and a CD player and small study area with a 486 computer with a graphical interface and CD ROM?"

You must resist the urge to say yes.

Okay. So you decide to sell. What's the first thing you have to do? Right. Decide upon a price.

Here is where you encounter the home price paradox.

You have looked at other homes, and you have said, "Can you believe they are asking $235,000 for that piece of junk?" But when it comes to your piece of junk, 40 thousand over market seems, well, fair.

This is all the more bizarre because you want to sell the turkey precisely because it doesn't work for you anymore, and you're tired of the basement flooding. Hence the paradox: everybody is asking way too much, which is infuriating and bad, except when it's you doing the asking.

Actually, it is not a good idea to ask too much because once a price is in your head, however ridiculous, any amount you accept lower than that will seem infinitely less. And that will lead to a huge disappointment.

And that leads to second thoughts. And there is nothing more damaging to your REM sleep patterns than second thoughts. You will lie awake nights, wondering if that far off sound you hear is the sound of real estate people laughing that you were stupid enough to price your house $20,000 below the market. If the night is quiet enough, and your anxiety high enough you might actually hear someone asking, "Didn't he wonder why it sold the first hour it was on the market?"

There is, of course, no way to win this one. If you don't get any offers, you lie awake and wonder if you're asking too much and if you will ever sell it; and if you don't, how long it will take making two house payments to deplete your life savings — which, for must of us, is about a month.

Finally, of course you must go through the pain of actually letting strangers walk through your home and literally, try it on for size.

There are two factors here that create a conflict. One is your house won't be right for most people, and it's hard to remember that it only needs to fit just one, and, as much as you may want to sell it, it is still yours, and you have a lot of you invested in it.

This is where the real flogging comes in.

It's hearing what people think of your choice in carpets, or drapes.

"Who picked the carpet? I haven't seen that color shag since I stopped taking LSD in college." Or, "Wow, orange counter tops. Haven't earned enough money to remodel the kitchen since the

'70s I see."

Kids are the worst: "Yuck! I hate this house. Let's go."

And there is always the chance that they will ask you the one question you don't want to answer. "I see these stains down here: has the basement ever flooded?"

"Flooded? The basement? Why would the basement flood? Dear, has the basement ever ... no, um, not that I recall. Well, we get some moisture down here when it rains for forty days and forty nights, but flood? Well there was that one time, but it was only, what's the word? Damp. Damp is what it was. Four feet of damp."

I think it's best to make up some benign cover story about why you are leaving the house. You have to drive too far to work, or you're getting transferred. You can always say, "I work for Key Tronic, and you know how that goes."

Nobody ever challenges that. Plus it sounds much better than saying, "Because the heat pump has puked a compressor again, the roof leaks and the kid's bedroom drops below freezing every time a north wind blows. Why do you think I'm selling it?"

No, I don't envy my friend, who is just beginning the process of selling his house. He's already having second thoughts. "Does having two people interested in the first day it's on the market mean I've priced it too low?" he asked, having second thoughts before his first ones are done.

"Absolutely not, probably," I said. And as he walked away biting his nails, I thought to myself, yeah, I think I'd rather be flogged than sell my house.

Line Dancing at Kelly's

I am standing on a dance floor, in a large group of people. On stage in front of me is a lady who is in a white blouse, black skirt and cowboy boots.

She is trying to teach us how to do a line dance to some country and western song.

"Right shuffle, left hitch!" she calls, and we all do a little hop with one knee up that makes us all look like some invisible force has simultaneously yanked up all our underpants. We are learning a dance called the Boot Scoot.

Or is it the shuffle? I forget.

The last time I danced like this, I was about 12 years old. I was in sixth grade, and I was so in love with Linda Sagstad that I would have done anything to get myself in a position where I got to hold her hand, including learn how to folk dance, which, among my buddies, was universally considered to be an activity for sissies.

"Right behind, step, stomp!" guides our instructor. I wish now I had paid more attention to the dancing and less to Linda 36 years ago.

A year or so later, my parents, along with everyone else's I knew, sent all their children to ballroom dance lessons where we learned the staples of the trade — the foxtrot, the box step, the waltz, and what we really came to learn: the bop. (Heel toe! Heel toe, step and twirl!)

I will confess, I never quite got the hang of the bop, because I was at least a head shorter than all of my dance partners, and to try to twirl a girl when you couldn't reach above her head was to put her at risk of facial lacerations from the cuff links my father made me wear or to make her have to unnaturally contort to get under my outstretched arm — a sort of spontaneous limbo move that put her entire lumbar region at risk.

But then came Chubby Checker and we began to twist, and I never again had to twirl a dance partner. Soon after came the Watusi and the frug and not only did I not have to lead and twirl, I didn't even have to know what I was doing myself. I got to just sort of shuffle around to the beat in my space on the floor, generally in the area of my partner who was similarly shuffling.

"Okay," She says. "Are you ready to put it all together? Let's do that much from the top."

Line dancing is what you'd get if a Solid Gold Dancer tried to invent close order military drill.

The group surges forward, hops (there goes that underwear, again) back, and everybody but me turns to the left. I turn right. I do not intuitively know my right from my left. I have to think about it for a moment, and a moment is not what line dancing affords you.

The lady facing me is surprised and can't move, and the people behind her can't move, but they do anyway and for a moment we are in danger of the dreaded domino effect.

Our instructor stops us and starts again. She's been through this before. She doesn't single me out for public humiliation for which I am eternally grateful. I'm thinking I may get the hang of it as long as I don't have to lead and I don't have to twirl anyone.

"Five, six, seven, EIGHT," and we're off.

I am concentrating on watching the instructor, which is okay until the dance turns us around and she is behind me. So next I watch the person in front of me.

Big mistake. He doesn't know what he's doing either.

I'm trying to repeat the cadence to myself which I think goes step, turn, hip, hip. At this point I look like a hula dancer who has wandered into the wrong bar, which wouldn't be so bad except that I think I may have dislocated my hip in the process of doing it wrong.

When we get done, I get this great sense of accomplishment, and I know why this form of dancing is sweeping the nation. I also know I need to exercise more.

We have gotten there early for the lessons, and as we learn, the bar fills up. About the time the band is ready to play, I know three dances, sort of. I say sort of, because my brain is wired up like a Milton Bradley Etch-a-Sketch, and every new step I learn erases an earlier one.

Oh, well.

It must be semi-formal night at Kelly's, because all the cowboy hats are black.

I have dug out my cowboy boots that I bought during my urban cowboy phase. I kind of wish I had a black cowboy hat so I looked a little more like John Travolta.

Right at nine, the band starts playing and there's a rush to the dance floor by really good dancers. They've been politely waiting for us klutzo beginners to get done.

It's like we've been playing three-on-three and then having the NBA suddenly take the court.

Wow! These people are good!

But wait a minute. These people aren't doing line dances. They're doing something else.

They're dancing with partners. They're moving around in a circle, everyone exactly in sync with everyone else.

And even though they are all doing exactly the same step, and everybody knows exactly what is going to happen next, the men are clearly leading. This is very bad news.

In unison, all the women twirl.

In a flash, I know that my night of dancing is over. Part of me hungers for a return to the formlessness of rock, to the comfort of what I know.

But a bigger part of me wants to learn this new symmetry and grace, even if it is pretty rigid.

The fact is, these people are having a lot of fun.

Besides, I already know the Shuffle.

Or is it the Boot Scoot?

Tax Time

It's about this time of year that everyone begins asking the big question.

The question that delineates the doers from the talkers, the roll-up-the-sleeves-and-get-it-done types from those subhuman, snivelling put-it-off types.

The big question is, have you done your taxes yet?

And if you've done your taxes, frankly, I don't want to hear about it.

I hate doing my taxes.

I don't know about you, but I put doing my taxes on about a par with having my prostate checked. I know it's something I've got to do, and I know it's for my own good, but it costs me money and to be honest, I don't much care for how the whole event feels.

Now, before I whine too much, I should tell you that I don't really do my taxes. My accountant does my taxes. I just give him all the stuff.

This is kind of an aside, but it is at this time of year that I often think if I were an accountant and saw nothing but tax forms from here until April 15th, I'd slit my throat. On the other hand, if you're an accountant, maybe this is the quarter of the year you live for.

"All right! A Schedule K-1 Form 1120 S, and this one has both qualified rehabilitation expenditures related to rental real estate activities **and** gross income from oil, gas or geothermal properties. Far out, man."

The night I do my organizing is Tax Night.

Every family sharing in the American dream, and a few that aren't, share tax night.

It is the night we sit down with all the 1099's and W4's and donation receipts and reports from banks that tell us A) how much interest they charged us, and B) how much interest they paid us.

"Last year, you paid us interest of $8,947 on your house loan. And on your certificates of deposit, we paid you interest of $46.23. It's a pleasure doing business with you Mr. Hurd."

To make my Tax Night easier, my accountant supplies me with a form to fill out that asks all the questions he needs answers to. "Did you or any of your dependents become blind or sterile last year while spending more than 50% of your time in a county that had previously received Payroll Interest Options Credits (PIOCs) resulting from federal cutbacks in defense spending (FCDSs) in the last 12 months?

Does my vasectomy count? Gee, I don't think so.

Which gets me to the heart of why I hate Tax Night. It makes me feel dumb.

Most of the year, I feel smarter than the government, but on Tax Night, they get me back.

So, I don't know about you, but I put it off.

When Tax Night comes, I become the perfect husband.

"You know, I think I'll go down and do a load of laundry," I say to my wife.

"Don't you have to get the taxes ready for Tom?" my wife will ask.

"Yeah," I reply, "but we need the whites done."

"Do the taxes," she says.

"Maybe I'll vacuum the whole house."

"After you do the taxes."

Lot of good that'll do me.

I begin my tax year, like all the books suggest, the year before.

I make a file folder and I write "Taxes" on it in big letters. And I swear, I promise myself that this year I am going to put all the pertinent information into it. Like all my many charitable donations.

"Okay, I'm giving Goodwill four old shirts, two towels and a broken down table and chair set we got for my daughter when she was three. Fair market value, $275. No, make it an even $300."

The form my accountant gives me to fill out shows what I gave last year. I'm always pretty surprised when I see those numbers. Probably about as surprised as the IRS.

Wow! I gave $12,000 to United Way last year? I must have been playing pin the decimal point on the number.

Anyway, at this time of year, I swear I will put all those blank receipts the Goodwill guys give me in my tax folder, so I can go right to them when Tax Night comes, and keep all my canceled checks and tax receipts and mileage reports, but somehow I never do, because you know, in the middle of June, who cares about their taxes, so when I go to my tax folder, it's empty, and I have to figure everything out from scratch.

This means I have to read all those forms I get from banks and investment firms and try to figure them out. Gross dividends? Yeah, okay, I found that, but now my form from the accounting firm wants capital gain <u>dividends,</u> but the forms from the investment firm say capital gain <u>distribution.</u>

Is a distribution the same thing as a dividend?

I don't know.

And inasmuch as it's the IRS we're dealing with here, the very question conjures visions of IRS storm troopers impounding my firstborn child and throwing me in prison, saying, "What a twit! Everybody knows a Dividend is not a Distribution, and ignorance of the law, or in your case, ignorance, period, is no excuse!"

Finally, like some sort of Kafkaesque numerical Halloween, Tax Night ends.

I have all the papers, arranged in piles, ready for my accountant. One pile is income, another pile is deductions, and a third pile is stuff I've been sent that has "Important: Tax information" stamped all over it that I don't know what to do with.

My accountant always takes about three minutes to go through the piles that have taken me hours to arrange and discards about half of it. "Don't need this, don't need that, hmmm, I wonder why they sent you this? You didn't buy stock in any third world companies that export oil to Cuba, did you?" And he tosses it.

He always asks for a few things that he needs that I haven't provided him with, and Tax Night is over for another year.

My relief is palpable.

We always have one last ritual though; I ask him what it looks like, and he bangs away on his ten-key for a few minutes, and when about 30 inches of paper have spooled out, he pronounces me okay. "If you have to pay, it looks like it won't be much."

I know he probably says that to everybody, but I don't care. For me, it's over.

Later I will sign what they give me and write a check for

what they say I owe, and the dirty deed will be done.

Except for going home and taking out a new file folder and, in big letters, writing "Taxes" on it and thinking ...

Well, you know.

How Much Fat Is There In This Infomercial

It is, without a doubt, the weightiest question of the day.

It's a question that suddenly seems to burn in the heart of every television-watching American. A question that cuts to the core of who we are as a people and a nation and who we want to be.

A question that reaches in and touches our collective personal identity and that everybody seems to be asking, all the time.

It is also a testament to the power and reach of that wonderful purely American invention, the Infomercial.

The question we are all asking is not will Boris Yeltsin stay in power, or will the Israelis and Palestinians find peace, or even why would Michael Jordan quit, but, "Do you know how much fat there is in that?"

We usually ask the question right when someone is about to stuff a Twinkie into his mouth.

Now the reason we ask the question at all is because we know the answer. Or, at least, how to find it.

And we know it because we have seen the "Stop the Insanity" infomercial, which has turned us all into a nation of label readers.

Infomercials are really long commercials. Like Ronco slicer-dicer commercials that have spent too much time on anabolic steroids.

They are Ginsu knife commercials expanded to fill five, ten, twenty minutes or more.

They are like Mary Kay and Tupperware parties coming at you from your television set, and you get to order, but you don't have to play the silly games.

And the "Stop the Insanity" infomercial is one of the all time great ones. It's the one with the lady who has the white-blonde hair cut in almost a pig shave, who used to be really fat and who is now pretty thin, and with her pig shave is pretty scary looking, and who is telling us that she has discovered the secret to being thin, and for only four payments of $19.95 or something like that, she will share that information with us.

But the thing is, she has already told us 90 percent of all we think we need to know, which is, if you are trying to watch your weight, you don't need to count calories, but fat calories.

And what's more, she tells you how to figure that out.

(For those of you who haven't seen it, it's simple. As it happens, every gram of fat has nine calories in it. If you figure ten to make the math easy, you read the label and multiply the grams of fat by ten, and then turn that into a percentage of the total calories to see what percentage of fat you are eating. Piece of cake, so to speak.)

The premise here is, it's not calories that count, but fat calories.

Apparently calories, like people, come in both good and bad varieties.

Which is why, all of a sudden, everybody is a fat calorie cop and wants to know if you know how many fat calories there are in everything you're eating.

"Excuse me, ma'am, but do you know what percentage of fat that lite and lean ham is you're eating?"

"Excuse me?"

"Let's see, 100 calories, five grams of fat, that makes, 50 fat calories ... 50, 100 ... That ham is fifty percent fat. What do you have to say for yourself?"

How about mind your own business?

But it's not that easy, is it?

Armed with that little formula, it's almost impossible not to go around telling people how much fat they are ingesting.

Even my daughter is getting into it. "This salad dressing is

40% fat."

"Hey look, you weigh 63 pounds, you're off the bottom of the growth chart, so for you 40% is probably not enough fat. Okay?"

"I'm not eating it."

"Fine."

"I'm having some potato chips instead."

It's not her fault. She's at that age.

The implied promise of the formula, if not the entire infomercial is, you don't have to diet to lose weight. You just have to not eat a high percentage of fat.

And in a country where we like our gratification instantly and our bodies to all look like what we see on TV, what could be more perfect?

You mean, I can eat all I want and not get fat?

Yes.

Well, maybe not. It might be if it was the only infomercial on television right now, but it's not. There is also Covert Bailey's infomercial. He's the guy who wrote <u>Fit or Fat</u>, and what he's saying is, you've got to exercise, so your body burns fat.

Exercise? You mean, like, sweat and stuff?

Yes. I'm afraid so.

Well, that's a drag.

Actually, it is entirely possible that the pig shave lady also was promoting exercise, but the fact is, once I got the fat formula, I tuned her out, so if she said anything about it, I didn't catch it. Well, like Paul Simon said, "A man hears what he wants to hear and disregards the rest."

Naturally, Covert Bailey has an exercise machine that will help us do just that. You could just walk everyday, too, but that's not nearly as dedicated appearing as ordering a machine.

But if you're going to order a machine to exercise on, that gets you into a whole new area of infomercials: stair climbing machines, Nordic Trak wannabes, machines that do 55 different exercises and give you biceps of iron and buns of steel, and then fold up and hide under the bed.

In fact, I think I've got one under there.

Anyway, it's all pretty confusing.

But that's okay, because when I get confused, I do what you do: I buy a quart of ice cream and some chocolate sauce, a bag of nacho chips and some bean dip and watch a little television.

Watching the Unwatchable: *Melrose Place*

I don't know how this happens.

You think you're doing great as a family, and then, all of a sudden the wheels come off.

We are television dysfunctional.

Now, I know what you're thinking: Every family is a little TV dysfunctional. I mean, who doesn't have a child who likes to watch "Full House" that makes the parents want to puke; or in every MTV family, there is always some clown who wants to watch the country music channel.

But this is worse. We are afflicted with the Family Television Viewing Incompatibility Syndrome.

I discovered it Monday night.

I was sort of watching Monday Night Football.

I say "sort of" because I was also trying to catch up on some Sunday newspaper sections I didn't read and an old Time Magazine or two.

My daughter came in.

"Can I change the channel? Thanks," she said. And before I could answer, she changed the channel to Melrose Place.

Now, those of you who like Melrose Place are thinking, yeah, okay, so what's the problem here? You get to spend an hour of quality family time, which in 1995 is defined as sitting in the same room with another family member watching television.

But you see, I hate Melrose Place.

In the Universal TV Program Viewing Hierarchy, Melrose Place is at the bottom level for me - in the category called Drives

You From The Room.

Unfortunately, it is at the top of the hierarchy — Immersion — for my daughter.

So there it was: clear as could be. Family Television Viewing Incompatibility Syndrome. Right in my family.

For a moment, I thought I could simply use willpower to stay in the room with my daughter as she watched. As a Melrose Place hater, I swore this year I would actually watch an episode all the way through.

After all, I should like the show. It's about people in an advertising agency, and I personally can find nothing wrong with Heather Locklear, except maybe her taste in husbands.

But then, not one minute into the show, in a scene that would do Hamas proud, some lady sets off timed bombs placed all around Melrose Place, blowing up all the pretty people and herself in the process.

Time out, my brain is saying. Where'd she get that lovely little detonator box with lights and buttons and all? The Beverly Hills Bomb Boutique? Bombs "R" Us?

"Here you go, ma'am. Our finest detonator box. Sets off four explosions in five second intervals. Just don't hook the wires backwards and you'll be fine. When this goes off, Militias everywhere are going to be <u>so</u> jealous. Will that be cash or charge, today?"

Now, besides the detonator box, right away there were two things wrong with the scene: first of all, we ad people are way too egocentric to blow ourselves up like this lady did — I mean, we're not Postal workers for Pete's sake, and second, if we are going to blow someone up, it's going to be our clients.

They're the people we hate.

Actually, that's a joke. We advertising people don't really want to blow our clients up.

Shoot them, occasionally, but not blow them up.

I looked at my daughter. None of this mattered to her. By the rapt way she watched the television, you could tell that setting off timed dynamite was a perfectly plausible Melrose Place story development.

There was no doubt she was at the top level of the Universal Television Program Viewing Hierarchy, which is Immersion. Must view at all costs.

This is where the viewer and the program are one. People schedule weddings and funerals around these shows. "I know I said I'd do your bypass surgery, but All My Children is on in a few minutes. I'm sorry. You'll just have to wait."

Remember how people used to talk about the cute things the Cosby kids said as if they were their own? Level one viewers. Trekkies? Right. Same thing. My daughter is a level one Melrose Place viewer.

Below that are Usually View programs. These are programs you like, and try to catch, but if you miss, well, you don't call your neighbor for a plot update.

Level three is Preferred Viewing, which is generally a choice of lesser evils, like choosing between KREM News and KXLY news. You know how that is — What's worse? Dennis Patchin yelling at us or watching KREM to see if they've fired their new sports guy yet?

Let's watch KREM.

In the middle of the scale is Benign Indifference. This is where I was with Monday Night Football. This is to television what rice cakes are to food. Filling but without anything that approaches satisfaction.

Below that is Negative indifference, which is like Benign Indifference, except you'd really rather be watching something else.

Then comes Surfing Stops which are programs you only stop long enough on to recognize your dislike for them and finally, at the bottom, level seven, Drives You From the Room. This is where it is impossible for you to remain in the room while the program is on without becoming totally rude and obnoxious.

Now as we all know, Family Television Viewing Incompatibility Syndrome is not a problem of values, or even taste. It isn't what you like, it is whether or not family members like or dislike the same thing.

I mean, those of us who find Melrose Place a level seven show, a show that literally drives us from the room — and we admit we are a small minority and that we are the ones missing the point — we don't mean to imply that the show is stupid beyond redemption and that the people who like it must be mentally defective or something to be drawn in by such tripe, not at all.

We just don't get it.

And when you've got a level one and a level seven person watching the same show, you are totally incompatible.

Televisionally dysfunctional, as they say.

If you like Melrose Place, I know what you're thinking; "Well, having Family Television Viewing Incompatibility Syndrome with one show isn't so bad: perhaps you can get some quality family time in watching other shows, like Beverly Hills 90210. Or Baywatch."

I've got a feeling it's going to be a long television season around our house this year.

Upgrading to an Upgraded Upgrade

It's like a fever that periodically sweeps over me.

I resist it, but like any fever, once it gets me in its grip, I am powerless to resist its debilitating force. My thinking gets foggy, and my mind and body weaken as the fever rages through my system.

What's worse is this time my wife has the fever, too.

We are looking at buying a new computer.

Now, it's not like we are venturing into the computer world for the first time, you understand, not at all. Our basement is littered with the unused carcasses of perfectly working computers from Apple II clones to early laptops to a Macintosh. So, strictly speaking, it's not a computer that we want - it's a new computer. One with a CD ROM attached.

An upgrade.

As you can probably tell, we are in the grip of the unstable mental condition the medical community now refers to officially as Upgradia Dementia.

Upgradia Dementia is the disease that makes us feel like happiness is just an upgrade away.

Upgradia Dementia is not a new disease. Some of our parents suffered with it in the 50's, but at that time, it was known by its earlier name: Keeping up with the Joneses.

Fortunately for our parents, to keep up with the Joneses, all they had to buy were cars and houses.

Today, we have to upgrade everything.

Like many diseases, you don't really catch upgradia dementia. You've always got it. It just isn't always active.

And the problem is, almost anything can activate it.

I tend to get it when I see a Lexus go by.

Upgrade! Upgrade!

In the computer world, upgradia dementia can be activated by a commercial showing how neat a CD Rom drive is.

Or by the "version" question.

This is where simply having the right software is not enough. You must also have the right version.

"And of course, we do all of our layouts in Pagemaker."

"What version?"

"Uh, 4.1 Why?"

"We have 5.0"

The unspoken message here is that <u>your</u> 4.1 is propeller driven while <u>their</u> 5.0 has afterburners. Never mind that most people can't figure out how to use all of 4.1, much less 5.0.

Or that to even run 5.0 you will have to upgrade everything from your keyboard to your printer.

It still activates the same response: Upgrade! I need to upgrade!

Computers aren't the only place we upgrade, of course.

As Americans, we have always upgraded our cars about every three years.

And who among us hasn't upgraded their personal sound system from records to tapes to CD's, and from little speakers to woofers the size of a small house and back down again.

And men are forever upgrading their power tools.

"I need a bigger, more powerful cordless screwdriver."

"Are you using larger screws than you used to, Dear?"

"No."

"Then why do you need to upgrade your power screwdriver which is already an upgrade from the 50 regular screwdrivers you have hanging in the garage?"

"Because I do."

And it's been my observation that about seven years into their first marriage, most women take a long, hard, critical look at their husband's thinning hair, spreading waistline, deteriorating personal growth and lifetime earning potential, bad spending habits, morning breath, and bad attitude about what constitutes "women's work" and consider a hubby upgrade.

And frankly, considering a husband upgrade isn't a lot different than considering a computer upgrade.

"Gee, I was told you would last a lifetime, but now I find that compared to today's models, you run real slow, you don't have much internal memory, you're subject to every virus that comes along, you can't multi-task, and that when I try to reprogram you to help with the cooking, housework and laundry like the newer models do, you give me a system error, not to mention that your hard drive is starting to crash when it shouldn't."

Sounds like time to upgrade to me. Or time to replace hubby with a new model altogether. Which they sometimes do.

Men have been known to do the same thing, of course. My brother, who lives in San Diego, says that down there, the prevailing sport among rich guys 60 and older seems to be upgrading to a trophy wife.

Clearly, a case of upgradia dementia.

And who among us who makes the daily trip to Sta-Fit or

one of the other fitness clubs isn't trying to upgrade our body? (Actually, technically, some of us have abandoned the notion of "upgrading" and would settle for simply slowing the process of deterioration, but that's splitting semantic hairs. It amounts to the same thing.)

But, as any of you who have bought computers, and computer software know, upgrading everything else in your life really pales compared to upgrading computers.

Computers were made to be upgraded.

So I suppose that before long, we will add a CD ROM computer to our collection.

Which begs the question a lot of us must want answered: does anybody want to buy a used Apple IIs clone?

You could upgrade it.

Financial Junk Mail

The 24-page brochure came in the mail.

It looked sort of like the National Enquirer.

In big block letters, the headline screamed: The Truth About The Economy!

Across the top was the name of the publication: "Straight Talk. A Special Report About Your Money." There was a $2.50 price on it, but I guess they thought I should get this special issue for free.

Above the name were smaller banner headlines. I was grabbed by every one.

"America's first family of finance tells all inside!"

"The truth about the banking system! Page 12. The truth about the IRS! Page 16. The truth about interest rates! Page 17. The truth about credit cards! Page 7. Inside: What the experts are afraid to tell you…"

And the real hook: look inside…free gift.

Free gift? I knew in an instant, I was holding a junk mail hall of famer. I felt unworthy. After all, I don't have any money. But being the junk mail junkie that I am, I figured, what the heck.

Now, usually when we get junk mail, we have some idea where it comes from, right?

For instance, I once attended a seminar on producing newsletters (big waste of money) from a company that I thought knew about newsletters. In fact, their expertise was not in newsletters, but in seminars, and so now I get junk mail from them addressed to Mr. Douglas Hurd for seminars entitled, "How to be an assertive woman in a male work place," and "How to manage employees you can't stand while you've got a raging case of PMS."

Interesting, but I'll pass, thank you very much. I'll post them on the bulletin board, but I'll pass.

But at least I know where that comes from. I bought their product once, so now I'm on their list. I mean it's like buying something from Radio Shack.

Radio Shack can't sell you a fifty-cent battery without getting your name so that they can send you four catalogs filled with TV antennas, diodes and coaxial cable connectors. When they ask me my name, usually I say. "Joe Zupan. Why?"

Now, unlike most educated and refined people, when it comes to junk mail, most of the time I read it. I toss it after I read it, but I read it.

The exception is credit card solicitations. Sometimes I wonder — are there any words in the entire English language that can get a letter from your hands to the wastebasket faster than "You're Pre-approved!"? or "8.9% Interest Rate!" I can't think of any. Somebody should tell the banks that.

But lately it seems, I have been getting tons of financial junk mail — you know, mutual funds newsletters and stock market reports and stuff that would indicate somebody somewhere thinks I have money to invest.

In point of fact, when I go to the bank and tell the teller I have to transfer money from savings to checking, they usually say under their breath, "You'd better not need to transfer much."

I suspect that it's not my bank balance that put me on their list, but my age. Being in my middle forties (okay, late middle forties), those savvy marketers probably know that all of a sudden, we baby boomers are able to see retirement as a reality; and so we are pretty receptive to messages about investing and not being broke twenty years from now.

So when the first family of finance wants to tell me the truth about the economy, I'm ready.

So I go inside to meet these people.

The first family of finance, it turns out, is the Dolans, Ken and Daria. Ken has wire rim glasses (quite studious, nothing flashy there) and a shock of white hair.

My first thought is if you've got so much money, Ken, why don't you invest in some Grecian Formula 16. He looks like kind of a cross between Joseph Kennedy senior and Ken of Ken and Barbie fame. Daria looks, curiously, like she might be related to Marge Simpson with her bullet-proof hair.

Now, I'm not sure what I expect the first family of finance to look like, but this isn't quite it. After seeing them, I wonder who gave them their title. Probably their manager. "I know; we'll call you the first family of finance! Those dilwads we mail to in places like Spokane, Washington will eat that up."

I move on.

I want the truth about banking, IRS, interest rates, all that stuff they promised on the cover.

Unfortunately, what I get is more teasers. "Three ways to audit proof your tax return! Page 30. I turn, breathlessly, to page 30, wondering if Tom Stevenson of McFarland and Alton who does my taxes knows about this, when I discover, there is no page 30.

And then it dawns on me. It's on page 30 of the book they want to give me for subscribing to their newsletter which I can get for $71 off the regular price.

Ahhh. So that's how it works.

I think about my financial condition, and I pass.

I don't think the first lady of finance should have bullet proof hair anyway.

I reluctantly toss their brochure in the garbage. It's good, but no sale.

Next is a lovely piece from General Electric, those nice people who want to bring good things to my life.

On the outside, it says, "To start the year with over $500 in GE Rewards Coupons, Open Immediately." Below the headline is a picture of a GE Rewards MasterCard.

"Hmmm," I think. What a nice way to say, "You're Pre-approved."

GE: meet the first family of finance.

Shopping for Furniture

Here's a question for you men who are newly married:

If money were no object and you could take your wife anywhere, where would she most want to go? Hawaii, in all its romantic splendor?

Sun Valley, with its mountains and romantic sunsets? Cabo San Lucas, with its pristine beaches and sun-drenched villas? Or Expressions Furniture, out on Sprague?

If you've been married longer than, say, two years, the answer is probably pretty obvious to you. Most wives will opt for the furniture store every time.

Nothing against us husbands, you understand. It's just that being able to choose between spending more time with a mere man (and for all that, a man who, in spite of all the curious odors and sounds he emits, she is committed to spending her whole life with) and spending some real quality time, not to mention quality money, in a real honest to God, non-warehouse type furniture store, it's no contest.

The man will lose every time.

Personally, I just don't get it.

Not the choice: I understand that.

No, what I don't get is, the whole nice furniture store thing. When I'm in a nice furniture store, I have one prevailing thought, which is, "You've got to be kidding."

I used to think that you are what you drive — you know, if you're driving a Mercedes you're probably more successful and richer than the guy who drives a Cadillac who is richer than the guy who drives a '73 Chevy Nova.

But the older I get, the more I think a much more accurate measure of your social standing is where you buy your furniture. Or your wife buys it.

When you're first married, and you're poor, and all your furniture is Early American Hand-me-down, you shop price. "No Frills, No gimmicks. No Quality!" I don't care; this is all I can afford.

"Hello. Welcome to Pressboard Heaven. Please don't sit in that chair. It might break."

Even here, at this tender age, your wife will ask the quality question: Is this real wood?

"Does sawdust count?"

After Pressboard Heaven, you move up to Unfinished Furniture. Now, I ask you: would your wife buy a new car if she had to put on the doors, hood and headlights, and then paint the whole thing? I don't think so.

But she'll buy furniture that way.

In the '60s the furniture continuum developed some aberrations.

First there was waterbed furniture, which was looked upon by our parents as being totally decadent, and consequently something we all had to have, and beanbag furniture which was okay as long as you were stoned, and on which you spent most of your time lying around food freaking on Lorna Doones.

But sooner or later, we all entered mainstream America, where having real furniture becomes important.

And this is where men begin to split from women.

For men, "real furniture" means a chair.

Some psychologists will tell you that all men aspire to their chair. Our fathers had their chair, and we want our chair. Preferably something you can sit in watching TV for six hours that won't cause temporary paralysis of everything below the lumbar section of your back, and something you can spill beer on and it won't stain.

So, our idea of furniture shopping is going to the Lay-Z-Boy store.

So when our wives say, "Come on, let's go furniture shopping," we husbands tend to reply, "Why? Is there something wrong with my chair?"

Now, we men know that sooner or later, we will have to replace the ugly green couch our parents bought when they were first married and gave to us when we went off to college. But we also know that shopping for furniture together just isn't all that much fun.

In the first place, our wives keep asking our opinion.

"Do you like this?"

"Yeah. Sure."

"Or do you like this one better?"

"Um, yeah."

"Which?"

"Either."

And then there are the multiple choice questions: "What about this couch with the fox-hunt mural fabric in the family room if we paint it a kind of sea foam green color?"

"Paint what, the couch or the room?"

And none of this is made easier by the fact that there is something sensual about a really good furniture store that women respond to, that men don't.

"Oh God, I love this fabric. Feel it. Doesn't that feel…good?"

"Yeah. Can we leave now? I think we should take you home before this feeling gets away from you."

I'm sure the sales people know that when the breathing gets deep and rhythmic, the Gold Card can't be too far behind.

Unfortunately, you may also need to deal with interior designers — they're the ones wearing scarves over their shoulders who describe everything as "darling."

"I've got to show you this accent piece that is a life-sized pig that is just darling. There. Wouldn't that just be darling next to the coffee table?"

Well, I realize I'm not qualified to judge, but "darling" is not the word that comes to my mind when I see a statue of a pig. I don't care if it is the star of the latest House Beautiful magazine.

There is an interesting paradox. The more expensive the furniture, the more trendy it looks, and the shorter its half-life. And the shorter its half-life, the sooner it gets sent to the recreation room.

Like the ugly green couch your parents bought.

But that's okay. The day will come when, like the good parent you are, you give your trendy, fox-hunt mural couch to your children when they go off to college. But in this case, it may go with one condition.

They gotta take the pig, too.

FINDING THE PERFECT ALL-PURPOSE-UNIVERSAL-CHRISTMAS-GIFT AND OTHER HOLIDAY TRADITIONS

Finding the Perfect All-Purpose-Universal-Christmas Gift

It's the day before the day before Christmas.

Which means that last night, in keeping with the ancient traditions of the holidays, wives all over the world asked their husbands the ritual pre-Christmas question that bonds the holiday to our spirit, and our families one to another: "Have you bought anything for your mother yet?"

To which we men all gave the traditional answer, "Me? Mom? I thought <u>you</u> were buying her something."

This marks the beginning of the annual denial of responsibility for buying Christmas gifts family argument.

"I thought you were going to buy something for my mother."

"She's your mother."

"Yeah, but you always buy something for my mother," we whine.

"Only since we've been married."

"Who else on my list haven't you bought presents for?"

And so it goes.

This argument is, however traumatic, catalytic, in that it initiates the male Christmas shopping season, which, like the life of some insects, is only 36 hours long.

So this morning, all over town, men are driving to work, looking like they are thinking deep thoughts about their work or business, but in reality, they are repeating the male pre-Christmas chant, "What am I going to get Mom? What am I going to get Mom?"

By noon today, the reality of the deadline of Christmas shopping will have sunk in, and the chant will have changed to, "What am I going to get everybody?"

And this is the point where we default the game of finding lots of gifts for lots of people and instead start looking for its diametrical opposite: the one-size-fits-all Christmas gift.

We start looking for the All-Purpose-Universal-Christmas-Gift. Or APUCG (Pronounced "A-Pug") as it is known.

Now, besides your in-laws, grown nieces and nephews, and their spouses, co-workers and the parents of friends of your children, A-Pugs are also what businesses give to other businesses, and are the sole reason why Hickory Farms continues to exist.

"Oh, look. A Hickory Farms Gift Pack from KGA with their special sinus-clearing mustard. Gosh, Thanks!"

(Have you ever wondered if a thousand years from now, anthropologists will ponder the religious or social significance of why we think it's okay to give someone a four-pound beef stick at Christmas but not at, say, their wedding? Just wondering).

All-Purpose Universal Christmas Gifts used to be no-brainers. You just got everyone a bottle of booze. The classy ones amongst us gave wine in little wooden boxes.

But then political correctness became all the rage, and alcoholic beverages were suddenly not correct.

(In spite of that, I have argued around our agency that we should still give those clients who change our layouts and re-size our headlines and disagree with us about our color choices for their brochures Christmas bottles of MD 20-20. I mean, what the heck, if they're blind anyway ... But we don't.)

So, if you're one of those guys still wondering what you're going to get those friends, relatives and business acquaintances on your Christmas list in the next 36 hours, allow me to help.

Books. Hardback books.

Now, for those of you who have already gone out and bought fifty one-pound bags of coffee from the Four Seasons or Starbucks figuring coffee makes the perfect All-Purpose-Universal-Christmas-Gift, let me say this: That was last year's gift. But, no sweat.

There's nothing in the Christmas Gift Manual that says you can't give two APUCGs.

People who get both coffee and a book from you will simply be overwhelmed by your generosity and Christmas spirit, and that's not such a bad thing.

Now a lot of you are thinking, "Wait a minute, I can't afford to be giving everyone on my Christmas list a twenty-five dollar hardback book for Christmas."

You don't have to. Because in the old Penney's store downtown, main floor, there is a bookstore that has hundreds of hardback books for three to five bucks each.

Now, I admit, this isn't an upscale B. Dalton kind of place. It's more like a literary Value Village, but who cares?

Why books?

Because hardback books are so classy.

They say: "I can read and I think you can, too."

They say, "You and I treasure the world of ideas, and if we just had more time, we would discuss weighty intellectual matters whose true home is in a hardbound book."

They say, "I know that you know that when people see shelf after shelf of hardbound books in a home, they are quietly impressed; assuming, naturally, that the owner has read all of them (faulty assumption, but who corrects anybody?), and I want to give you the gift of making that impression on people who visit you."

It's another way of saying, "Let's face it, we're both intellectual phonies, but who cares? It's Christmas."

And for three bucks each, they cost less than beef sticks or coffee and do less damage to your breath.

Now if there is a down side to all this, it's that you can wander all over the whole store and never see a title or author you recognize. But that's not altogether bad either, because when you give a book, the presumption is you know it's a good one. Just like when you give a coffee blend, you're presumed to have tried it and liked it, or that you can vouch for the bottle of wine you give.

Imagine your joy when your brother-in-law opens your present: "Wow. A book: <u>Fourth Century Etruscans and Their Pottery</u>. Thanks."

Do you think your brother-in-law is going to read it? Not a chance.

Will it go on his bookshelf? Probably.

So, does that mean we men who give All-Purpose-Universal-Christmas-Gifts want to receive a hardback books for Christmas?

Sure. As long as they're from B. Dalton.

Less Than Perfect

I know this is the season when we're supposed to be filled with love and charity for all, but I'm having a problem with someone.

This is someone I want to like, someone I should like, I even used to like. But all of a sudden he's getting on my nerves.

In fact, I'm coming to hate this person.

To make matters worse, I only just met his wife, and I already hate her — purely by association.

Who is this person? Probably someone you're coming to hate, too. Jim Palmer.

You know, the guy in the commercial who says, "So if you have credit that is less than perfect, call The Money Store."

Jim Palmer and his commercial is getting to be like an obnoxious party guest who doesn't know when the party is over, and it's time to leave.

This is unfortunate, because I used to like Jim Palmer. He

was my hero. Here was a guy who made a fortune playing base-ball, and then made another fortune being photographed in Jockey underwear.

Having once been described as the poster child for the ath-letically-challenged, I can't relate much to his baseball career. But I think that most all men can admire a guy who can make a lot of money doing nothing more strenuous than standing around being photographed in Jockey shorts.

Nice work, if you can get it.

But he's wearing out his welcome.

"Is your credit less than perfect?" he begins.

"No, Jim!" I'm now screaming back at the TV. "My credit is spotless, because my daddy told me never to miss a payment or the Sheriff would come and repossess my car, my stereo and my first born male child, and I believed him. Half the banks in America want to give me a Visa card, my credit is so perfect, Jim, so get out of my living room, and hustle your deadbeats some-where else! "

Like I said, he's starting to get on my nerves. I might add, the guy from Camp Chevrolet who says much the same thing isn't too far behind.

But even though I really want Jim to go away, and I find him annoying and his wife is, well, "unwatchable," I think is the chari-table way to describe her, I do know when I hear advertising writing genius, and this commercial is it.

It's in the phrase, "Less than perfect."

I mean, does that not speak directly to all the little insecuri-ties you carry around, bypassing all the filters and defense mecha-nisms you erect just to function normally in society?

When you hear those words, doesn't a voice from deep within you cry out, "Yes! I am less than perfect. I admit it. I try, lord knows I try to be perfect, but I just can't get there with my lim-ited abilities. I'm not a bad person, but I am less than perfect. Can I have some money?"

Me, too.

I like "The Money Store" too, although, at least ten years ago a local Ford dealer was trying to get the word "dealer" out of their name and referred to themselves as "The Ford Store" as in, "Pick up your new Mustang at the Ford Store." So that is hardly a new idea.

It didn't stick.

Still, if you are trying to talk to people with botched credit, "The Money Store" probably is less threatening than, "First Federal Intransigent Financial Corporation," or some such.

But "Less than perfect." Wow. That's pretty close to perfect ad copy.

The only problem is, it's wasted on The Money Store. Because now, none of the rest of us can use it, when there are so many applications.

"Are your thighs less than perfect? Send for the world famous Thighmaster!"

"Is your whole body, possibly even including your genetic code, less than perfect? Call Jenny Craig Diet Centers."

See how it well it works? Did I say the odious word "overweight" and make you feel bad?

No. I said, "less than perfect" and you filled in the blank.

And most advertisers don't care how imperfect we are. In fact, the more imperfect, the better, because the inference is if you heed the call to action, you <u>will</u> be perfect.

And isn't that all that we really want in life? To be perfect?

That, and to have a high disposable income.

"Is your income less than perfect?" Does that resonate or what? I don't know about you, but I'd be tuned into the rest of the message. "Join the exciting and growing field of computer theft."

And the line doesn't have to be just about ourselves to be effective. It can be about someone else, and it works just fine. The opens up a whole world of commercial possibilities.

"Is your husband less than perfect? Well, now you can have the husband you've always wanted, even if the one you chose is less than perfect.

"He can be trained. Just send your husband to Doug's Husband School.

"In no time at all, your husband will be leaving the toilet seat down and shutting cupboard doors, and — yes — actually putting dishes in the sink and running water into his empty milk glass.

"In our advanced course he'll learn to pick up after himself and wipe his feet when he comes in from outside. Our husband graduates have actually gone on to do the laundry, plan a meal, and shop at Lamonts for the kids clothing.

"If you're expecting a little one, we can even teach your husband how to change poopy diapers, although that costs more. You can have the husband you deserve, even if the one you chose is less than perfect. Call the number on your screen. Hair transplants, bowel resections, and cosmetic surgery not included."

And if that doesn't work?

Well, you could always go to The Husband Store.

Getting Ready to Get Ready For Christmas

"Are you getting ready for Christmas yet?"

I was asked that by my bank teller because I was moving some money from savings to checking the other day. She wasn't being nosy, you understand, just chatting.

Like when you get a thousand bucks in traveller's checks and they say, "Going on vacation?" To which I always reply, "No, just going over to Nordstrom to buy a tie." They never know quite what to do with that. Some just smile and say, "That's nice," while others give you that, "And how long have you been through with your electroshock therapy?" look.

I thought about her question for a moment and said, "No, I'm not getting ready for Christmas yet, but I am getting ready to get ready."

Moving money from savings to checking is one of the key signs you're getting ready for Christmas. But as it happens, I was moving money for a more immediate, pedestrian reason: I was overdrawn by $400 dollars.

But I have been getting ready to get ready for Christmas.

It starts with getting ready to pay for it all.

Now, I <u>know</u> that it's better to give than receive, and I <u>know</u> that when Christmas Morning comes, if I haven't given lavishly, I will feel really bad about it. And I <u>know</u> that every year I resolve to do better in this department next year, and give more gifts and more <u>thoughtful</u> gifts (you ladies are saying, "A man? Give a thoughtful gift? Are you a genetic aberration, or what?"). And I <u>know</u> I should give more to the relatives out in the twig section of the family tree; and I know I would feel better on Christmas Day if I did. But what they don't tell you about it being better to give than receive is giving is also a lot more expensive.

So I have to get ready to get ready for that expense. I wish I didn't, but I do.

I train for Christmas by reading my checkbook register.

The Gap: $117!? It's like taking a hit to the solar plexus. Ooooph.

Mariposa: $67.50 Oomph!

50 bucks? "Hey, what'd you buy at Joel's for fifty bucks?" I ask my wife.

"Napkins, Dear." Oh, Jeez.

Now, remember, this isn't Christmas spending yet. It's just spending spending. After a while, when I get so I can look at a check for $125 to Wilson's Leather without flinching, I know that I am done getting ready to get ready, and it's time to move the Christmas money into checking.

To ease the pain, I move as much money as I think it's going to take to pay for all our Christmas gifts.

I usually do that three times before we're done. Sound familiar?

The next thing I have to get ready to get ready to do is put up the Christmas lights.

My daughter starts me on this by asking, "Can we put up the

Christmas lights today?"

Note the pronoun: Can <u>we</u> put up the Christmas lights.

I answer something like "Sure. Why don't you get them out?"

To which she inevitably replies, "Me?" and gives me a look that says if I keep talking nonsense, she'll have to send me back for more electroshock treatments.

There is a law of nature somewhere that says that the day you put up the Christmas lights, the temperature will drop to below 10 degrees, your dog will eat your only pair of work gloves, and the rest of your family will decide that putting up lights is man's work and holler if you need help.

Not wanting to rush things, I have to get ready to get ready to put up the lights. This requires studying the front of my house for about a week and trying to remember how I did it the year before.

You'd think that after a year or two I'd have it down, but I don't.

Every year I have to be re-trained, which is complicated by the fact that I can never quite remember what I did or didn't do the year the wires and the screen door got all tangled up and I almost electrocuted the paper boy.

The actual getting ready, by the way, is quite short in that it does not include testing the strings before I put them up, which would violate my macho self-image, not to mention deprive my wife of being able to ask, "Why didn't you test them before you put them up?"

Actually, it doesn't matter. Because after I do get them up, I always have to take them down and turn them around because I never get all the plugs going in the right direction so they all plug in together.

I also have to get ready to get ready to go get the Christmas tree. This involves preparing myself emotionally for the trauma of skinned knuckles, a car full of pine needles and losing a tree wrestling match with a fat, bushy Douglas fir that looks like it needs to spend a little time in Tree Weight Watchers.

I also have to get emotionally ready for the task of getting the tree in the stand and having the traditional "Is it straight?" discussion.

This is where I lie on my belly on the floor, and with pitch dripping on my bald spot, try to hold an eight-foot tree in a vertical position so my wife and family can see if it is straight.

"Tilt it to the left."

"Oomph."

"That was right."

"Oomph."

"More."

"Humph."

"What was that popping sound? "

Just the sound of my cervical vertebrae exploding under the pressure.

Of course, all this getting ready to get ready adds a layer of stress to the holidays. Which is why, when someone cheerfully asks, "Are you getting in the Christmas spirit yet?" I want to shout, "YES! Merry Christmas! NOW GET OFF MY BACK!"

But I don't. Instead I smile and usually say, "Not yet, but I'm getting ready ... to get ready."

Rules For A Successful Thanksgiving

This being the week before Thanksgiving, I think that someone, and it looks like it's going to have to be me, should review the rules for a successful Thanksgiving, so we can all give thanks for what we have without a major family fight.

Now, I know that all you couples who have been married a long time are rolling your eyes back and saying, "Do we have to go over the rules again?"

Yes.

Even though you may be settled into your Thanksgiving routine, there are lots of young couples out there who may be experiencing the joy of their first married Thanksgiving.

The joy begins when they realize that both sets of parents will be expecting them.

"When do you want to leave for Thanksgiving?"

"Since it's a four-hour drive, I'd like to leave Wednesday night."

"It's not a four-hour drive to my parents' house."

"Who said anything about going to your parents'?"

So Rule #1: Talk. Decide in advance whose mother you are going to disappoint and get on with it.

It is okay to negotiate this point. There is nothing in the rules of a successful Thanksgiving that says that just because you show up somewhere, you are morally or legally obligated to stay for four full days. This point can be useful in reaching a negotiated settlement.

"Okay, but if we go to your mother's, we get to leave Friday."

"Night."

"Morning."

"Noon."

"Agreed."

Rule #2: The spouse must call the soon-to-be-disappointed mother. A lot of young couples refer to this as the revenge rule. ("Fine. We're going to go to your parents — you call my mother and rip her heart out.) But in fact, revenge has little to do with it. The real purpose of the rule is to deflect potentially lethal (lethal to your marriage, that is) comments from the disappointed mother. ("This was his doing, wasn't it? Does he have a job yet? Listen honey, if this isn't working out, you can come home. We'll just put this whole marriage thing behind us, like it never happened.") If the other spouse calls, none of that happens.

Rule #3: Since Thanksgiving is really about being together with family and not about food, don't bring up your mother-in-law's cooking ability as a reason not to go there.

"What your mother does to a turkey qualifies as substance abuse. And her feeding it to the kids is child abuse. The moment that bird hits the plate, we could all be placed under arrest by

Child Protective Services."

"Dad says a turkey should be well cooked."

"Well, that doesn't mean it has to be so dry it sucks all the moisture out of your brain when you eat it."

Not fair. Not fair at all.

Which brings up Rule # 3.1: Since Thanksgiving is about being together, it is considered bad form to point out that you don't like getting together with your in-laws.

You will learn that some things are better left unsaid.

Rule #4: Be nice and help. This is easier for the wives than the husbands. In fact, right now most of the new husbands listening are thinking: What? Have you been to my in-laws at Thanksgiving?"

I know what you mean. There is nothing that can make a new son-in-law feel quite so useless as being around a family getting Thanksgiving dinner ready. This is because everybody has a pre-assigned role except him; someone mashes the potatoes, dad carves, mother becomes project foreman.

To the outsider, it's a little like stumbling into a surgery at Sacred Heart.

"Carving knife."

"Carving knife."

"Fork."

"Fork."

"I can't save his legs! I've got to amputate! Stand back, this is going to get ugly."

The only thing worse than feeling useless is if they ask you to carve the turkey. "Sure, why not? Got a clean chain saw handy?"

There is something about carving a turkey in front of your mother-in-law that guarantees shredding it to bits.

But even setting the table can be a problem. That's because on Thanksgiving, you don't eat on the regular plates. You eat on the <u>nice</u> plates.

The rule here is: You should view this "is the glass half-empty or half-full" situation as a compliment to your importance, and ignore the inverse message, which is all the rest of the year, you're not worthy enough to eat off plates with little roses painted on them.

For your part, you wives must resist the urge to humiliate your husband into feeling like a ten-year-old by telling him — so everyone can hear — to be careful with the nice plates. It's hard, but you must trust him not toss them onto the table like a bunch of family heirloom frisbees.

To new husbands, I would offer this bit of advice on rule four: clear the table. When the meal is pretty much done, carry the dishes into the kitchen.

Don't put them into the dishwasher, which undoubtedly has secret loading instructions which only your mother-in-law knows, and shares with no one.

But it is amazing how many of your personality flaws will be erased in the eyes of your new in-laws by the simple act of clearing away the dirty dishes. Assuming you don't break any.

This action has the added benefit of disengaging you from table conversation, which, if you sit there long enough, will inevitably turn to why you don't have a child or a job, or both.

The final rule, of course, is to give thanks. Give thanks for all you have, for your family, for the football on TV that passes the time, and give thanks that Christmas, with all its family traditions, is still a month away.

The Day After Thanksgiving

Right now, at this very moment all across the Inland Northwest, thousands of people are waking up and thinking, "Why did I pick a career in retail?"

Or put in career counselling, college catalog-ese, "fashion merchandising."

Maybe it was because you were a sucker for an ad:

"Can you count? Can you make change or at least read a cash register that will make change for you? Can you run a label across a scanner? If so, you could join the exciting world of fashion merchandising."

"You mean, can I be a retail store clerk?"

"We prefer calling it, "Minimum Wage Sales Associate.""

Or maybe you chose retail because you like working most weekends, some evenings and starting today, days, weekends and evenings for about thirty days, during which time you won't see your family, unless they go out shopping where you work.

I have friends in retail who observe a Thanksgiving weekend ritual called, "The saying of goodbye to daddy," which is not unlike the sending off of Submariners on patrol. "Say goodbye to daddy, Celeste. You won't see him again until Christmas Eve. Or, if it's a particularly good year, Christmas Morning. Goodbye, goodbye. Write when you can. Leave notes on the kitchen counter."

Well, whatever the reason, if you work in retail, it's showtime.

But it's not like you'll be alone today. Because custom and ritual dictate that all the rest of us, at least those of us who were smart enough to choose a career field where we get today off, are going to come visit you.

And if we don't today, we will by Sunday.

Today is to my credit cards what New Year's Day is to the calendar and the first day of school is to my daughter's social life: both an ending and a new beginning in the ongoing circle of life.

It is the low water mark for my Visa card balance that rides up and down on a spending holiday tide.

Like a person who knows he is going to gain ten pounds over the Thanksgiving holiday so he looses ten pounds in advance, I spend the months from roughly April through October trying to get my credit card balances in shape for the spending binge that's going to take place in the next 30 days.

This is the best time of year for my credit cards. They're lean. They're ready. "Put me in, coach," they all seem to say.

All in good time, I reply. All in good time.

Actually, when I go shopping today, I don't buy much.

I look.

This runs contrary to my wife's day after Thanksgiving shopping philosophy, which is "lookers lose." Or as Julius Caesar once said, "You see, you want, you buy."

Now, there are some rules we must all follow today.

The first one is if you're a man and you're single, you don't have to shop at all. You get to stay home and watch football on TV. Some married men do this, too, especially where they gather in families where they can all lie about in overstuffed LazyBoy loungers and look like beer-drinking, football-watching walruses.

If you have a teenage girl, the rule is you must connect her to a friend and then let them fly around the mall on their own. Teenagers must never be seen actually shopping in a family cluster if they are to maintain even a shred of social standing among their peers.

If you're newly married, you probably shop together. All day.

If you're not newly married (anything over, what, three weeks?) the rule is the men get to take a periodic TV break to go to the TV department to watch football.

This is kind of an aside, but wouldn't selling televisions in Sears at this time of year be the pits? I mean, you'd have to face an army of bored married men standing around looking at your televisions and try to figure out which ones are in the market for a TV and which ones are simply killing time.

"Can I help you?" "Yeah, go find my wife and tell her I'm tired and I want to go home. I think she's in Zales."

I wonder what would happen if one of them got on the intercom and said, "If you're not buying a television, will you please clear the area and go find your wives." I'll probably never know, huh?

When shopping today, everybody must observe the personal interest sensitivity rule, which roughly translated states, "be sensitive to the fact that today is not the day to indulge your particular personal interests."

It is considered bad form to ask your wife and kids to watch you fantasize about a new set of golf clubs if they don't golf, for instance. On the other hand, if your wife wants to go look at percale sheets and floral print bath towels while you contemplate a new set of woods, that's perfectly acceptable.

It is also wise to remember that shopping is a union activity, and the international order of men shoppers has included in our contract a one hour coffee break for each hour of shopping. We realize that our contract isn't quite as good as the teamster's contract, but it was the best we could do.

The final rule is don't hassle the sales people. After all, they probably didn't realize what they were getting into when they signed up for fashion merchandising.

Christmas Shopping Paradoxes

I suspect that the worst thing about being a single or divorced man would be that you would have to do your Christmas shopping without a wife along to tell you when you were making a bad choice.

"Honey, your mother is 78, and she lives alone in an apartment. I don't think she needs a McColloch chain saw."

"Are you sure? It's got a 14-inch bar and a chain brake."

"Trust me on this."

I was thinking about this because this is the weekend I am going to have to do my Christmas shopping.

Like most men, I would rather be flogged than go Christmas shopping alone.

That's because of the Christmas Shopping Paradoxes.

The Christmas Shopping Paradoxes are those quirky laws of nature which make shopping difficult for women and almost impossible for men.

The first Christmas Shopping Paradox states, "everybody on your list already has everything."

For proof of this paradox, I cite the success of the Pendleton Shirt Company.

Everybody loves Pendleton shirts. So what do you get someone who has everything? Right. Another Pendleton shirt.

Now, how many of you are going to give your father-in-law a Pendleton shirt for Christmas? Right. And how many of you are thinking about it? I believe that's the rest of you. And this in spite of the fact that all of the fathers-in-law in question probably have several Pendleton shirts from Christmases past they haven't even taken out of the box yet.

The second Christmas Shopping Paradox is the "I don't want, or need anything" paradox.

This states that at the onset of the Christmas shopping season, everyone on your list, when asked what they want for Christmas, will honestly reply that they really don't want or need anything. (The exception to this rule is children, who want and need everything.) You can test the validity this paradox on yourself.

When asked what you wanted for Christmas, how many of you answered, "Oh, I don't want anything for Christmas."

I don't know about you, but I spend 11 months of the year, thinking bizarre thoughts like, "You know what I really need to buy myself is a three-ton floor jack just in case I ever want to change the transmission on my car."

Right.

Or, "You know, I really need one of those fancy $129 wine bottle cork removers they advertise in the Sharper Image catalog." (Never mind the fact that most of the wine I drink comes in boxes or in bottles with screw-on caps.)

But when Christmas comes, and somebody might just buy me something like that, I go blank. I honestly can't think of anything to put on my Christmas list. So when asked what I want for Christmas, the answer is usually, "I don't know," or worse, "Nothing."

And I suspect you're the same way.

(The risk of saying "nothing" is that I might just get nothing for Christmas, which isn't what I want either.)

In any case, there is the paradox: Just when you need to buy presents for people, no one can seem to think of anything they want.

Some help that is.

The third Christmas Shopping Paradox is anybody you'd really be good at buying for won't be on your list. (This paradox has an inverse version: everybody on your list will be somebody you are not good at buying for.)

For instance, I'd be great at buying presents for a young couple moving into their first house from an apartment. In that situation, you can just go into Eagle Hardware and buy anything on the east wall of the store.

"Wow. Stanley inch-and-a-half, double-key, double-throw, dead bolts! How did you know? Thanks, man."

See what I mean? Easy. Unfortunately, the Christmas Shopping Paradox keeps anybody like that from my list.

The exception to this rule is married couples — especially younger married couples buying for each other. This is why you go through a phase in your marriage where the gifts you give each other are not so much for your spouse as for both of you. Together.

"What do you want for Christmas, Dear?"

"A lamp for the living room. What do you want?"

"A trailer hitch for the car."

"I was hoping you'd ask for rain gutters over the front door."

"I was hoping you'd ask for heavy duty shocks for the Blazer." "Can we have both?"

"Sure."

"Done."

I wonder if my mother-in-law would like rain gutters? Nah, she's already got rain gutters.

But even here, if you stay married long enough, you run out of things to give to each other.

The final Christmas Shopping Paradox is, the longer you shop, the less there will be to choose from. This is not just less in the absolute — "I'm sorry, we're all sold out of Mortal Combat. Perhaps your child would like "Rape and Pillage" or the newest video game for seven to ten year olds, "Drive-By Shooting" —

but also in a conceptual sense. The more stuff you look at, the less right any of it seems to be.

And that's why you want to have your wife with you. Women don't go into Christmas shopping sensory overload nearly so quickly as we men do, so if you take your wife with you, you actually have a shot at choosing some nice gifts.

Okay, acceptable gifts.

The only thing I haven't figured out is, if I'm shopping with my wife, when am I going to buy her <u>her</u> Pendleton shirt?

Shopping on Company Time and Other Time Honored Christmas Traditions

This being Christmas Eve day, it is the day that the Christmas traditions really begin.

Now, I know that some of you are saying, "Wait a minute. What about the traditional Christmas tree decorating fight, where entire families get to get into the spirit of the holidays by offering each other traditional Christmas Tree greetings, like, "What are you putting that there, for? It looks stupid there." And, "Are you going to help, or what?" And of course, everybody's favorite: "That isn't how you're supposed to put on tinsel."

You're right. Certainly, the Christmas tree decorating fight is one of the traditions of Christmas.

But starting today, Christmas Eve day, so many of our individual traditions sync up that you can almost feel the spirit of the event sweep across us.

This very moment, men in bed, men shaving, men on their way to work, men everywhere are all having the traditional Christmas Eve day wake-up thought: "Oh my God! I've still got 75 presents to buy, and I'm out of time! How did I let this happen? I'm dead meat."

This gives way to tradition number two, which is telling the boss you've got some errands to run, and doing your Christmas shopping on company time. This is generally not a problem, because your boss is out Christmas shopping, too, unless your boss happens to be a woman, who, if she is normal, will have completed her Christmas shopping last Saturday and is apt to be very unsympathetic to your plight.

But today, even the best of shoppers and planners will have the traditional attack of the "Christmas Uh-ohs," which is what you get when, from out of the blue, you realize that you forgot someone on your list.

The uh-ohs can strike any time, anywhere. "Ladies and gentlemen of the jury: A man's life is at stake here. A man unjustly accused of murdering his ... Uh-oh. Uh-oh. I forgot to buy a present for Uncle Harry. Your honor, could we take a short recess please? Say until next Tuesday?"

When the uh-oh's strike, normally the victim stops what he is doing and looks straight up.

Now, that's not so bad if you are sitting at a desk somewhere, but it can be very dangerous if it happens to you when you are driving, or for that matter, at the wrong place in the mall. I once got a case of the uh-oh's at the top the stairs at NorthTown, and almost got knocked down the stairs by a shopper following too close who rear-ended me because she couldn't stop in time.

A sub-set of the uh-oh's is Christmas sock panic.

I never encountered Christmas sock panic until I got married because in my family we didn't have Christmas socks. We had a fireplace, and we had a mantle, but we just didn't do socks.

I always sort of figured that socks were a Dickens invention that went away shortly after the turn of the century.

Wrong.

Imagine my surprise when, on my first Christmas Eve with my wife's family, I am introduced to the tradition of everybody getting up out of bed in the middle of the night, and, in their jammies, stuffing everybody's Christmas sock.

In the first place, I didn't bring anything to stuff, and in the second place, I don't sleep in jammies.

So it is that every year, at just about noon on Christmas Eve day, I traditionally enter Christmas sock panic. Fortunately, Christmas sock panic is really no big deal, because everything you need for a Christmas sock can be purchased at Payless. Three bottles of industrial strength Oil of Olay, Lady Shick razors, 250 count generic aspirin, deodorant, a few CD's and some Penicillin for baby brother who's now 18 and doing things we don't want to know about.

Today is also the day you get to have the traditional "when are we going to open the presents" conversation.

Now, let me ask you a question: If, during your wedding ceremony, the minister or priest or whomever had said, "And do you, Herman, promise to have and to hold, to open your presents on Christmas Eve, to love and to cherish, in sickness and in health…" how many of you would have said, "Wait a minute, wait a minute! Go back a minute. What was that part about opening presents on Christmas Eve? We never talked about that. If we open presents on Christmas eve, what do we do on Christmas Morning? Watch cartoons? No way. I love you, Dear, but I'm not going through life opening presents on Christmas Eve. Sorry. It's Christmas Morning or the wedding is off."

Yeah. I don't know what it is that makes Christmas Eve openers attracted to Christmas Morning openers, but they are, and hence the discussion.

This usually leads to some sort of compromise that satisfies no one.

"Fine. The kids can each open three presents Christmas Eve, but not the big one from Nana. And you and I will each open two, but I get to open an extra one if I happen to choose the underwear from Penney's that Mom always gives me because that doesn't count."

Finally, with all the last minute shopping and uh-oh attacks, you have the traditional last minute wrapping frenzy. It is not unusual here to run out of a few of the crucial wrapping necessities:

"Tape! I need more Scotch Tape."

"We're out of Scotch tape."

"Shoot, and I'm out of duct tape, too."

"I bought some for your Christmas sock; we can use that."

"You bought me duct tape for my Christmas Sock? Was I a bad boy last year or something?"

Finally, ultimately, Christmas Eve arrives, and you must put everything else aside, and, hopefully, with whatever family you have, simply stop and enjoy it.

I say hopefully, because in something like 12 hours, the Christmas Day traditions will begin.

Merry Christmas, everyone.

Christmas Present Recycling

'Tis the season to be jolly. 'Tis also, I'm afraid, the season when some of us recycle.

Not just recycle glass and aluminum like good little citizens, but actual Christmas presents, like bad little elves.

Like all Christmas present recyclers, I feel awful about it when I do it. (Of course, that's offset somewhat by the fact that I feel awful about having to spend a big chunk of my weekend shopping for somebody on my list when I know that what I will find will not be any more cherished than what I already have in a box in the basement: A Revereware genuine plastic crock pot with daisies on the outside.)

And I'm sure I speak for all of us when I say we don't mean to recycle.

It just sort of happens. I mean, we don't plan for it, or anything. It's not like we open our presents on Christmas morning and exclaim, "Wow, a Crock-pot! Thank you. This will be perfect to give to somebody I don't like very much next year."

Not at all.

But what happens is some presents just don't get into the "return to the store for something I want" pile because you think you might use them sometime. But then along with the Christmas lights, they go into deep storage, where they are completely forgotten.

Until next Christmas.

So just about the time you're pulling out the Christmas lights and coincidentally wondering what you are going to get for some of the people way down on your Christmas list, there in front of you is this perfectly serviceable, still in the box with the instructions, crock-pot.

Or Rand McNally Atlas you didn't need but couldn't return because it was something your mother-in-law got free for joining the AAA or something.

Or a hand-painted collectable porcelain dinosaur you got stuck with at the office Christmas party gift exchange last year that is just about the ugliest thing you've ever seen, and you think, "Hmmmmm. Who would know?"

Besides yourself, of course, but if you're this far into the thought process, let's face it: you don't count.

Now, while you're answering that question and not coming up with anybody except your wife, it usually doesn't occur to us recyclers to also ask, "Why would I want to give something to somebody else that I couldn't find a use for myself?"

The answer to that is: Well, for openers, you're lazy!

Recycling Christmas presents does not come without a price in guilt and apprehension, however.

In the expediency of the moment, it is easy to forget that by the time people are actually sitting around the tree opening presents, you will not only be gripped by the normal apprehension surrounding gift giving ("Did I make a right choice? Will the color be right? Will they like it?"), but you will also have an overload of doubts that you have correctly remembered what you got from whom the Christmas before, and you are about to be discovered as having recycled a gift back to the original giver.

"Why Doug, you're breaking out in hives. Whatever is the matter?"

"The matter? Nothing! Would it be okay if you didn't open that big box over there?"

Now if you should happen to receive a recycled gift, one that you gave a year ago, custom dictates that you don't recognize it.

"Oh, a crock-pot! Just like the one I gave you last year. Just

<u>exactly</u> like the one I gave you last year. In fact, it's even got the same recipes I put in yours last year. Isn't that a coincidence?"

"Well, we liked it so much ... "

So if are going to give in to the temptation to recycle, someone must know absolutely and for certain who gave you what last year.

If you're a man, this is not you.

It is probably the family genealogist.

"Who is this 'Lucinda' that's on our list?"

"Okay: Remember your brother's second wife's daughter by her first husband?"

"I thought that was Emily. Amelia."

"Actually, that was Rose. Emma was your sister's step-daughter by her third husband. Anyway, Rose married Ed who had an older son who married Lucinda. We went to their wedding, remember?"

"That's who that was? I thought that was somebody you worked with. So what does that make Lucinda to me?"

"Um, 33rd on your Christmas list."

"Think she needs a crock-pot?"

Now, I should add here that not all Christmas gift recycling is bad. My daughter has decided that maybe some of the stuffed animals she has received, accumulated, loved and abandoned over the years should be re-gift wrapped and recycled to a child less fortunate somewhere. Sort of her own private Toys for Tots program.

And I think that's great.

And, frankly, I'm not so sure that recycling what you got in the office gift exchange right back into next year's office gift exchange isn't such a bad idea, either.

Especially if what you got is the world's ugliest porcelain dinosaur.

So how do you keep the gifts you give from being recycled? Well for starters, select your gifts with love and attention to their personal needs, wants and tastes.

And never give anybody a crock-pot.

The Mother's Day Covenant

Remember just before you got married, and they took you into that little room with the witnesses and you signed all those official looking papers, and everybody laughed and the guy who married you said that this was the real wedding, that signing those papers was what really made you married, and the ceremony was just for show?

Remember that?

Did you read that document? Or did you just sign, motivated by the love of your bride and out-of-control hormones?

Neither did I.

Neither does anyone.

But we should have because down near the bottom, in very small print, in the section titled "Hallmark Holidays," is a little agreement we all entered into called The Mother's Day Covenant.

And Mother's Day is Sunday.

What the Mother's Day Covenant says is, "Whereas the party of the first part is legally joined in social and emotional contract with the party of the second part, said contract being entered into voluntarily and without restriction, the party of the second part, hereafter known as "Husband" does agree to..." Maybe I'll just tell you: It says since she agreed to go through childbirth and generally ruin her body, you agree to get her a Mother's Day present.

I know what you're thinking. "Like what?"

But here's the catch in the covenant — you can't ask.

At least you can't ask her. Because the covenant requires that she answer, "Oh, you don't have to get me anything," which, at the very best gets you back where you started and at the worst, you might just believe, which skips you immediately to the Violations and Penalties section of the Covenant, which I don't have time to get into right now, but we all know the penalties for getting nothing for the mother of your children on Mother's Day are pretty severe.

There is nothing in the Mother's Day Covenant that says that you can't ask people you work with what they are getting their wives or mothers for Mother's Day. You should remember, however, that if you ask an actual mother what she hopes to get, she will know what you are up to and the esteem in which you are held by that person will diminish severely.

On the other hand, if you're an average white, balding, middle-aged male, you're not held in any esteem anyway, so what have you got to lose?

But before we get to the gift buying and cover minimums and maximums set forth in the covenant, I feel I should review section 12: Duties and Responsibilities. It says right here, "So long as there are minor children in the household, the organizing and buying of the Mother's Day presents, the giving of said presents and all activities for the day notwithstanding pre-existing family traditions," etcetera, etcetera, etcetera, here we go, "...shall be the responsibility of the father."

There.

Meaning, it isn't enough for you to just duck into the nearest Rosauers and buy a card, like you're thinking of doing right this moment, but you have to be sure that the kids (kids — mother — remember?) are presented with a opportunity to buy a gift as well.

And, if you have boys, the chances are better than eight to one that they will ask one of the most difficult questions you will face during their entire childhood: "Like what?"

If your children are still in day care or at school where they have made gifts for their mother, those count (see section 13, paragraph 9, Gifts, Alternatives and Exceptions) and by all means you should use them.

If your children are older than that, but not yet old enough to think for themselves (for girls that's age 12 or 13; for boys, 27), you've got some gift buying to do.

And, I should note here that it is considered very bad form to wake your children up on Sunday morning and go do it then. Besides, it is doubtful that you'll find just the right gift in 7-11 which is about the only thing open at that hour.

"A loaf of Snyder's Bread and a quart of 2% milk. How thoughtful."

So where do you go to buy your Mother's Day gifts?

Well, let me give you a short list of places you don't go. You don't go to Big O Tires. There is nothing they sell at Big O Tires that qualifies as a Mother's Day gift.

And you don't go to Ernst, Home Base or Eagle Hardware, either. I know that some of you have been eyeballing one of those electric hedge trimmers and thinking, "You know, Mother's Day is coming up…" but forget about it.

You can go to Falco's or Stanek's, but only for flowers. For instance, it's not considered an appropriate Mother's Day gift to buy a bale of steer manure for her garden, even if she is a master gardener.

Being a mother and all, she gets quite enough of that during the rest of the year, thank you very much.

It wasn't all that long ago when taking mom out to brunch was considered the height of appreciation. But this gift had its origins in a time when mom cooked every meal every day of her life, which may no longer be the case.

Plus, there is the whole dichotomy of food-as-a-gift, thing: "Let's see: you love me, so you are treating me to a high-fat breakfast of eggs, sausage, bacon, biscuits and butter, pancakes and syrup. What's wrong with this picture?"

Of course, she would never say that, because part of the covenant dictates that whatever you give her she has to accept with grace and appreciation. That's her part of the bargain.

Plus, she has to buy the cards you send to your mother. (You still have to sign them, of course.)

So, what gift will my daughter and I get for my wife on this Mother's Day?

Well, being a man, and understanding my obligations under the Mother's Day Covenant, I've had a long talk with my daughter about that, and we've agreed that we'll figure that out ... sometime tomorrow.

Finding the Perfect Father's Day Gift

I know what you're thinking right now:

"Father's Day. I have to get whatshisname something for Father's Day."

And if you are newly married, the perennial Father's Day question: Do I have to get something for my father-in-law?

Well, let me clear that up right now: If you're a wife, getting something for your father-in-law is your job.

If you're a husband and it's your father-in-law, hey, he's not your dad, is he?

Now, if you're a woman, I realize that this may not seem fair, but think about it: do you really want to leave present buying to your husband?

"Honey, I found a great present for your dad for Father's Day at the General Store: a graphite core, full rear-boot, high performance HO brand slalom water ski."

"My dad doesn't water ski."

"Yeah, I was thinking about that. Since he doesn't ski, maybe he'd want to leave it in our boat."

You see what I mean.

If you are young and newly married, deciding the in-law thing is real important because you are establishing traditions that you will adhere to until you get old — or divorced, whichever comes first.

If you are a young mother, and this is the first year your husband is a father, and you're wondering if you have to get your husband something for Father's Day (after all, he's not your father) the answer is: yes.

Never mind the fact that he may have asked the same question about you for Mother's Day and come up with the opposite answer.

Unfortunately, just because you married a clod doesn't change your Father's Day responsibilities.

Which gets us back to the original question, what to get whatshisname for Father's Day.

The problem with Father's Day is, it is a guy-oriented thing generally administered by women. It easier to figure out what to get your father, therefore, if you understand some of the unwritten, unspoken and even unconscious rules men live by.

For instance, there is the rule of multiple tools, which states that a man can't have too many of the same tool. Scientists think this rule evolved to protect man from the effects of his "lost it" gene: that curious propensity men have for losing whatever tool they happen to need right at the moment they happen to need it.

Plus, as protection against the lost it gene, we men like to have tools squirrelled away in different parts of the house, which is why there is a screwdriver and pair of pliers taking up space in your kitchen junk drawer.

So, don't let the fact that your father already has a set of socket wrenches keep you from getting him more. A man can't have too many sockets.

Now, another great Father's Day gift is the current cool tool.

The cool tool changes from year to year, and you can usually tell what it is by watching television.

This year it is the detail sander. The man in your life hasn't sanded anything in years? Doesn't matter. Using it isn't particularly important. What's important is having it. And if he ever actually sands something for you, well, consider that a bonus.

Another category is the techno-upgrade class of Father's Day presents.

For instance, if you have a home computer, you may want to get him a CD ROM drive. Or maybe a month's subscription to CompuServe. Or a faster modem.

This may have a side benefit for you. If you're getting to that point in your marriage where he's sort of in the way in your life, get him the computer game Myst. You won't see him for <u>months</u>. "Wow, Myst. Thanks." "You're welcome, Dear. Bye bye."

Are there presents you shouldn't get?

Of course.

You may have seen advertising for candy for Father's Day. Wrong. No father should have to go back to work Monday and explain to his buddies that he got a chocolate hammer for Father's Day.

"Wow, Irving, do you drive little chocolate nails with it?"

And personally, I've always found a gift of 18 gallons of exterior latex house paint and a roller to be a distressing gift. "Happy Father's Day. Bye, bye."

Contrary to what the advertising flyers for Penney's and Shopko would have you believe, most men don't consider clothes as a gift. Clothes are something else. This is probably due to the childhood trauma of going shopping for school clothes with our mothers.

So what is it we want?

Well new body parts for the ones we have worn out through abuse, disuse or just plain bad luck would be nice, but I suppose that's not very practical. "Wow. A new set of knees! Oh, and look: a brand new rotator cuff muscle and a full head of hair. What a wonderful Father's Day." But let's face it; unless you're Mickey Mantle, that's probably not going to happen.

It really doesn't have to be that difficult.

I would say that when it gets right down to it, what we want for Father's Day is pretty much what mothers want for Mother's Day — to be acknowledged for what we bring to the family table and forgiven for what we should but don't.

And one of those high-pressure electric power washers, would be nice, too.

New Year's Resolutions

It is the new year.

A time for new beginnings. A time for resolving to change, and to do things differently.

This is one of two times a year we engage in a little honest reflection.

Not the philosophical kind of reflection where we ask deep questions like, "What is my purpose on earth, and how am I supposed to accomplish it on my meager income?", but the other kind of honest reflection, the mirror kind of reflection, where we actually <u>look</u> at our reflection in the mirror, and we say, "Whoa, I look like hell."

The other time of year is three months from now when the warming weather and longer days activate swimsuit panic time, which is when we realize that in just a matter of weeks, we might actually have to appear in public in a swimsuit, and naturally, we panic.

It is this time of year when I lean in closer to the mirror and study the hairline above my temples and I wonder: is that where it was a year ago? Or like a perverse tide that only goes out, has my hairline receded again this year, moving inevitably backward toward the circular patch of non-hairy scalp on the back of my head? Yes. No. Yes. And I think: Next year, I'm putting Rogaine on my Christmas list.

It is a time we resolve to improve ourselves.

"This year, I'm going to get thin," we say. And then we amend that to, "Well, thinner, anyway."

Actually, I suspect that's what women say. We men do not aspire to thinhood; rather, we resolve to "get in shape." And being the more self-delusional of the species, we're never too specific, you understand, about what that shape is.

It is somewhere south of where we are but north of being a cover guy for Muscle Magazine. Most of us don't aspire to be something completely different; we'll settle for simply what we were when we were say, 18. Or 23. Or 35, even. It all kind of depends on where we are now, if you know what I mean.

This works well for us, because "getting in shape" is an amorphous goal that encompasses muscle tone which, as we all know, is invisible; and improving our "wind" - the aerobic ability to climb a flight of stairs without getting winded and wanting to die (which is also invisible), and in extreme cases, losing weight, which is not invisible, but which we men normally choose not to see.

"I'm not fat; I'm just in need of some control top panty hose."

The bottom line is, because getting in shape is not defined by a specific poundage loss or waistline, we can declare ourselves in shape and quit whenever we want.

But, in this moment of a mixture of post-holiday guilt, introspection, New year's resolution making and mental self-flagellation, we resolve to get in shape, and we join a health club.

Now, the older and wiser among us know that if we can just put off signing that health club contract until, say, January 15th, the odds are great that the urge to hurt ourselves like this will pass, and we won't have to face the urge to actually exercise until after next Christmas.

Of course, by next Christmas we may be dead of heart failure, but that's a risk we're more than willing to take.

Now, during this period, while we are focusing on what our new toned up, slimmed-down and aerobically fit bodies will look like and feel like, what we forget is exercise is a lot of work.

I mean, there is a reason why we have chosen eating over exercise for a decade or so: exercise hurts!

But in we go, human lemmings off to a sea of exercise machines.

And what a sea it is. Machines that isolate and exercise every conceivable muscle in your body. Machines that adjust to your exact size and strength. Machines that you need a degree in mechanical engineering just to figure out how to sit on without hurting yourself. Treadmills and stair climbers and stationary bikes that are so confusing to operate you also need to be semi-computer literate, as well.

There is nothing that will sap your resolve to exercise quite as much as being made a fool of by a recalcitrant treadmill that is waiting for the exact sequence of instructions from you before it will go. Everybody else is pushing up their heart rate walking or running while you stand there pushing nothing but buttons. "Enter weight, calories per hour or time," it tells you. What? Where? how?

Most men, of course, won't ask directions, so they just stand there a while looking stupid, and then, frustrated, move off to something low tech they understand how to work - like barbells.

In our zeal to shape up, we also tend to overlook another blindingly obvious fact: we are going to have to do this exercise thing in front of other people.

If you're a man, that means that everybody will be able to see exactly how much weight you can't seem to lift. This, in an environment where your goals, not to mention your manhood, is measured in weight lifted and repetitions.

Now the fact is, nobody who is really into exercise as a way of life, cares what you can or can't lift. But that doesn't help much when we're faced with looking like a wimp.

So, inevitably, in an effort not to look like exactly what we are, namely winded, balding, out-of-shape, middle-aged men, we overreach our ability to perform, and in the process, if we don't do permanent bodily damage, then we do damage that at least *feels* like it is going to be permanent, with the result being, anywhere from three days to three weeks after we start, we are still unable to move without looking crippled, so we declare ourselves fit, and we never go back.

At least, until next year at this time, when we start the whole process all over again.

Doug Hurd is a graduate of the University of Washington and Whitworth College. He is a writer and account executive for WhiteRunkle Associates, a Spokane advertising agency, and a columnist for The Edmonds Paper, in Edmonds Washington. When not writing advertising for his clients or commentaries for KPBX he can usually be found playing or coaching volleyball. He splits his time between Spokane, Washington and Laclede, Idaho. He is married to Jeannie, his wife of 24 years. They have a daughter, Allyson.